# CREATIVE ABSTRACT
# Mixed Media

## The beginner's guide to expressive painting with watercolor & more!

### KATE REBECCA LEACH

**DAVID & CHARLES**
—PUBLISHING—

www.davidandcharles.com

# Contents

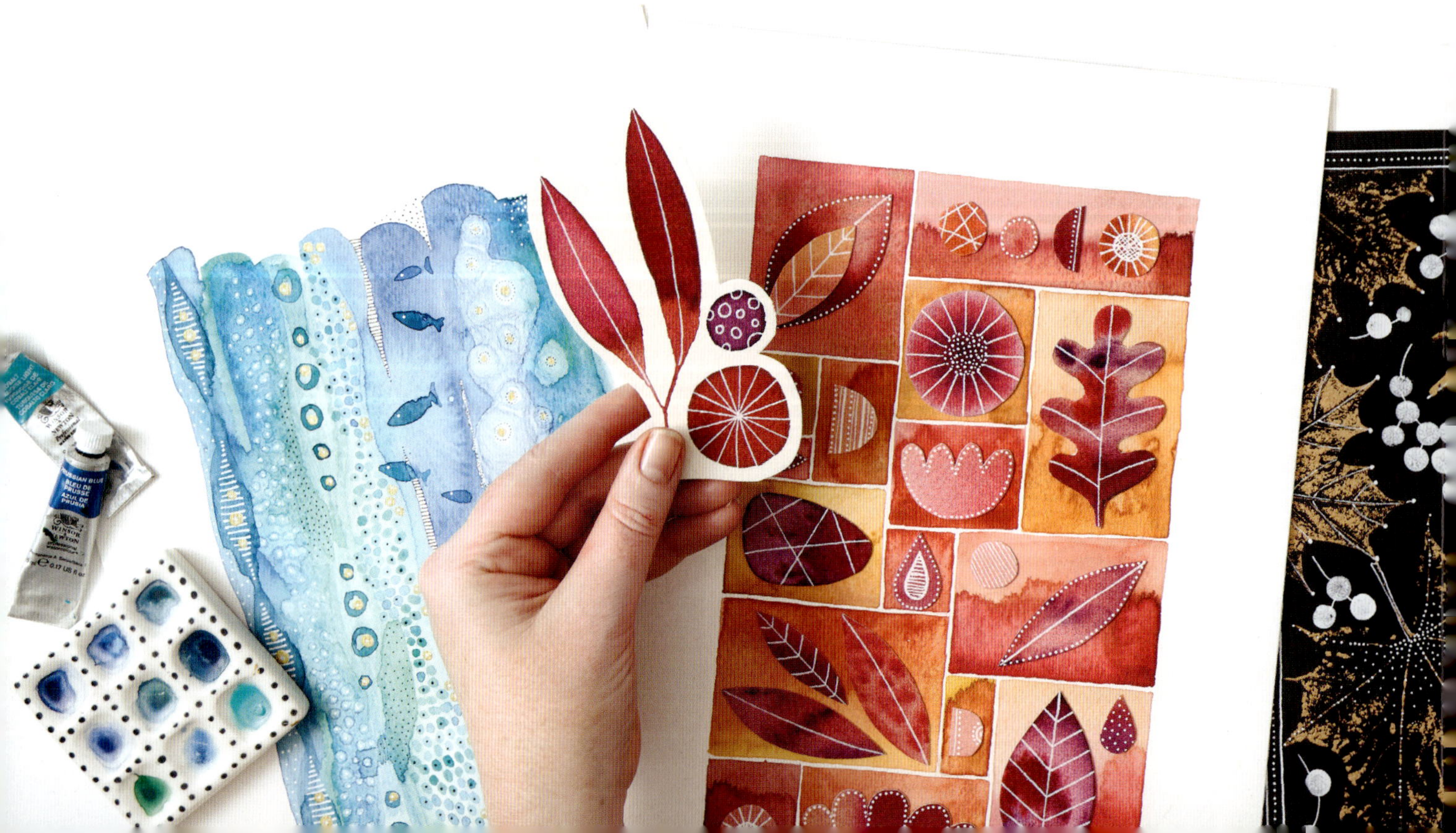

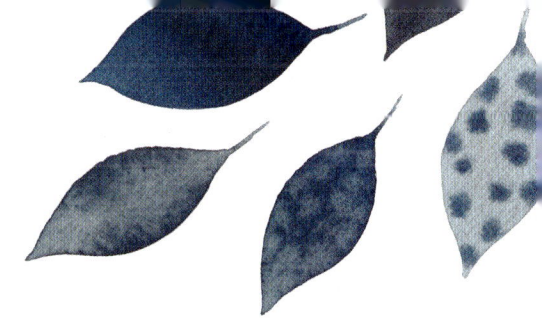

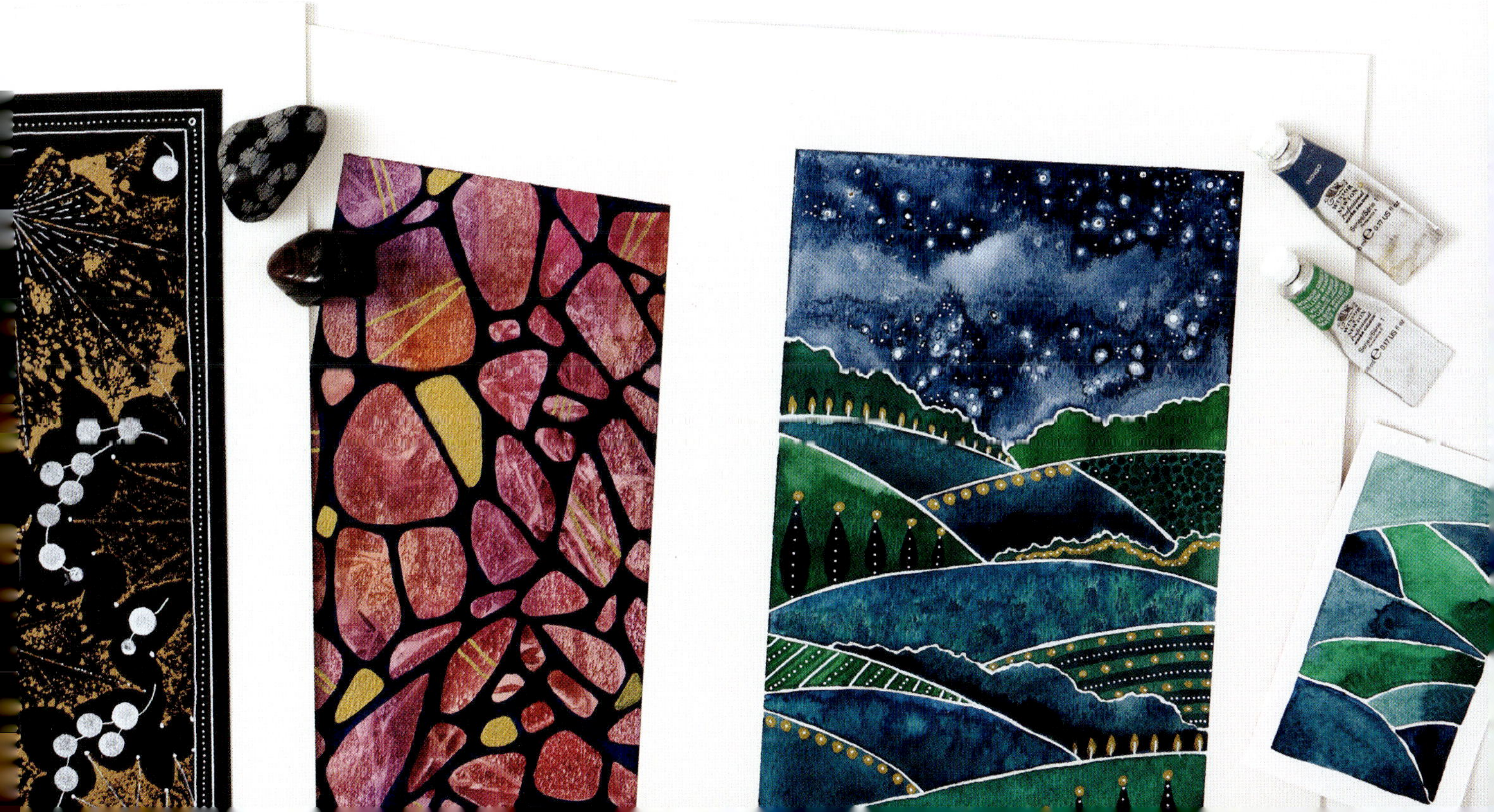

# Introduction

As I sit here, writing the introduction to my second book (a sentence I thought I'd never type), I'm reflecting on my creative journey over the last four years and feel an amazing sense of gratitude for an incredible transformation of my life. As some of you may know (and for those that don't), I've always been an "artistic" person, from my love of art and design, and appreciation of culture and history, to my somewhat eclectic dress sense!

As a child, I was never happier than when painting, drawing, or making, and this is something that has stuck with me through my teens, 20s, 30s, and now into my 40s! My creativity has had times of abundance during my school, college, and university days, where I was lucky enough to gain a degree in textile design and surface pattern, through to 20-plus years of dormancy. As some of you may have experienced, life can get in the way, and a corporate day job led me away from my true artistic calling.

Fast forward to lockdown 2020, when a brief period of furlough allowed me the time and headspace to begin creating again, and I've never looked back! Art is something that morphed from a mindful hobby (and a way to calm my busy brain) to a way of life, and, I'm delighted to say, now my vocation. I've become an author, designed my debut fabric collection, and licensed my work across the globe. As I write these words I am in my last few weeks of employment in the corporate world, before I take the exciting (and slightly terrifying) leap into life as a full-time artist, illustrator, tutor, and writer!

Since finishing my last book I've explored and experimented with a host of different media, which I can't wait to share with you here. From crackle paste to salt, and collage to gold thread, I've (literally) embellished my watercolor work with a host of exciting new techniques. I'll be sharing my favorite materials, top tips, and 13 new projects with you to explore. I hope this book will take your work to heady new heights and allow you to create something new, exciting, and – most of all – fun!

Happy painting!

*Kate*

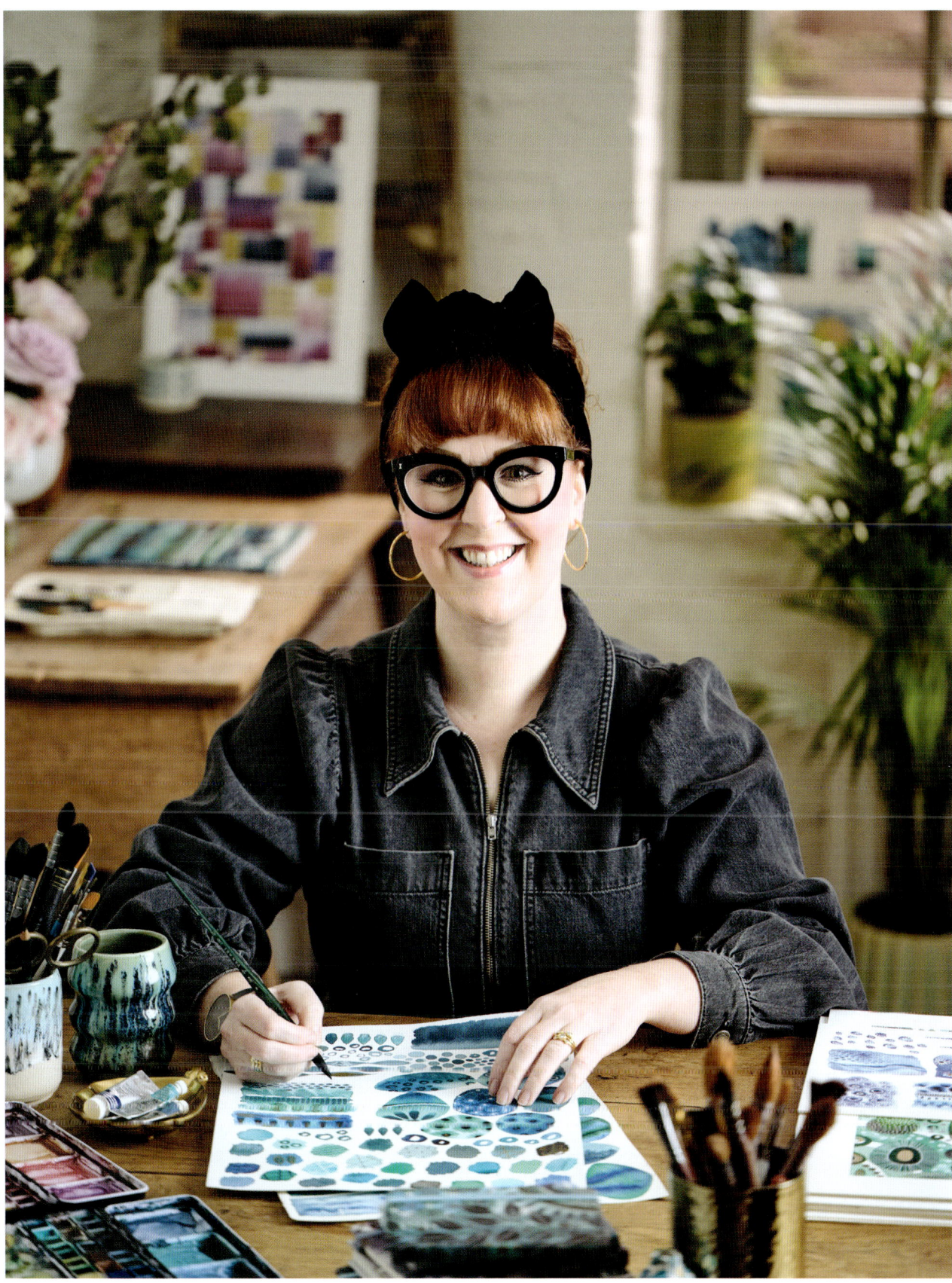

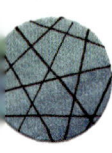

# What is Mixed Media?

Hmm, this is a tricky question to answer as I'm sure many artists will have a slightly different viewpoint, but for me the following definition from the Tate art institution sums it up nicely:

**Mixed media is a term used to describe artworks composed from a combination of different media or materials.**

**The use of mixed media began around 1912 with the cubist collages and constructions of Pablo Picasso and Georges Braque, and has become widespread as artists developed increasingly open attitudes to the media of art. Essentially art can be made of anything or any combination of things.**

The reason I love this definition is one line in particular: "art can be made of anything or any combination of things". I love the freedom this approach offers. It allows me to "go with the flow ", and I feel free to use any art materials I can lay my hands on. As a creative, I don't like to have set rules and techniques that I must abide by. I simply want to play, explore, and at times make a mess!

I remember teaching a watercolor workshop once, where one of the participants was a real traditionalist and scolded me for using inks and pens over my work, as this wasn't "pure" watercolor. I had a fantastic chat with them later in the session about my philosophy on art; rules are there to be broken, and I considered myself somewhat as a free spirit! For me (and I hope you'll join me in this as you explore the book), there is joy in painting and then figuring out what is needed to enhance the piece. I may grab some gold drawing ink, a handful of salt to create texture, or even collage over parts of my painting to add a new and exciting dimension to it. The sky's the limit, and it's so rewarding to try new things!

## MIXED MEDIA ELEMENTS IN MY ART

Mixed media may feel new or daunting, but don't let the title put you off – it's just a case of using more than one type of art material in your work. For some artists this may be metal, plastic, fabric, wood, and more, but for me I use a pared back selection of materials that I can easily work with at my home studio with limited space (I'm a neat freak so can't cope with lots of mess!).

I always begin with painting and then add new materials on top in separate layers to add visual interest, texture, contrast, or simply decoration! An analogy I like to use when teaching is the following:

**"Think of your painting as an outfit – for me, it's a black dress! I like to think of my mixed media embellishment as the jewelry and accessories that bring the outfit to life!"**

Here are some of the key ways I use mixed media in my art:

- Alcohol and salts – using them with wet paint to create a range of fantastic textures and effects
- Collage – vintage or painted papers
- Colored or metallic inks
- Crackle pastes
- Gel and paint pens
- Gold thread or foil to add metallic highlights
- Markers, pastels, chalks, and graphite
- Printing – using print techniques to create textures and interesting marks

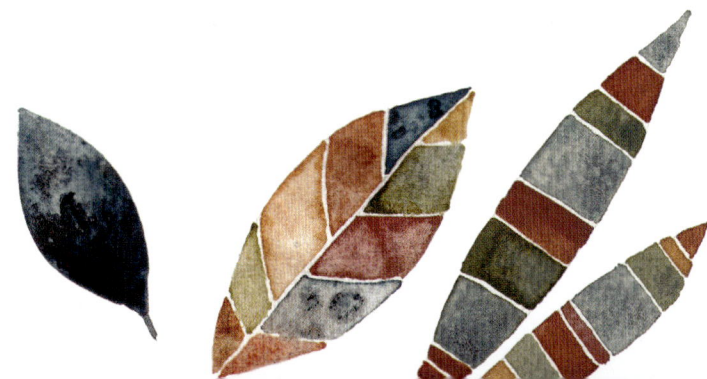

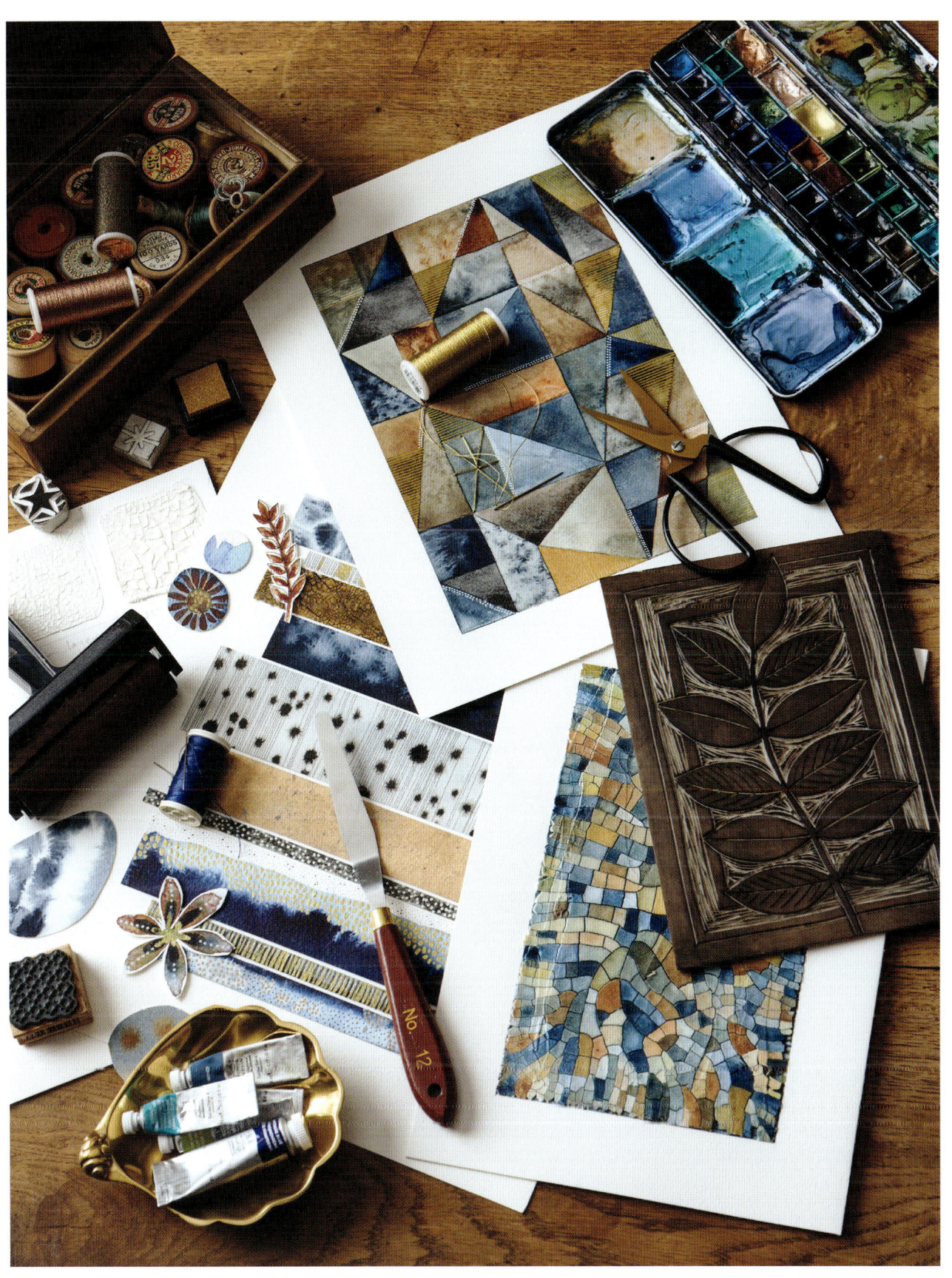

# MY INSPIRATION

People often ask me where I get my inspiration and ideas from, and it's a tough question to answer! I think as an artist or simply a creative person, I look at the world a little differently to some. I try to take in everything (and I really do mean that) – from the interesting texture of peeling paint on an old shop front, to little beads of dew on a leaf during a frosty winter walk. Inspiration is all around us – for me it's just taking the time to be mindful, go for a walk, and slow down, really noticing the infinite colors, patterns, and textures that surround us.

That said, life is busy, and time is always short, so dedicating some time whenever you can is great. A simple 30-minute walk in nature can fill you with ideas and get you raring to paint! Some of my favorite ways to get into a creative mindset are:

- **A walk outside:** Great in the garden, at a local park, or on a trip to the beach to watch the ocean.

- **A museum or historic site visit:** Look at vintage textiles, amazing architecture, or simply the textures of buildings that have stood the test of time.

- **Travel:** For me there's nothing more inspiring than exploring a new town, city, or country! I love to take a small sketchbook with me or simply snap some photos to use for inspiration when I return home.

- **Reading:** A book can transport you somewhere else – whether it's to magical lands or halfway across the world – in a single page; the more I read, the more I find that it feeds my imagination.

- **Music and podcasts:** I love to listen to something while I paint and it can often influence my work, whether it's the loose watercolor marks of indie music or the intricate details inspired by listening to a gripping story!

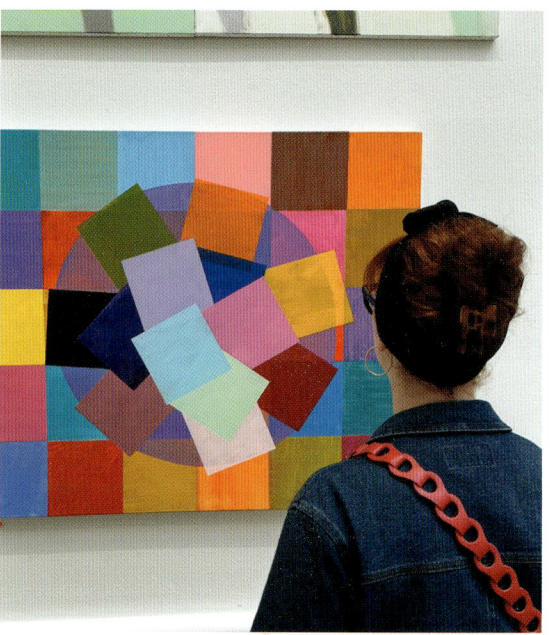

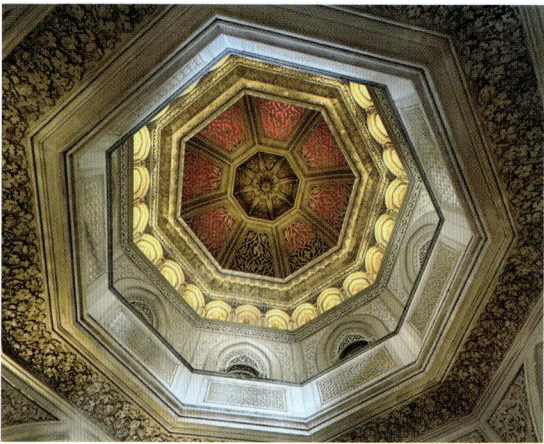

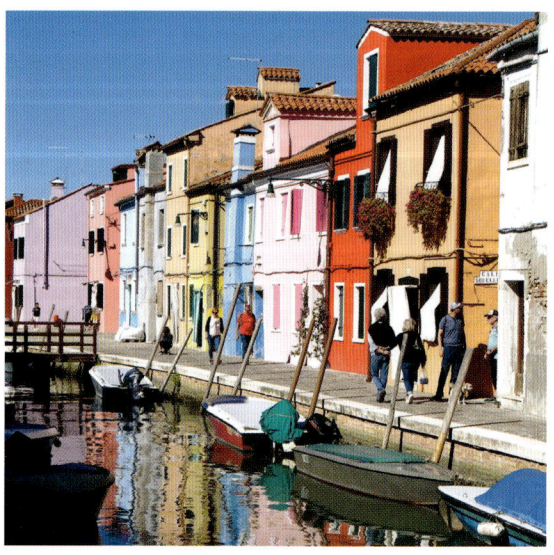

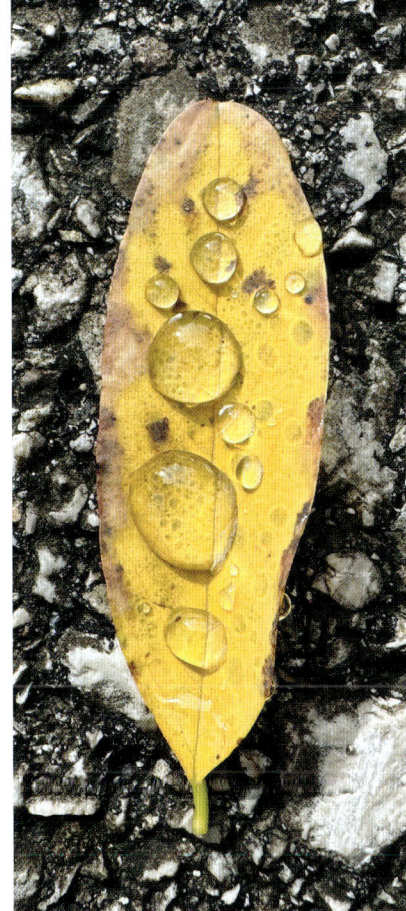
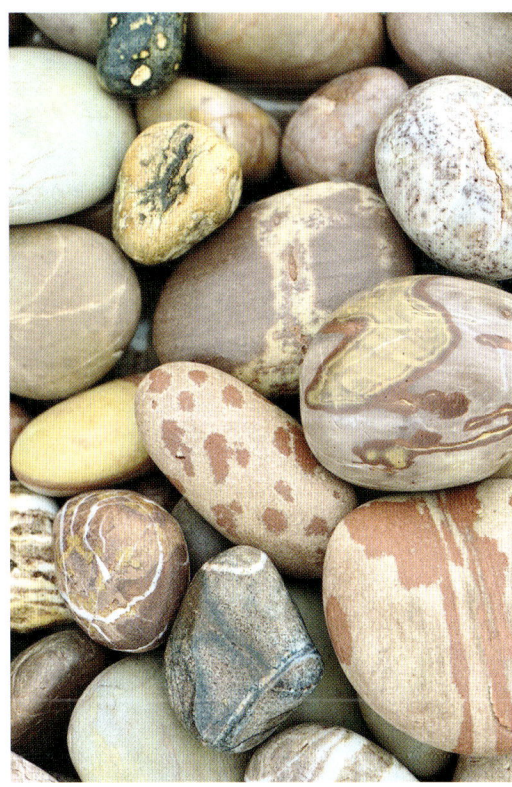
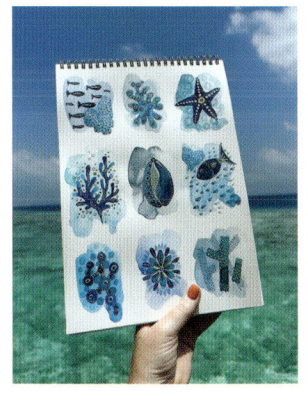
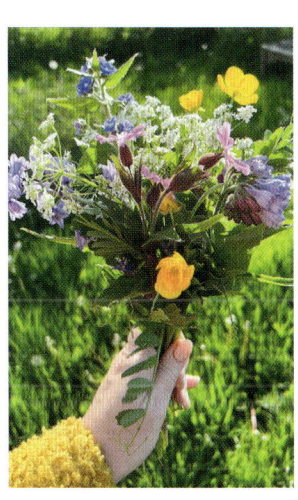
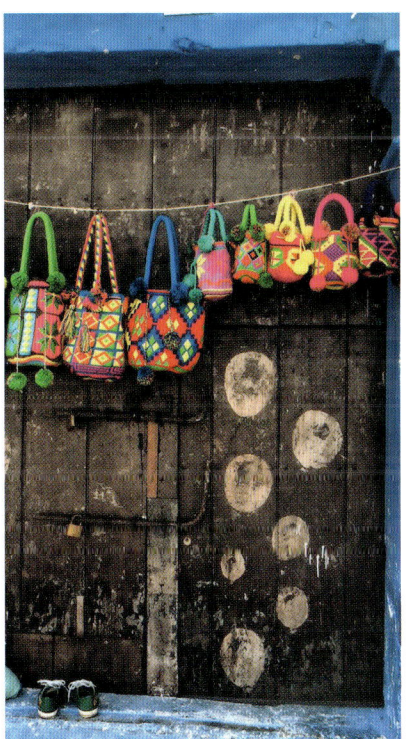
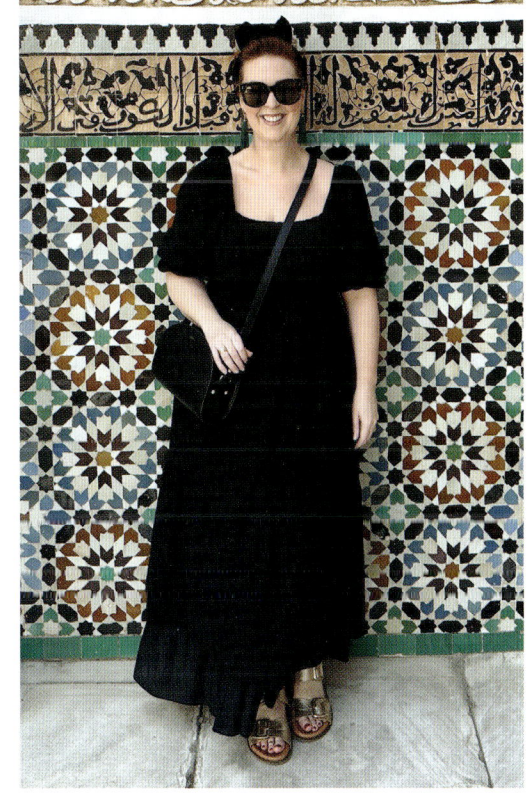
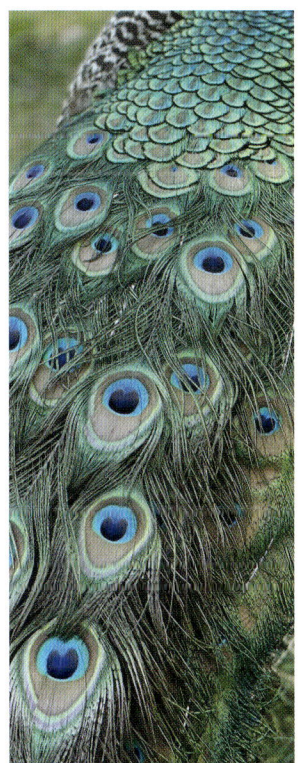

# Materials

I found the subject of materials to be a minefield when starting out! The vast array of paints, papers, brushes, and more seemed incredibly hard to narrow down to a basic kit. Don't be daunted – I started out simply with a small set of watercolors, a pad of paper, a brush or two, and a jar of water, and it stood me in good stead. Over the last three years of research, trial, and error, I've found my favorite materials. Here are my recommendations for your kit.

## PAINT

Most paints can be bought in a set, which provides a useful collection of basic colors as you're learning. Paints can also be bought in individual colors, allowing you to buy an empty tin and create your own set (see Selecting a Color Palette).

### FORMAT

Watercolor paint mainly comes in two formats – tubes of liquid paint, and small square or rectangular "pans" of dried paint. I prefer pans, as they're economical, portable, and easy to use. But I also have a variety of my favorite and most-used shades in tubes – I'll often mix a generous quantity of these in my palette before I even begin painting.

### QUALITY

Many brands come in a choice of grade – either student or professional. Student paints are a great price, but contain far less pigment than their professional counterparts, so lack the same depth of color. I recommend buying the best paints you can afford – they last for ages, especially pans! My first painting sessions started with an old set of Winsor & Newton's student range, Cotman. I quickly progressed to their professional watercolors, which are the paints that I have used throughout both of my books.

## TIPS FOR BUYING PAINT

- **Refill and reuse:** When using a set of pans, you may run out of one color more quickly than the rest. If so, buy that color in a tube and use this to refill the empty pan, letting it dry in the pan. Never throw away an empty pan – it can be filled and reused (as I'm self-taught, I didn't know this for my first year of painting!).

- **Shop around:** Many art shops and online suppliers offer great prices on basic sets, often saving you up to fifty percent. Paint is the one material that I believe is worth spending a little extra on – you'll get better results and will not regret it.

- **Experiment:** I use mainly Winsor & Newton professional watercolor pans and tubes, but I enjoy exploring other paints from time to time. For example, I've used Kuretake sets. These oversized pans are available in a fantastic array of colors. Their thicker paint can be used more like a gouache, which can give interesting results.

*Top Tip:* Look for paint that is lightfast, such as Winsor & Newton. Your painting will retain its true color and vibrancy when proudly out on display.

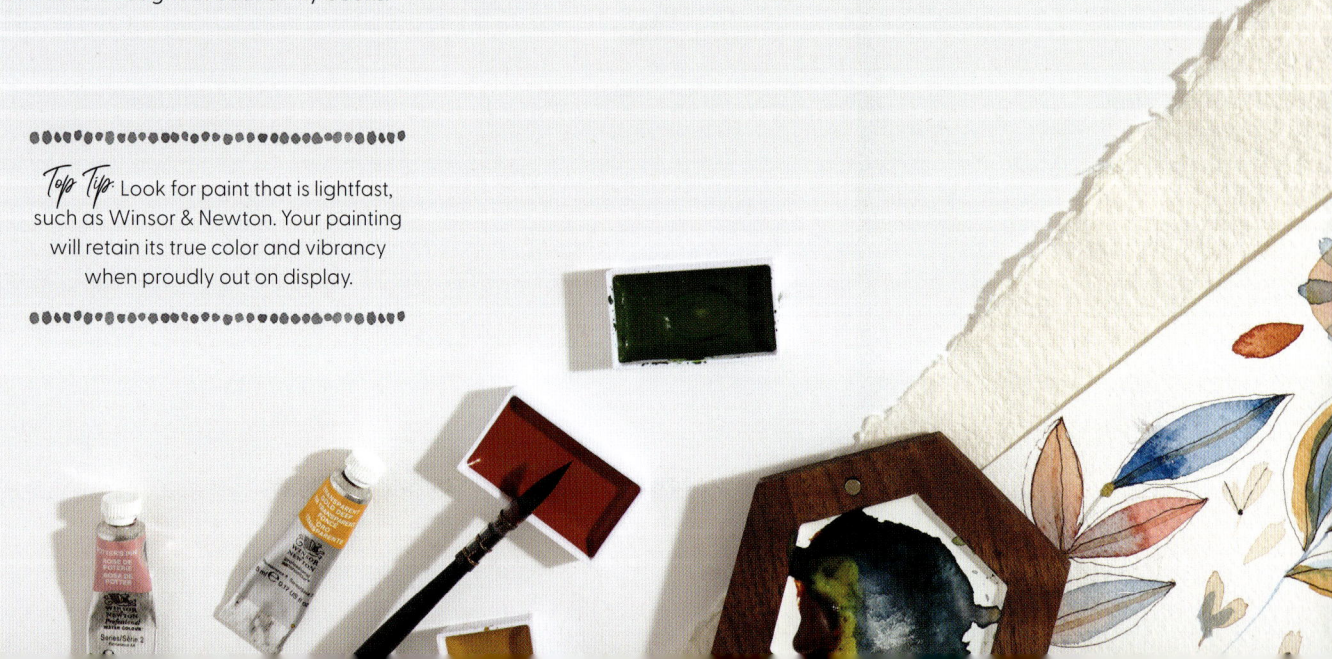

# PAPER

Quite literally the foundation of your work, your paper dictates how colors blend, how the water washes across the page, and how the paint pigments settle. The right paper can help to create a variety of patterns through its texture alone.

## TEXTURE

Watercolor paper usually comes in three main textures.

- **Smooth:** Also known as "hot pressed", the very smooth surface allows you to create small and intricate details.

- **Cold pressed:** Also called NOT, as in *not* hot pressed, this is my preferred paper. Its pleasing texture reveals the natural properties of watercolor, and it is suitable for beginners.

- **Rough:** The most heavily textured paper used in watercolor, this feels similar to the thicker, grainier texture of handmade paper and is ideal for loose abstract pieces.

## WEIGHT

All watercolor paper, whatever the texture, is labeled to show its weight. The measurement used is "gsm" (grams per square meter). I recommend starting out with 300gsm paper – it's sturdy and good to practice and experiment on.

## FORMAT

Paper comes in many formats – here are the four main types.

- **Loose sheets:** Inexpensive, so ideal for building muscle memory, practicing techniques, and generally having fun!

- **Sketchbook:** Spiral binding keeps the pages flat and stable as you paint. It keeps all your work together, so it's great for trying out new techniques and ideas. As you grow your skills, you can flick through to chart your progress!

- **Pad:** Pages of paper glued along one edge. The pages can be kept together, or removed to give you loose sheets.

- **Glued block:** The pages are glued along all four edges, with a small opening that lets you lift away each finished page. The top page is kept taut by the pages beneath, so it is less likely to buckle or ripple and is a budget-friendly alternative to watercolor board.

- **Watercolor board:** A very rigid board with a sheet of watercolor paper adhered to one side. This allows you to use lots of paint and water, and the paper won't buckle or bend (which can happen with thinner paper). Look for watercolor board covered with cold-pressed paper.

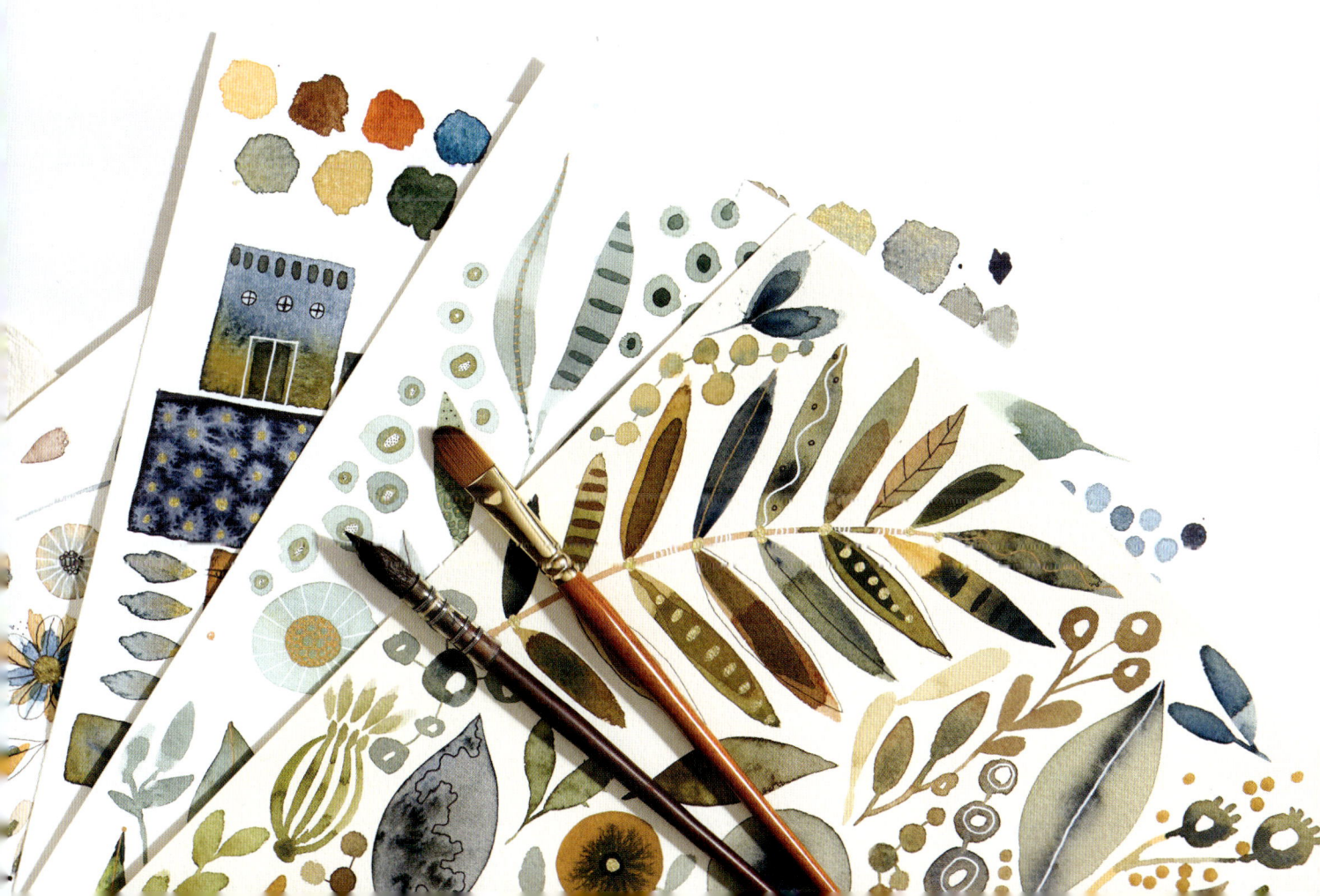

## MASKING SUPPLIES

Where your paint doesn't go is as important as where it does! I use a couple of products to create everything from tiny details to sharp, bold borders.

### MASKING TAPE

Good tape is an absolute essential in your beginner's tool kit! Used to mask off simple shapes and create soft torn edges, it's also a must for preserving a crisp white border (see Core Watercolor Techniques: Masking Borders). I use FrogTape Delicate Surface Painter's Tape – Yellow in 24mm (1in) and 36mm (1½in) widths. The tape can also be used to cover simple shapes or areas you want to protect from paint.

### MASKING FLUID

Once you have some experience with masking tape, you may want to experiment with masking off more complex shapes. This is where masking fluid comes into its own! For example, you might want to retain clean white shapes, free of paint, in your design but still use bold watercolor washes. Masking fluid would be applied to those shapes first. Once dry, you can paint over the paper and the masking fluid, then remove the fluid once the paint is dry.

## BRUSHES

I feel as if I've tried most of the many, *many* brushes out there! Early on I purchased several, but used only a handful on repeat. A few basics available from art suppliers is all you need to get started. Here is what I use and recommend.

### QUILL BRUSH

This is a great all-round brush. Its full "belly" and fine point allow you to make both full, sweeping marks and delicate details. Quill brushes hold lots of paint or water, meaning you can paint for longer before returning to your palette.

**I use...** my new favorite brush is the Da Vinci Casaneo quill brush. It's a lovely shape and holds masses of paint/water. I have sizes 0, 2, and 4 –the 0 is great for fine details, 2 is my everyday go to, and 4 is good for bold marks and washes.

### ROUND BRUSH

This is another great all-round brush for mark making and adding details. Sizes 0, 4, and 8 provide a useful range for getting started.

**I use...** Daler Rowney round brushes – I've built a small collection over the years.

### FILBERT BRUSH

The wider flat side and narrower edge of this versatile, sturdy brush create lots of interesting marks. The bristles form a flattened oval head, which I use to create my raindrop spots.

**I use...** an ancient Daler Rowney filbert brush – a keepsake from my art student days! Size 3 or 4 is the most useful.

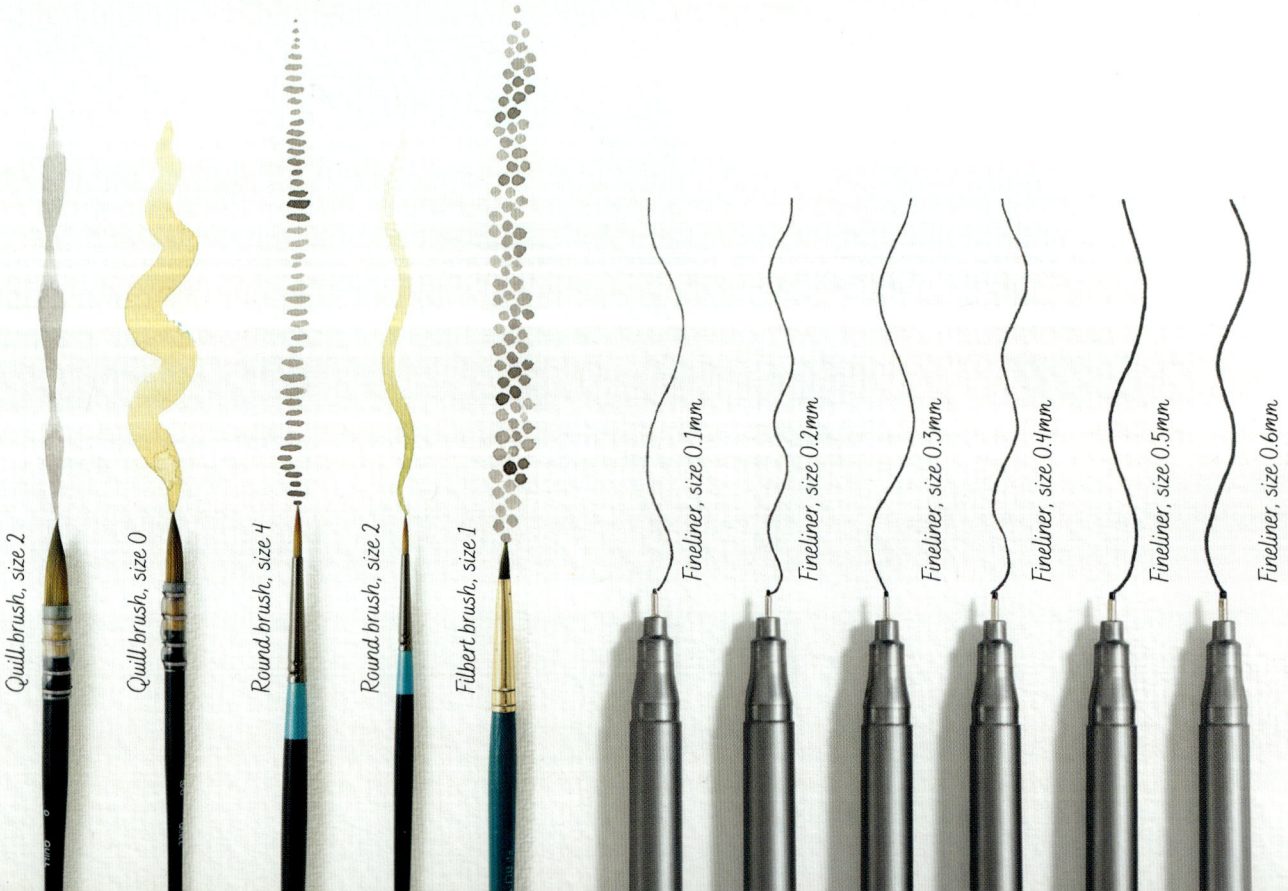

Quill brush, size 2

Quill brush, size 0

Round brush, size 4

Round brush, size 2

Filbert brush, size 1

Fineliner, size 0.1mm

Fineliner, size 0.2mm

Fineliner, size 0.3mm

Fineliner, size 0.4mm

Fineliner, size 0.5mm

Fineliner, size 0.6mm

# INK AND PENS

In addition to paint, there are other mediums that play nicely with watercolor, allowing you to add refined details and embellishments to your art.

## METALLIC INK

As I've already mentioned, I love to embellish my work by painting metallic details and highlights over the watercolor base. There are fantastic metallic watercolors on the market, but I find that metallic inks create the best color and shine! I enjoy the Winsor & Newton metallic inks. The thick metallic pigment and clear liquid solution separate in the bottle, so shake well to combine before use. Use a filbert brush for spots, or a small round brush for other details.

*Top Tip:* Metallic ink can be used sparingly. Rather than dipping directly into the glass jar, I use the lid to hold just the right amount and ensure a good mix of pigment and liquid.

## PENS

Much like metallic inks, pens can be used on top of your finished painting to add texture, new color, or details. I use a range of pens to add lines, dots, details, and more. These are the best pens I've found:

### White and metallic gel pens

Uni-ball Signo gel ink pens flow well and add nice opaque coverage, even when working over darker colors. I use the size "Broad", which is actually only 1mm! This size allows for well-defined line work as well as delicate details.

### White paint pens

Posca paint pens are fantastic for dots, dashes, and other embellishments. I wouldn't be without them in a range of sizes to suit the scale and style of the piece I'm working on.

### Black fineliners

These are a great tool to include in your kit – they make adding details easy and precise. I use a range of sizes, from ultra-fine 0.1mm for very delicate lines, up to 0.8mm for larger dot work.

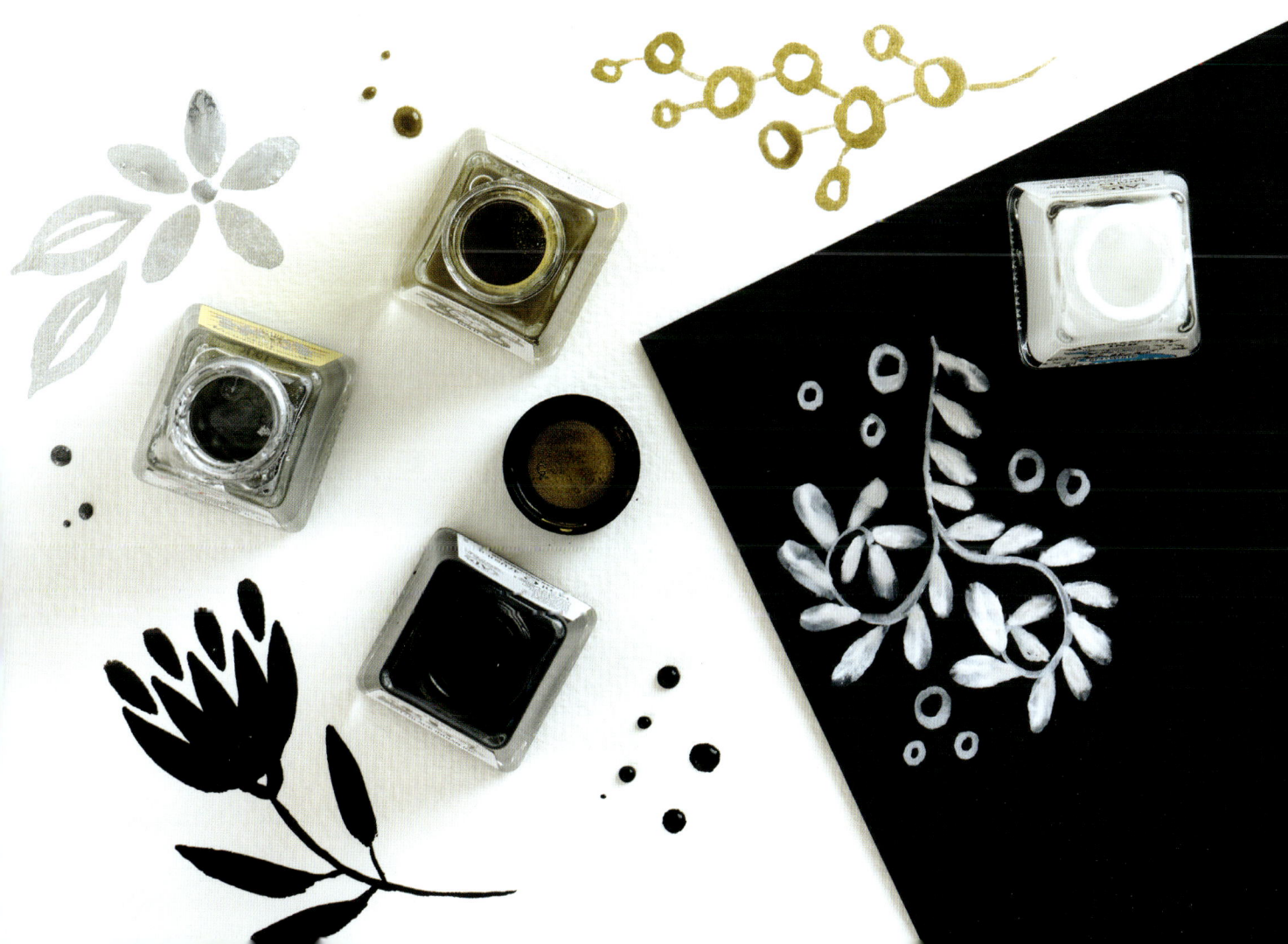

# MIXED-MEDIA MATERIALS

While my obsession with all things watercolor continues, I love to discover new materials and techniques to help my work develop and enable me to grow as an artist. Bringing mixed-media elements into my work offers a range of fantastic new opportunities; below are some of my favorite new materials.

## DOUBLE-SIDED ADHESIVE SHEETS

When I found these in Hobbycraft (my local arts and crafts store), I was thrilled! I love collage, but can't stand the messiness of glue or the edges of my collage pieces curling up. These sheets can be stuck to the back of your watercolor paper, basically turning your sheet into a giant sticker. You can paint on your watercolor paper, cut out your chosen shapes, then peels off the backing and stick the cutout to your piece/background. Clean, quick, and gives a great result!

## DOUBLE-SIDED TAPE

If you can't get your hands on double-sided adhesive sheets, plain old double-sided tape works really well for collage. It normally comes in a range of different widths – I try to find a wide roll, which allows me to use it on large collaged elements.

## ALCOHOL

Now I'm not talking gin or vodka here – you'll want to use pure alcohol, often called 100% Pure isopropyl alcohol or rubbing alcohol. When this is added to wet watercolor it will give fantastic effects, removing color and adding texture to the piece.

## SALTS

Salt is a great way to add texture to your watercolor; simply sprinkle it onto your still-damp watercolor painting and let the magic happen! I've tried a range of salts in my work – I'd recommend trying fine salt, sea salt, and course rock salt, as they all give different effects.

## PRINTING INK

This slow-drying ink is perfect for making multiple prints, whether you're using rubber stamps, found objects, or lino blocks. It comes in a myriad of colors but I tend to stick to classic black and gold for most of my work.

## RUBBER STAMPS

I always have an eraser or two in my studio, and they are great for carving into to make customized rubber stamps. I use these in my artwork and they also come in handy for making unique gift wrap by printing on brown paper!

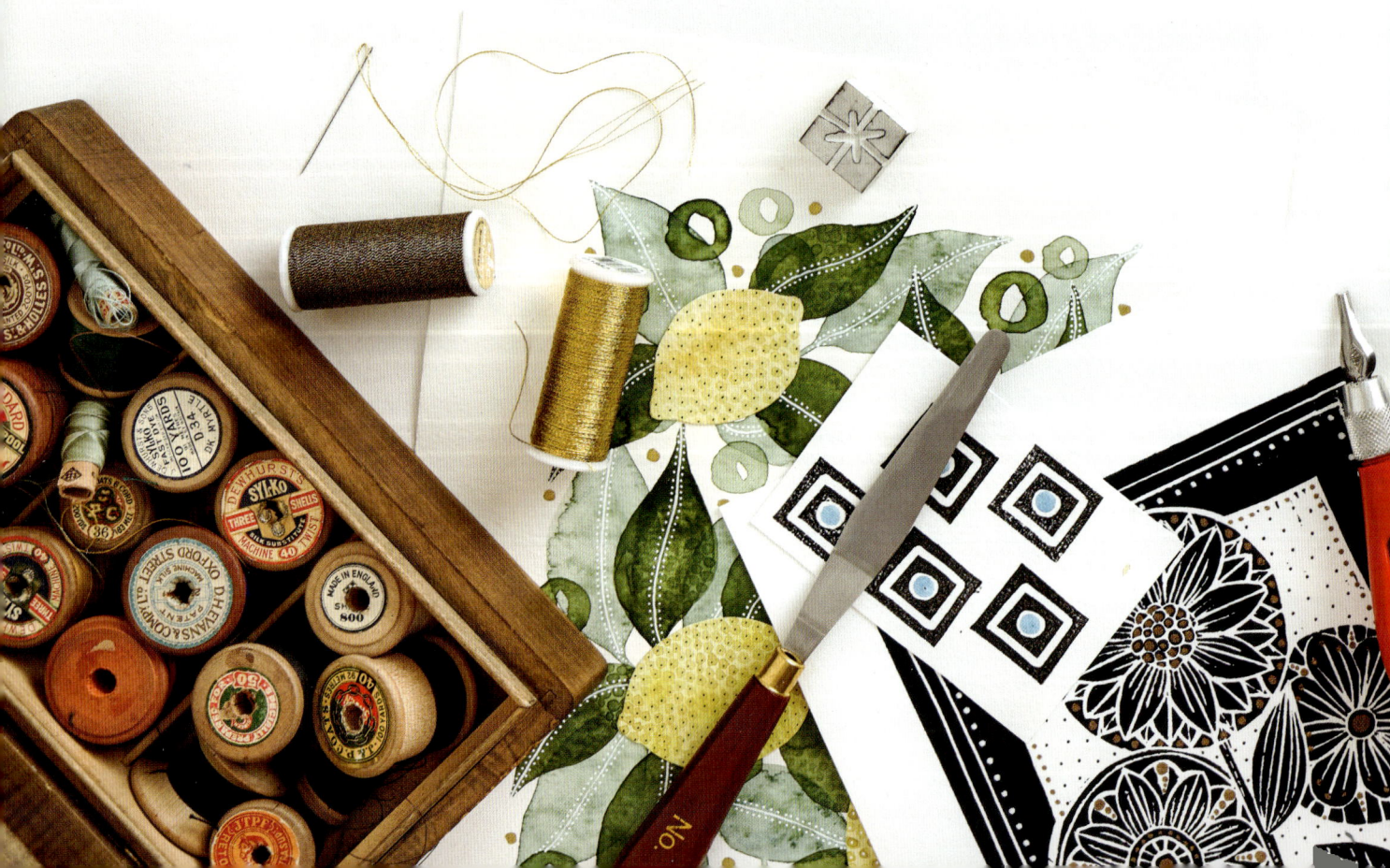

## THREAD

I'm not a sewing expert, so I tend to opt for threads that appeal aesthetically rather than look for a certain type/brand. For my sewn embellishments, I tend to use metallic thread of a medium weight (anything too large will make sewing through the paper harder). If in doubt practice with test paper before diving in on your final piece.

## FILM

For one of our projects, we'll be using simple plastic wrap that can be found it most kitchens in homes all over the world. In the UK we call it clingfilm, but it may have a different name depending on where you are reading this. The brand doesn't matter, you'll just want a thin plastic film (the kind you use to cover food). It should have a sticky/clingy texture to it that will help you to create some fantastic textures when used with watercolor.

## CRACKLE PASTE

I've tried many forms of crackle medium, including pastes, sprays and gels, but to create a textured crackle effect that is ideal to paint on, I use Golden brand crackle paste. This can be spread thinly to create smaller cracks or applied more thickly to give large and distinct "platelets" (cell-like shapes that remain between the cracks).

## VARNISH

There are two types of varnish that I use to finish my crackle-paste pieces: liquid varnish and spray varnish. Both help to seal the crackles and stop them flaking or peeling away, and both have benefits and drawbacks. Spray varnish is quick and easy but can be messy! Liquid varnish is good but needs to be applied carefully to avoid reactivating the watercolor and merging the colors. Both types have gloss and matt options.

*Top Tip:* We will look in more detail at using these materials in a techniques section that precedes each group of projects.

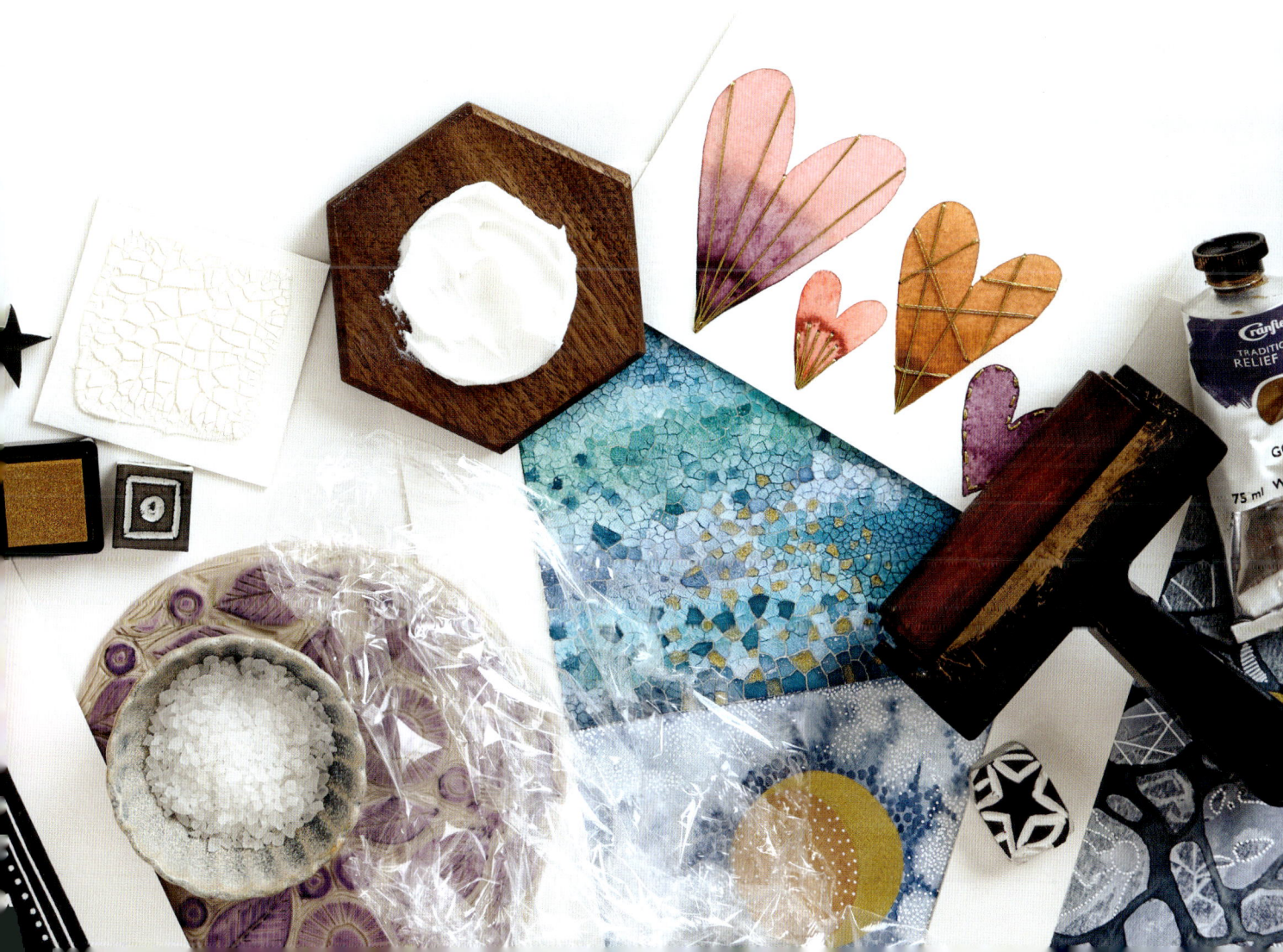

# Selecting a Color Palette

Over the years I have read or heard about many principles of color mixing, rules for how to use color "properly", and guides to what colors work best together. Having studied art at college and university I was taught these guidelines, but over the last two decades my color philosophy has changed rather a lot!

My color choices can be determined by the piece I'm creating, a client's request (if I'm painting a commission), or simply my mood on the day! I tend to go with my gut and lean into the colors that call to me when I sit down to paint. Later in the book you'll see my suggested palettes for each project, but I'd always encourage you to break free from "having" to use certain colors, rather opting for the colors that bring you joy.

As I like to work in analogous palettes (more on that over the next pages), I split my paints/pans into two different metal palettes, one for warm colors and one for cool. I often get asked if they come this way – they don't! I start with a store-bought set of paints and an empty tin. I then move across the colors I want until I have a good split. This leaves plenty of space to add new and exciting colors to each set! In the photo below you can see my 'cool' set – all of my favorite blues and greens with a few accent colors.

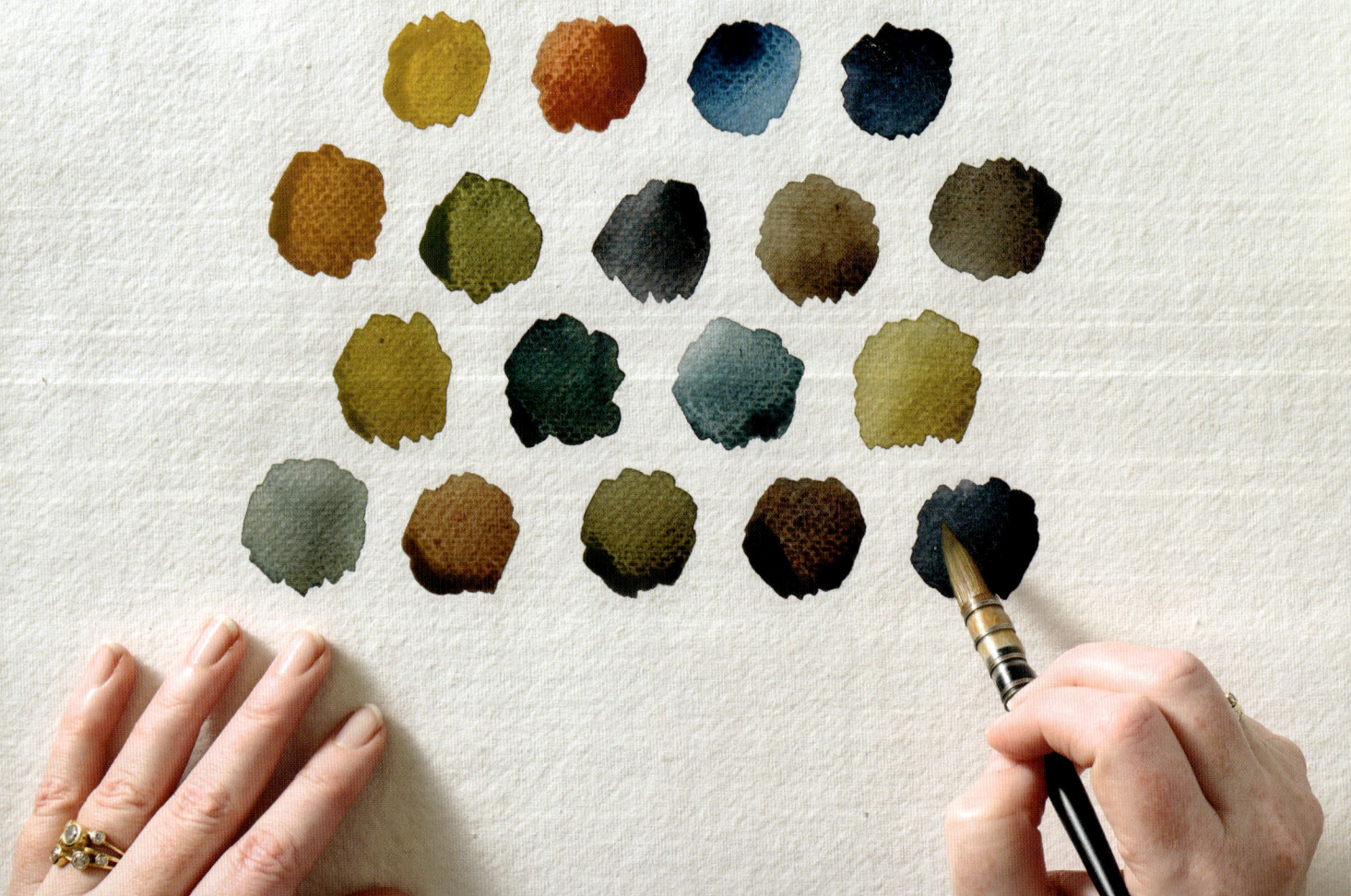

# HARMONIOUS PALETTES

While I don't tend to stick to the "rules" of painting (I consider myself a bit of a painting maverick!), I did recently read about a method that I feel I may have inadvertently been using all along. It's called "the mother method", and its definition is as follows:

**The mother method is a painting technique that involves mixing a small amount of a single color, called the "mother color", into every other color in a painting. The goal is to achieve color harmony, which is when a group of colors work well together and are pleasing to the eye.**

Those of you that have read my first book or follow me on social media will know of my deep and longstanding love of the color Payne's Gray. It's a soft and sophisticated blue-gray that appears in almost all of my work! I often joke that due to my water jar constantly having a Payne's Gray hue, it manages to sneak into every color I use. I do believe this helps my palette stay harmonious – and it may be the mother method working it's magic.

## MY 'HERO' COLORS

There are a few key colors I reach for again and again; you'll find them in much of my work.

- Payne's Gray
- Indigo
- Burnt Sienna
- Yellow Ochre

*Top Tip:* Many watercolor purists paint with two water jars: one for clean water and another to rinse their brushes between colors. I prefer to use one large water jar as I tend to work in analogous palettes (colors of the same type), so I never mind if there is leftover color in my paint water!

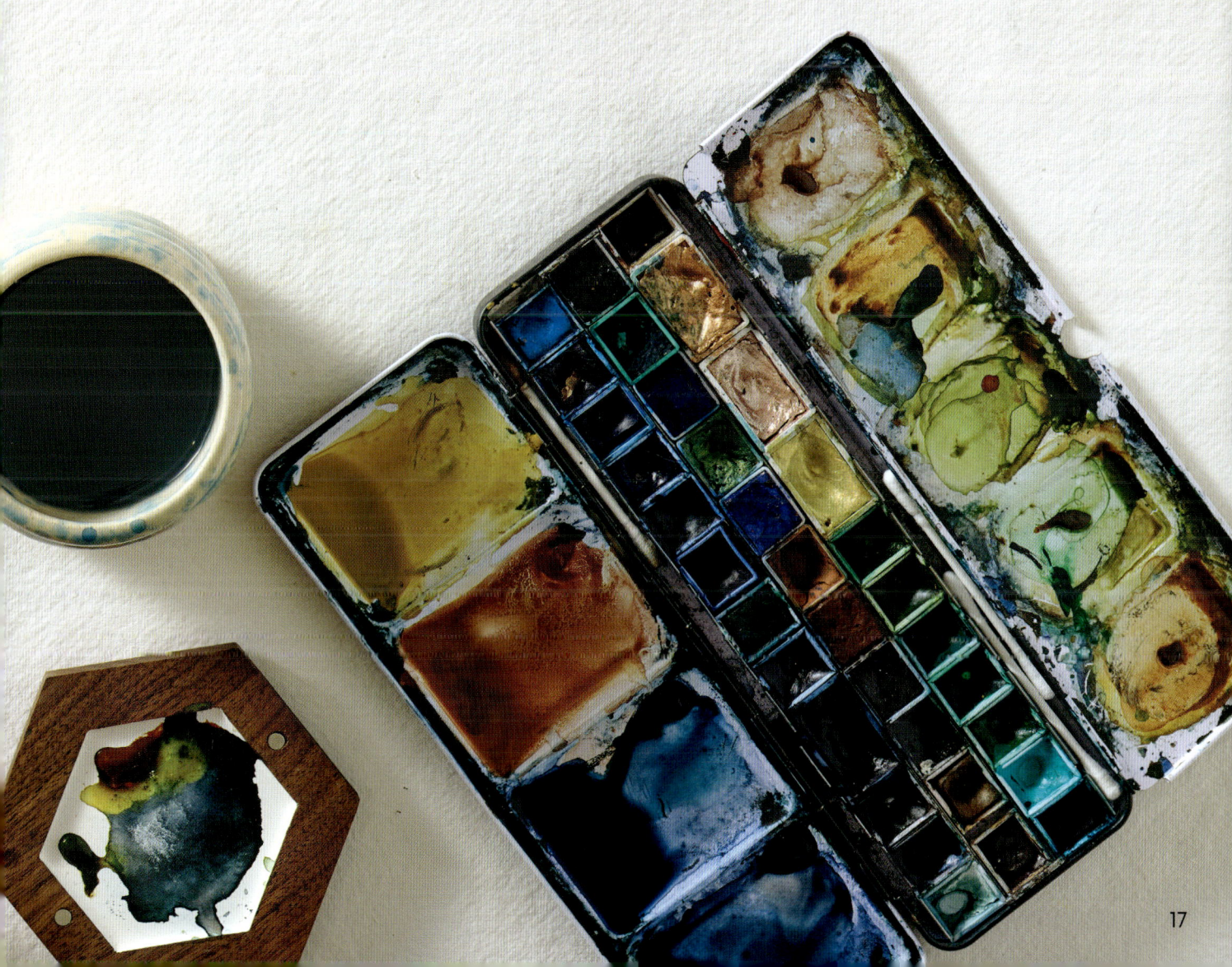

# COLOR MIXING

When preparing to write my books, I noticed that although I haven't referred to the color wheel since my university days, I tend to favor colors that are adjacent on the wheel – these are often referred to as "analogue" palettes. Analogue palettes are a safe bet when creating a harmonious look that's pleasing to the eye, with no one color standing out too prominently. I often use a pop of metallic (gold in particular) to help add highlights and contrast.

*Top Tip:* An example of an analogous palette is using pink, red, and purple together – as they are similar colors from the same side of the color wheel, they can be intermixed and will still look harmonious!

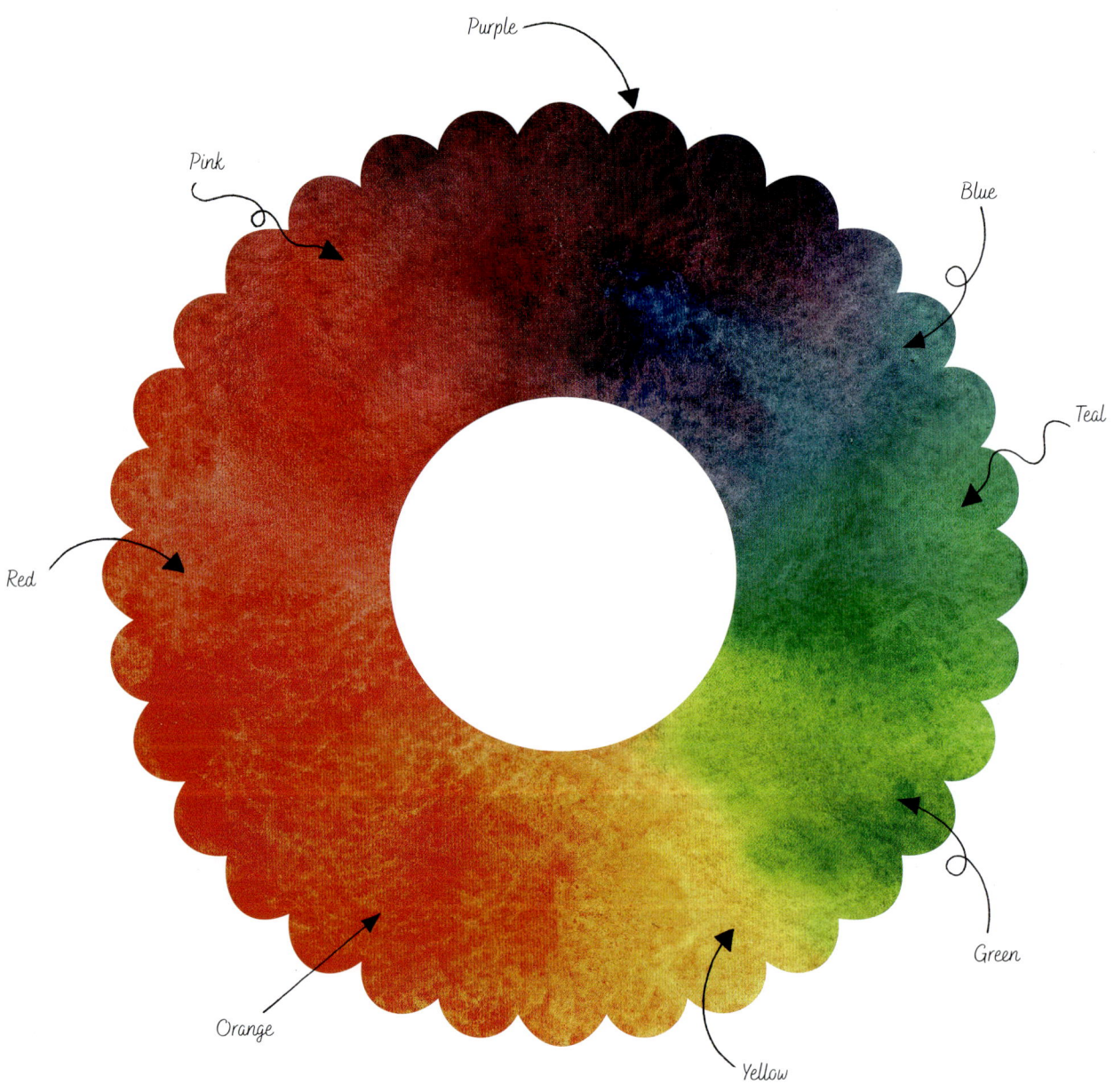

Purple

Pink

Blue

Teal

Red

Green

Orange

Yellow

## SOME OF MY FAVORITE PALETTES

The questions I get asked most at workshops and on social media are about my use of color. I'm often asked to share some of my favorite color combinations, so here are four of my most used palettes. I start with a few analogous colors and then color mix to expand the range: see my mixing recipes below each color!

### Dark & Stormy

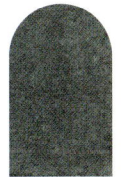 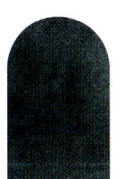 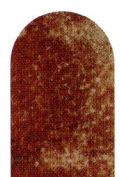 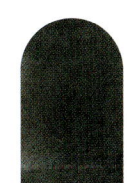 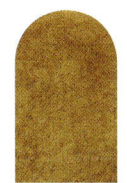 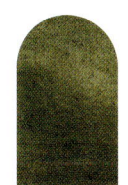 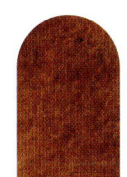

| Payne's Gray | Indigo | Burnt Sienna | Indigo + Burnt Sienna | Yellow Ochre | Yellow Ochre + Indigo | Yellow Ochre + Burnt Sienna |

### Underwater

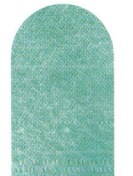 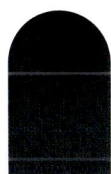 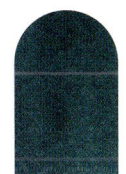 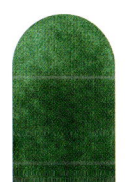 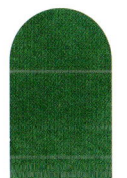  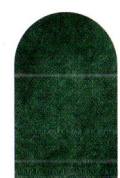

| Aqua | Indigo | Aqua + Indigo | Hooker's Green | Hooker's Green + Aqua | Hooker's Green + Indigo | Hooker's Green + Indigo + Aqua |

### Purple Haze

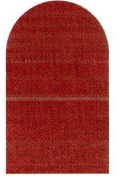 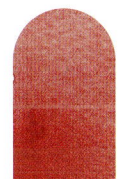 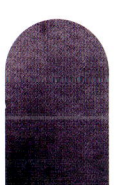 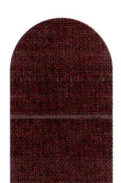 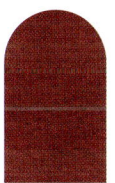 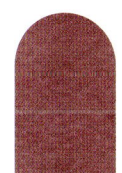 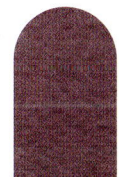

| Permanent Magenta | Permanent Rose | Winsor Violet | Permanent Magenta + Winsor Violet | Permanent Magenta + Permanent Rose + Winsor Violet | Previous mix + water | Permanent Magenta + Winsor Violet + Water |

### Autumnal Warmth

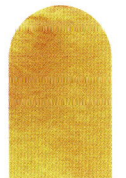 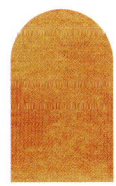 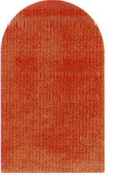 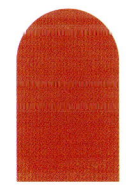 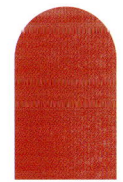 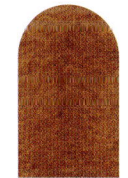 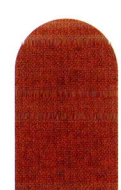

| Cadmium-Free Yellow | Winsor Orange | Cadmium-Free Red | Winsor Orange + Cadmium-Free Red | Alizarin Crimson | Burnt Umber | Burnt Umber + Alizarin Crimson |

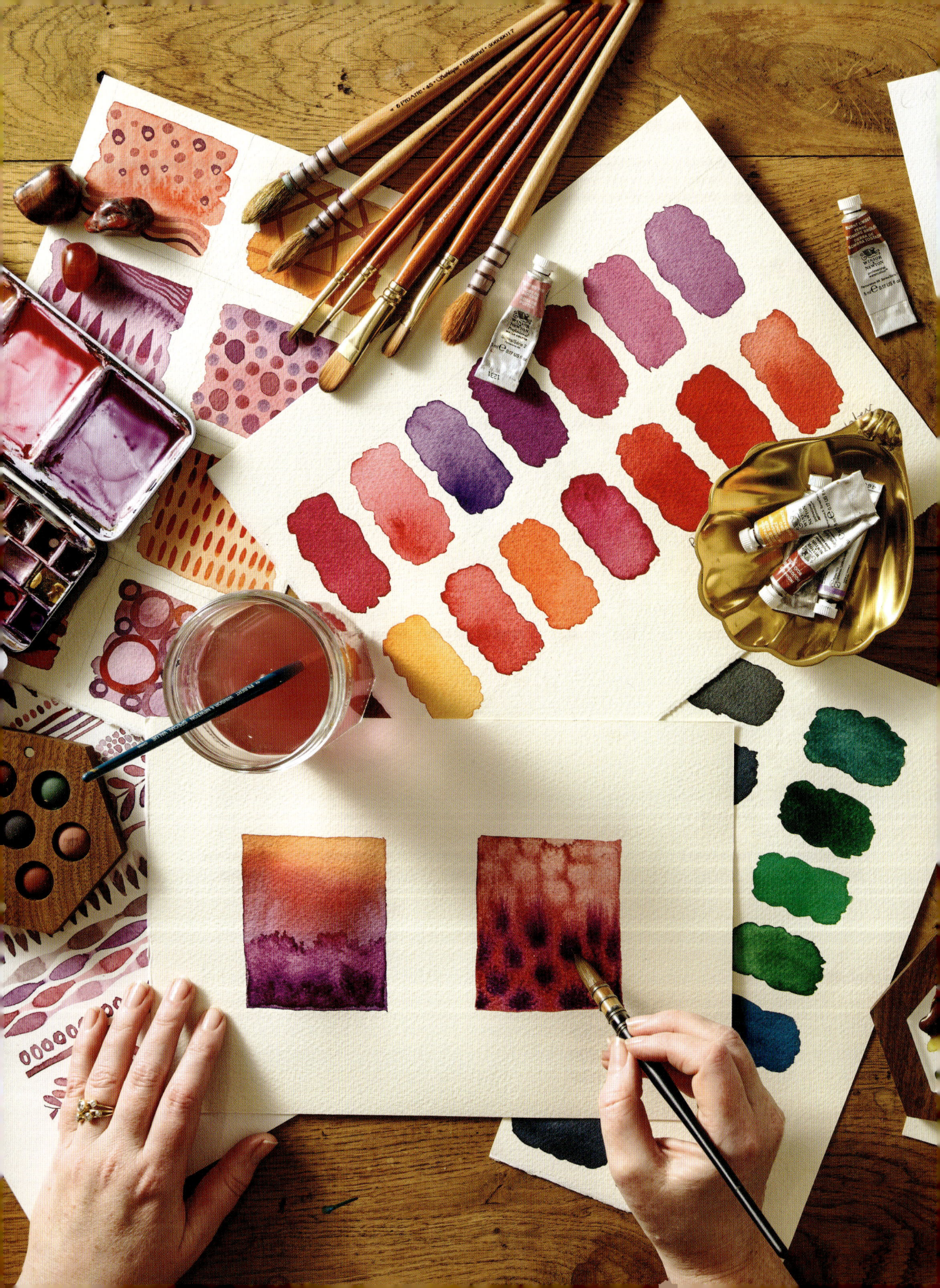

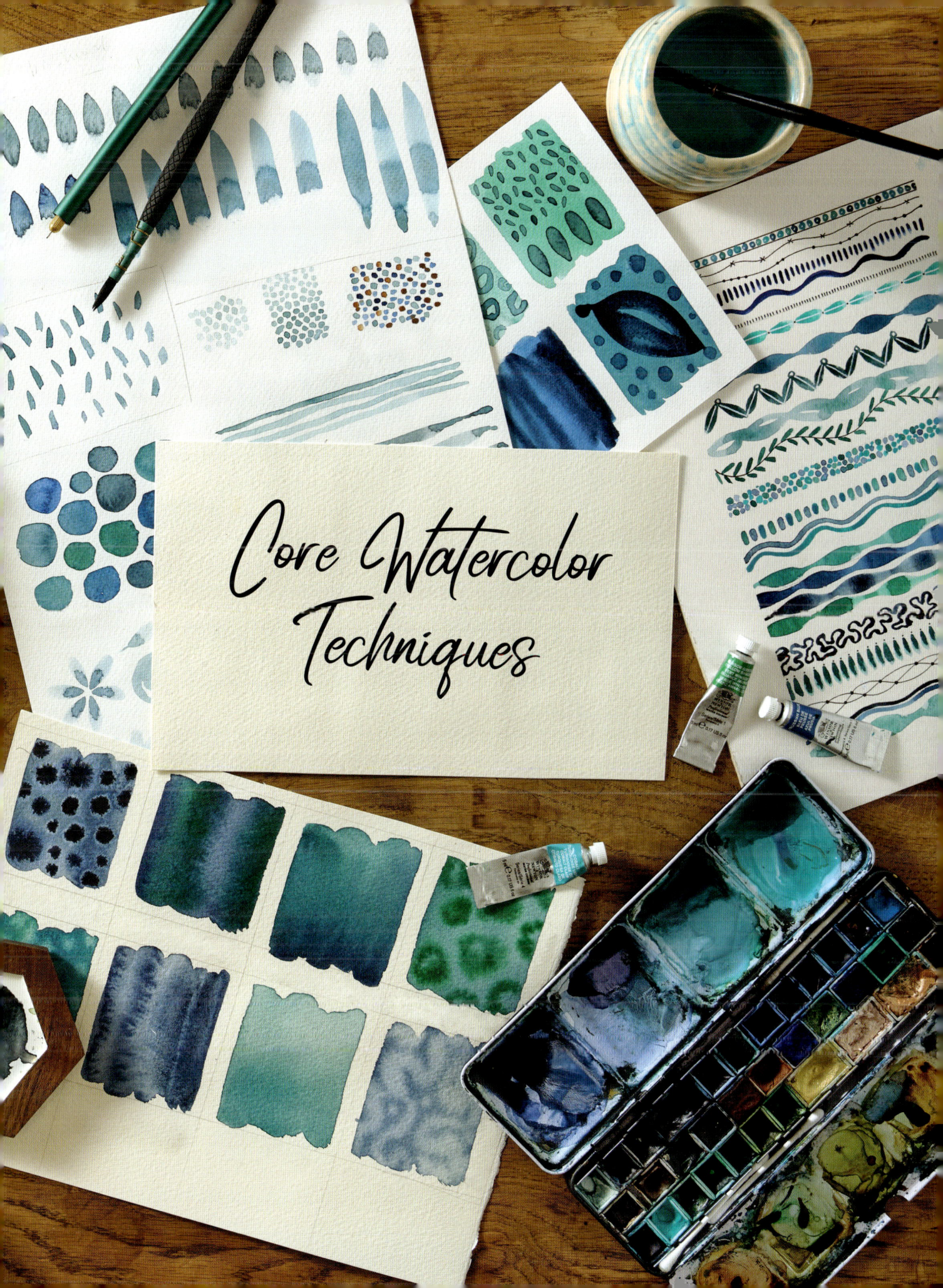

# Core Watercolor Techniques

# WET ON WET

This is the technique of putting down a layer of water or wet paint and then, rather than waiting for it to dry, working straight into it. It gives interesting effects as the new paint reacts with the wet layer beneath. It can create beautiful merges of color, shapes in the paint as the pigments move, and textures that form as the paint dries.

### PAINT ON WATER

1. Paint a square using clean water, and add a color along one edge.

2. Choose a second color to flood the opposite edge.

3. As the paint settles, the water will allow the two colors to merge together.

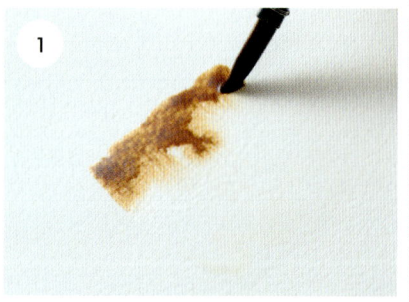

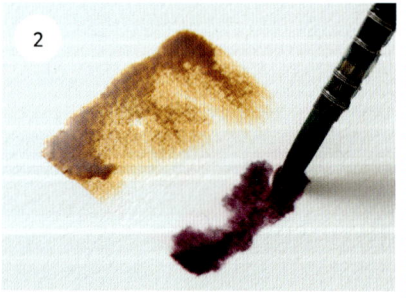

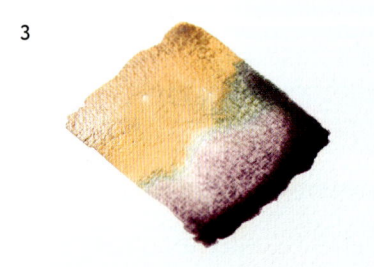

### WATER ON PAINT

1. Paint a square of color, using plenty of paint for a bold effect.

2. Once the square has settled for a few minutes – but is still wet – drop in dots of clean water from the end of your brush to create water blooms.

3. The paint will dry to a textured effect.

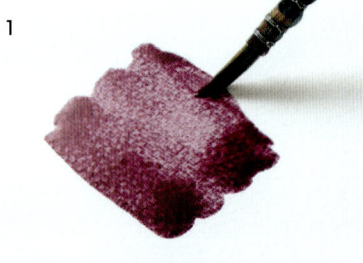

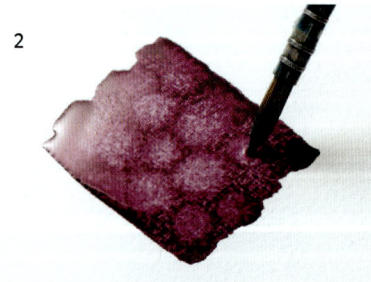

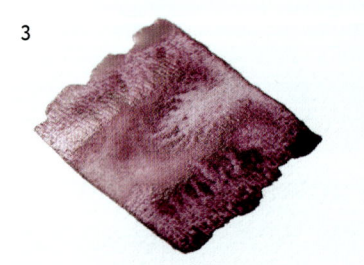

### PAINT ON PAINT

1. Paint a square, making it nice and wet. Here, I've added more paint on one side for interest.

2. From the end of your brush, drop in dots of a second color.

3. New shapes will appear as the new color moves across your base color.

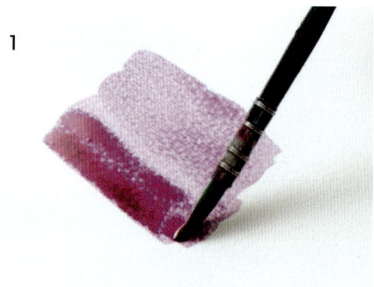

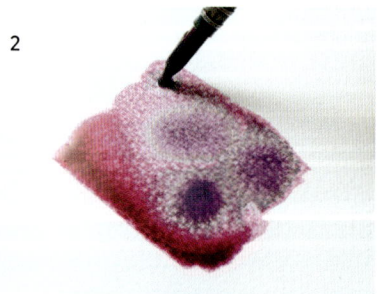

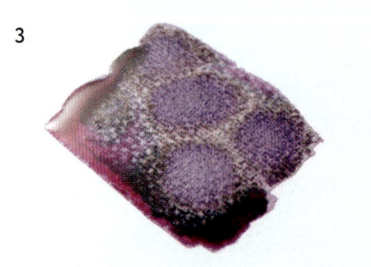

# WET ON DRY

Wet on dry is as simple as it sounds: adding wet paint to a layer of dry paint. This lets you create defined shapes and stops colors from mixing. It's a great way to add details and texture to a dry wash that looks a bit flat – you can see here how simple shapes can add lots of visual interest.

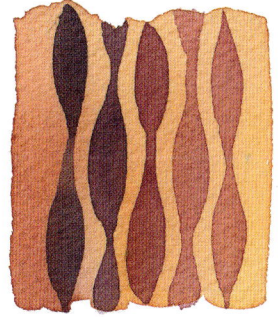

Wavy brush lines made with a quill brush

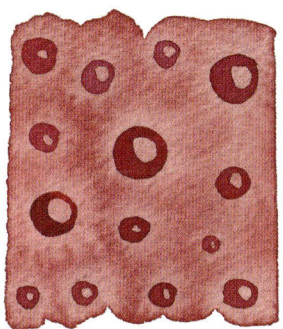

Loose watercolor circles inside water blooms

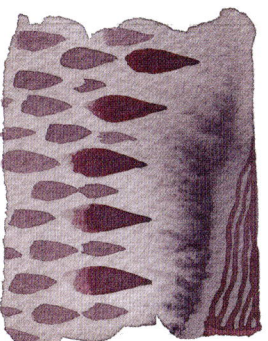

Teardrop brush stamps with wavy lines

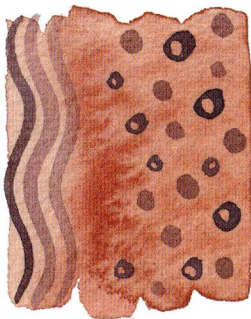

Wavy lines and watercolor circles

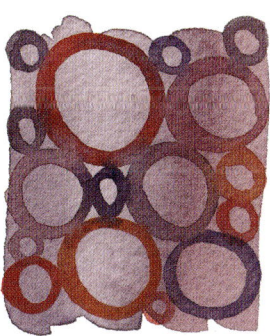

Large circles with smaller ones to fill gaps

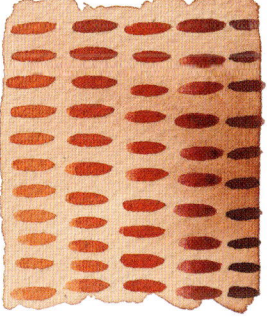

Rows of brush stamps made with a round brush

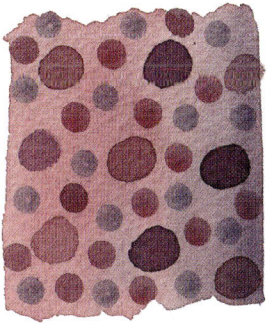

Freehand painted circles with cotton bud (Q-tip) stamps

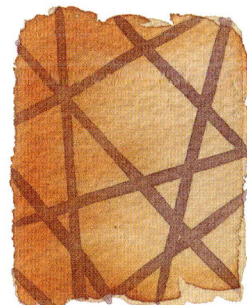

Freehand painted grid lines

## ADDING WET-ON-DRY DETAILS

Start with a square of fully dry watercolor, then paint wet details. The dry base allows for defined marks.

Here, I have accentuated dried water bloom by painting soft watercolor circles. Once dry, I added a center to each one.

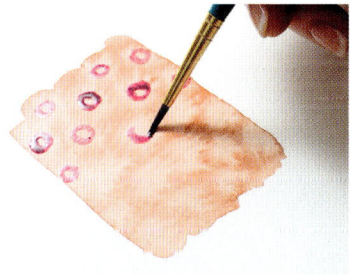

Accentuating dry texture

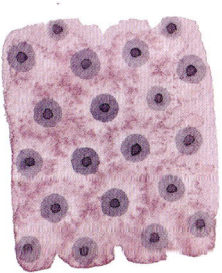

Layered circles and spots

# MARK-MAKING DIRECTORY

Mark marking transforms watercolor paintings into mixed media. Brush marks, pens, and inks can all add texture, detail, highlights, and contrast. These details accentuate the areas of the work you love, and can "save" any areas that need a helping hand.

## STAMPED SHAPES

Most of the stamped shapes, patterns, and textures in the projects in this book are created using basic equipment. Here are some simple ideas.

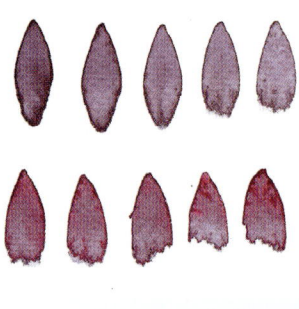

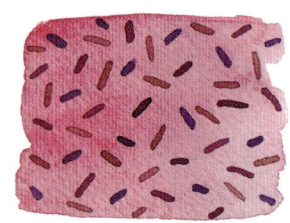

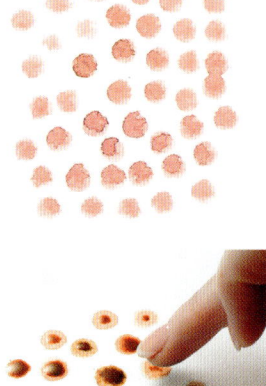

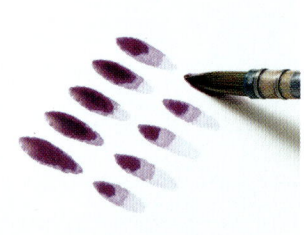

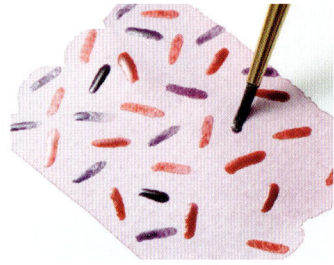

*Brush stamps*

*Stamping across a plain, dry wash*

*Fingerprints*

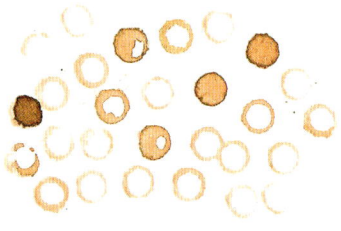

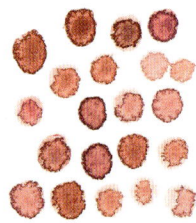

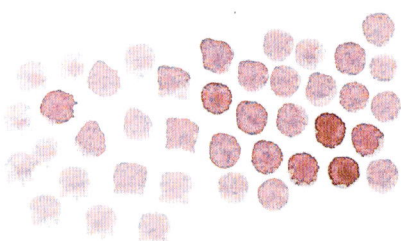

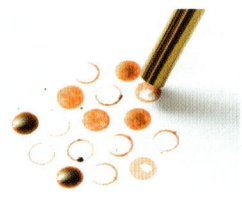

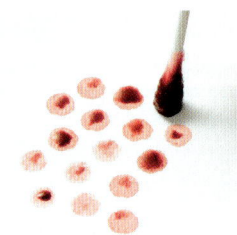

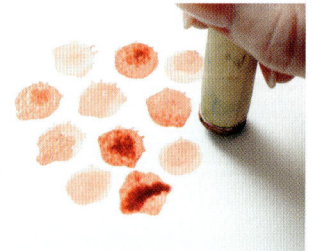

*Metal drinking straw circles*

*Cotton bud (Q-tip) marks*

*Foam stamp marks*

## PAINTED SPOTS AND CIRCLES

Lovely soft, organic circles and spots work beautifully in all sorts of compositions, from decorative borders and sea pebbles to the center stamens of abstract flowers. Here are a few of the basic spots and circles I like to use in my work – try them out and experiment with a loose, wet paint mix and different brushes to discover more of your own!

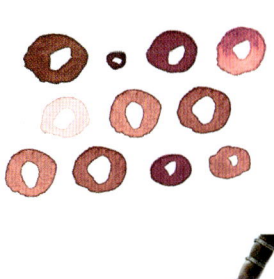

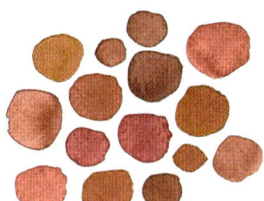

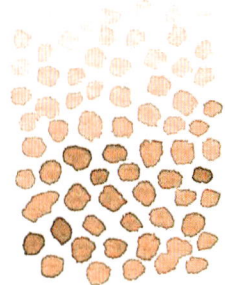

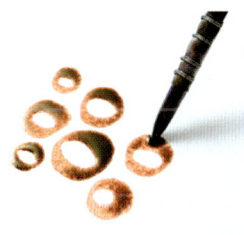

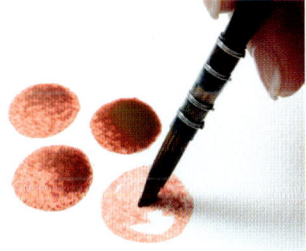

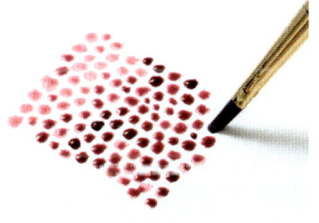

*Loose circles with brush*

*Painted in circles*

*Raindrop spots*

## LINES

You can make interesting lines by loading a quill brush with lots of very watery paint, then using either the tip or the base of your brush, and by varying the pressure on the brush as you move. Have fun and play, and soon these movements will become intuitive!

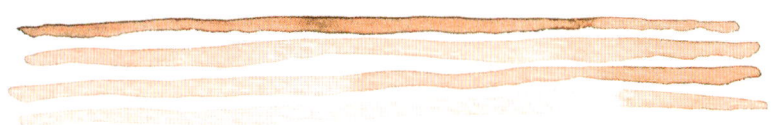

*Painted lines*

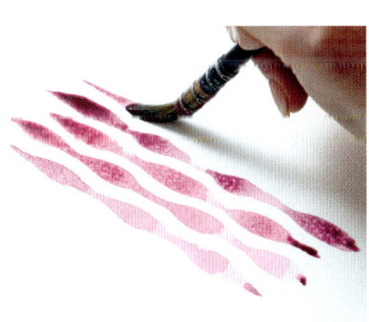

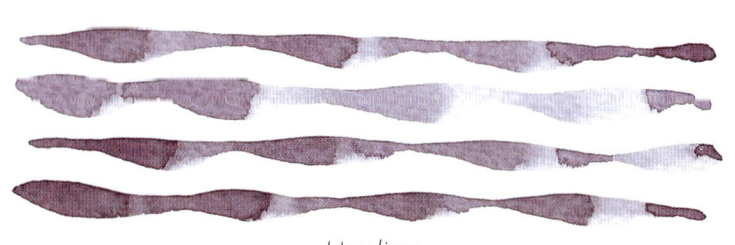

*Wavy lines*

## BASIC MARKS WITH PENS

Pen marks can be made on most surfaces and backgrounds, and although simple can create a dynamic effect.

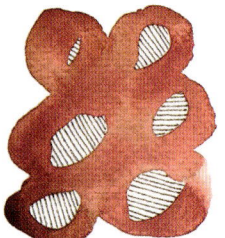

*Black line work:*
black fineliner pen

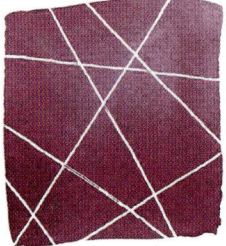

*Intersecting lines:*
white gel pen

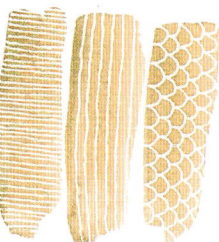

*White line work:*
white gel pen

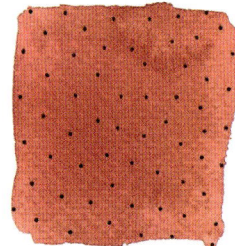

*Black spots:*
black fineliner pen

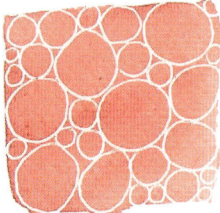

*Circles in various sizes:*
white paint pen

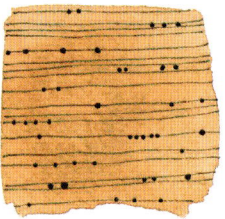

*Stripes and dot work:*
black fineliner pen

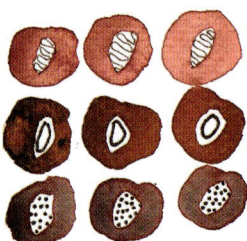

*Spots, lines, and circles:*
black fineliner pen

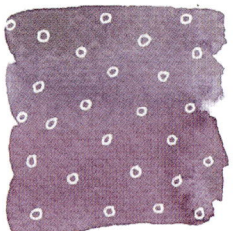

*Small circles:*
white gel pen

## PEN MARKS GUIDED BY BLOOMS AND BRUSHWORK

Be inspired by the paint effects in your work – whether they were intentional or a happy accident!

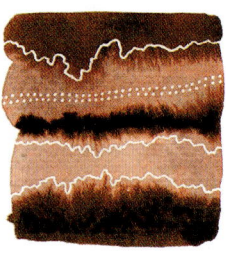

*Fault lines and dots:*
white gel pen

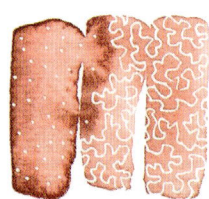

*Dots and squiggles:*
white gel pen

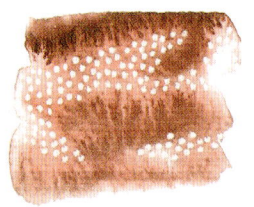

*Large cluster spots:*
white paint pen

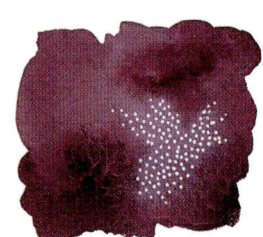

*Spot clusters:*
white gel pen

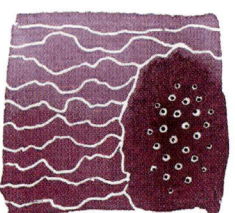

*Lines and spots:*
white paint pen +
black fineliner pen

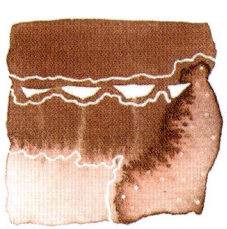

*Fault lines:*
white paint pen

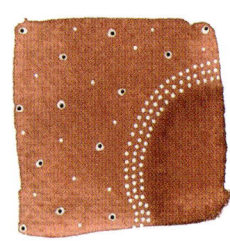

*White dots, rows, and spots:*
white gel pen +
black fineliner pen

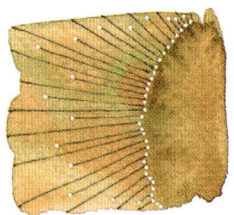

*Sunburst lines with spots:*
white gel pen +
black fineliner pen

# MASKING BORDERS

I use masking tape mainly for creating crisp borders around my paintings. The border gives your artwork room to breathe and allows it to stand out against the clean white paper. I use lots of strong colors and textures, so the contrast is all the more vibrant, but even the softest colors and textures benefit from the straight line created by a masked border.

## TIPS FOR MASKING YOUR BORDER

- **Selecting a size:** Choose the best width of border – and therefore masking tape – for your painting.

- **Testing your tape:** After much trial and error, I found a tape that doesn't lift or tear the paper when removed (*see Materials: Masking Supplies*). However, always test your tape on a scrap (or the back) of the paper before using it on your artwork.

- **Creating a strong bond:** Ensure that each strip is well adhered to the paper by firmly rubbing the inner edges and corners of the tape.

- **Checking the corners:** Take special notice of the corners where the tape overlaps. This is the area where paint is most likely to bleed under the tape.

- **Removing the tape:** To remove the tape safely, without ripping the paper, peel it away slowly, pulling it toward you at an acute angle. If you pull the tape "up" rather than across the page, it can lift and ruin the paper below.

- **Using heat:** If your tape proves difficult to remove, run a warm blow-dryer over it to melt the glue slightly – this should make it much easier for you to peel away.

## CREATING CRISP BORDERS

1. Starting with the long sides, align the outside edge of the tape with the edge of the paper for neat, vertical borders. Repeat for the short sides, overlapping the tape at each corner to ensure no paint seeps underneath. Use your fingertips to smooth down the tape's inner edges and corners.

2. Paint your piece – don't flood the tape with water or paint, but don't be afraid to work right up to and over it.

3. When the paint has completely dried, remove the tape from the short sides first, gently pulling it back on itself to avoid damaging the paper.

4. Now remove the tape from the long sides to reveal a lovely sharp border!

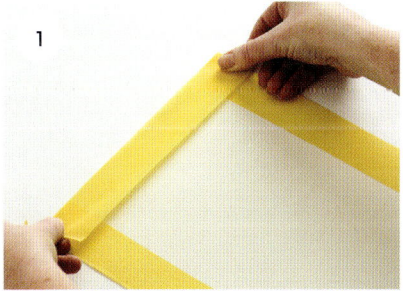
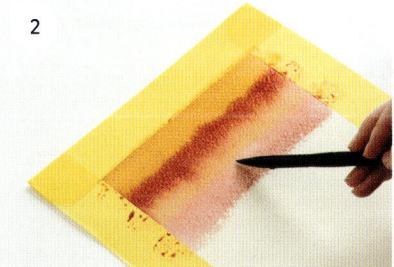
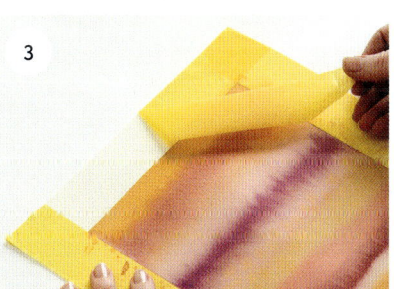
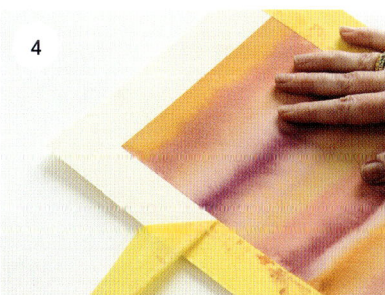

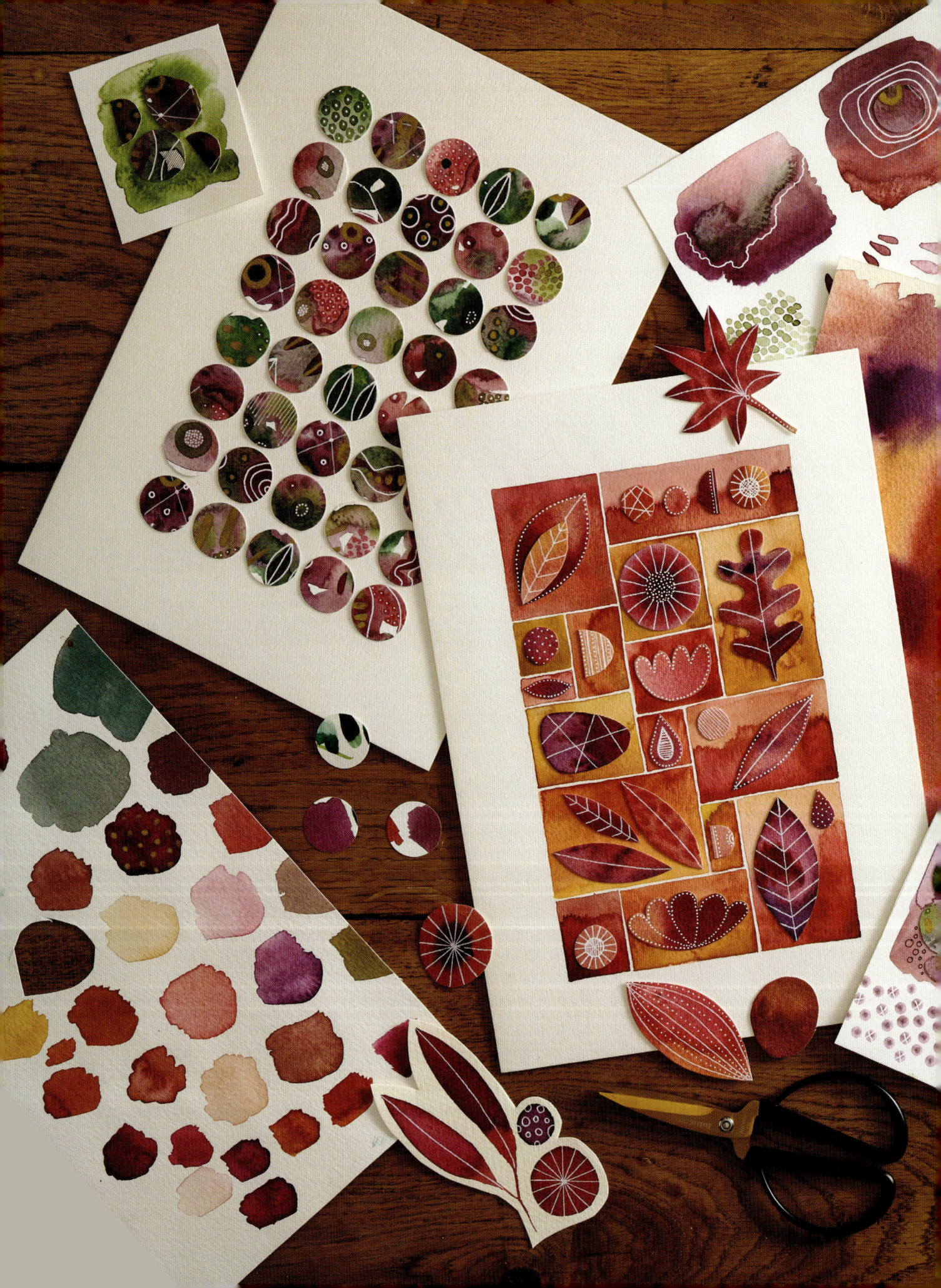

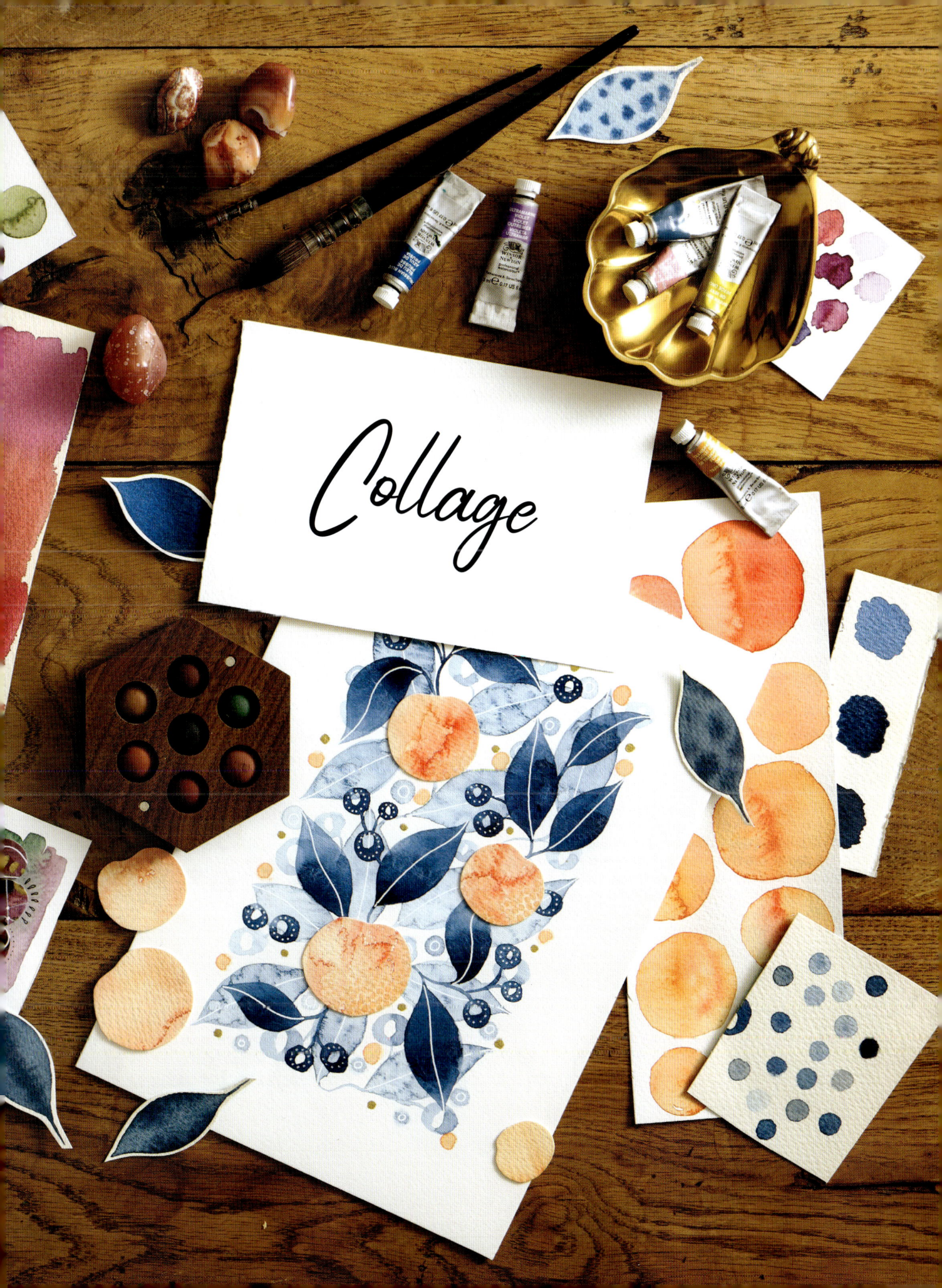

Collage

# Collage Techniques

Definition: *The word collage comes from the French verb* **coller**, *which means "to glue".*

Ok, so I'm going to start this techniques section with a confession. Don't worry, it's nothing dark and sinister! Rather I'm owning up to not being a collage expert, which might come as a relief if you're just starting out with collage too. There's lots of information available in collage books and on the internet, and I don't have the knowledge (or the space in the section) to go through all of the technical terms and techniques, so instead I'm going to give you the inside track on what works for me. Rightly or wrongly, the information in this section is what I like to use and reflects the way I use collage in my artwork. I hope you find it useful!

## GETTING STARTED WITH COLLAGE

My first foray into collage was back at school when I used to use acrylic paints. I remember peeling the dried paint off my palette and being amazed by the cool texture and colors that each peeling contained. I even created an abstract piece of art by sticking my discarded paint onto a canvas. I loved the myriad colors and textures!

Fast forward to my current art practice, and I have rediscovered collage through a passion for recycling. I love the idea of giving a second life to discarded work, and due to all my workshops over the last few years, I had many test sheets leftover from demonstrating techniques. These had great textures and colors but no composition. I decided to recycle them to create new work, and my collage era had begun! Sometimes I create background colors and textures to use for my work, but much of the time I use abandoned pieces that I have lying around in the studio.

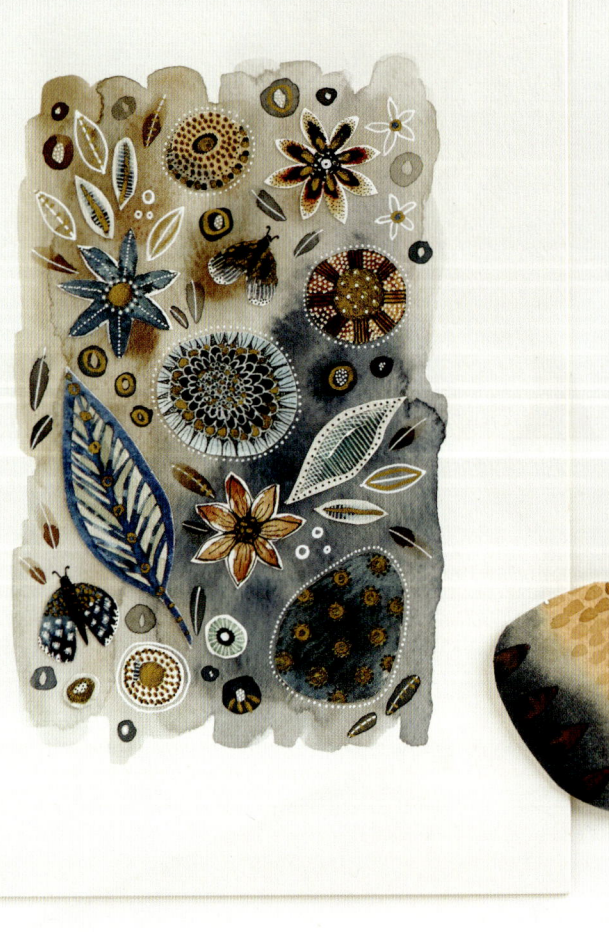

## COLLAGE MATERIALS/PAPERS

To start your collage journey you need materials, the first being your items to collage – what I call "collage fodder". Your collage fodder could include fabric, found objects, plastic, natural materials such as leaves and wood... you name it, you can use it! I work mainly with papers, and here are some of the papers I like to use most:

- Painted paper – this is what we will use in the projects over the following pages
- Printed papers – marks made on paper with a gelli plate or rubber stamps
- Old test sheets or experiments
- Old magazines, book pages, or newspaper print
- Handmade papers

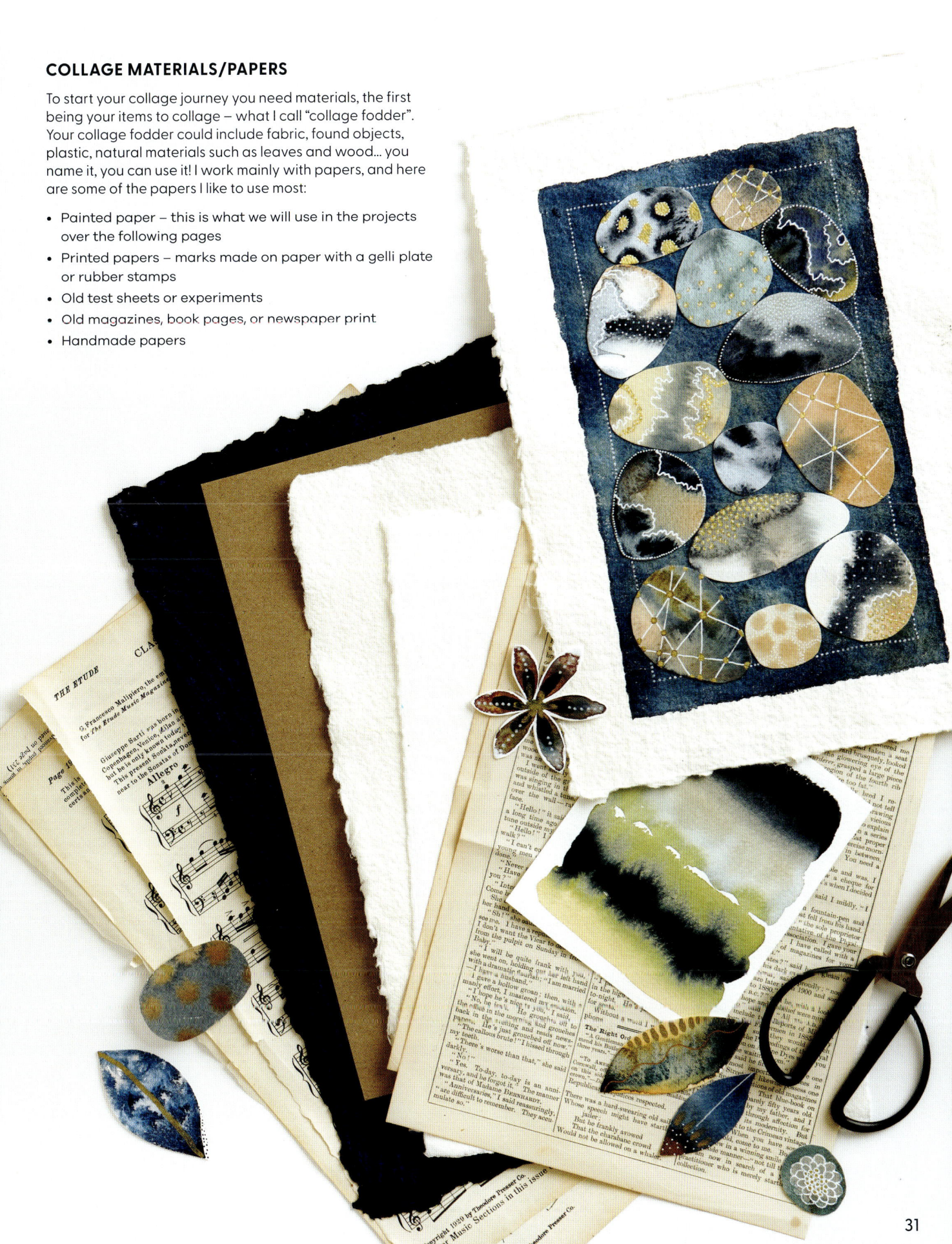

## CREATING YOUR SHAPES

Once you have your collage fodder, there are various options for how to apply it to your paper. Do you want distinct shapes or are you using them to create a background? As we work mostly with paper and scissors for the projects in this book, this is what I'll show you here, but remember that you can collage with all sorts of materials! You might like to try the following cutting tools:

- **Scissors:** Choose large and small depending on how intricate the cutting needs to be.

- **Craft knife or scalpel:** This is a good for details but requires a steady hand!

- **Utility knife:** Also known as a Stanley knife or box cutter, this is good for harder to cut and thicker pieces.

- **Ripping/tearing:** A great technique for creating organic shapes and rough edges.

- **Punches:** These small devices help you to punch out distinct shapes. I've used a circle punch in the projects but you can get all sorts of shapes like stars, flowers, hearts, trees, and more.

*Top Tip:* Plan what you want to achieve with your piece. Do you want straight or rough edges? Textured paper or smooth? Do you want your collaged pieces to stand out or blend in? What percentage of the piece will be collage materials?

## CUTTING OUT PAPER SHAPES

### MATERIALS

- Watercolor paints and your choice of paper
- Pencil
- Double-sided adhesive sheet or tape, if using
- Scissors

### METHOD

1. First paint a watercolor background from which you will cut your shapes. Leave it to dry completely.

2. Decide what shapes you'd like to create, and draw as many as will fit onto the painted paper. You can draw on the back of your work, but it will be easier to see any lovely effects that you want to include if you draw on the painted front.

3. If you are using a double-sided adhesive sheet or tape to apply your collage elements, apply it now (see opposite), then simply cut out your shapes following your pencil guidelines.

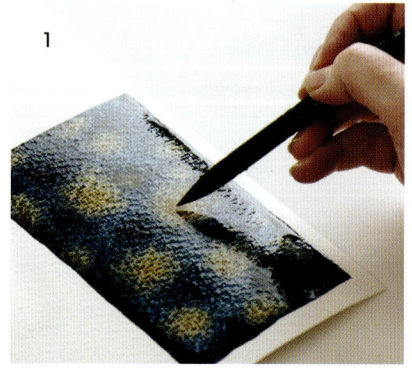

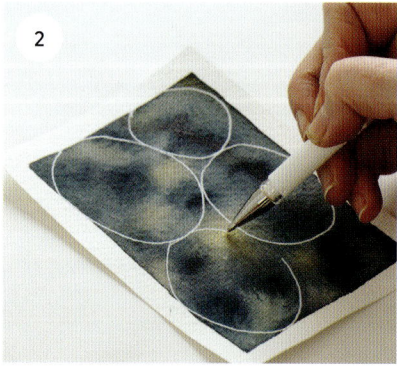

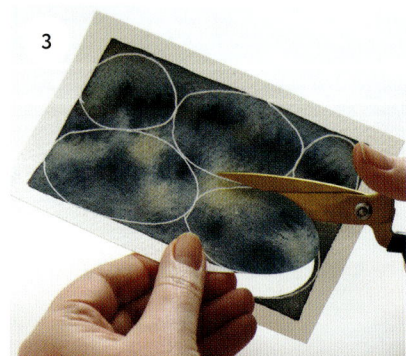

## ADHESIVES AND GLUES

I know a lot of artists will use glue sticks, liquid glue, or even wallpaper paste to attach their collage materials. These are good when you are building up many layers or if you're using transparent papers like tissue or fine handmade papers. I prefer to attach my pieces using double-sided adhesive sheets or sticky tape, so this is what I will show you here. It gives a lovely finish with no glue bubbles, mess, or lifting edges.

*Top Tip:* If I'm adhering large pieces (attaching old book pages to artboard before painting on them, for instance), I also like to use spray mount. Feel free to find what works for you!

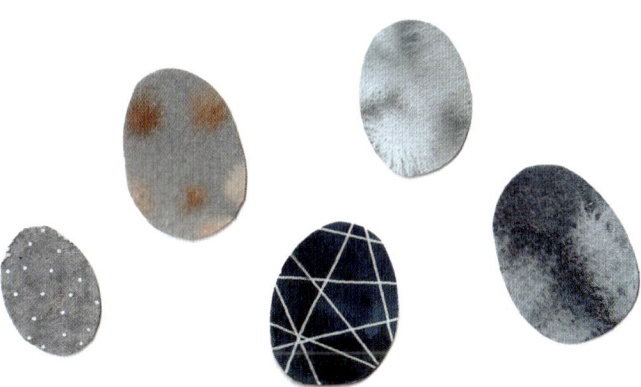

## BACKING WITH DOUBLE-SIDED ADHESIVE SHEETS

### MATERIALS

- A painted background that you want to use for collage shapes
- Double-sided adhesive sheet

### METHOD

1. Start by removing the paper backing from the adhesive sheet.

2. Align the sticky backing with the back of your watercolor paper and smooth down.

3. Once the full sheet has adhered firmly, you can draw and cut out your shapes (see opposite). Then peel the backing away from your 'sticker' – and it's ready to stick onto your work!

*Top Tip:* If you can't find sheets, simply apply double-sided tape, butting the strips up closely together to fill the paper.

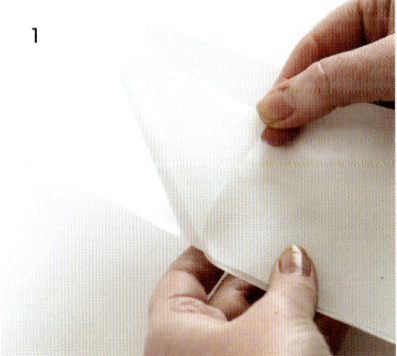

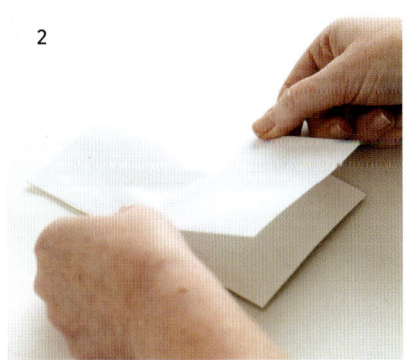

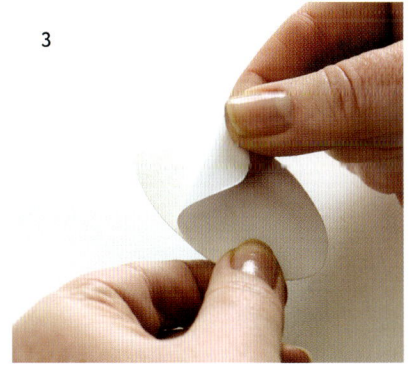

# Graphic Circles

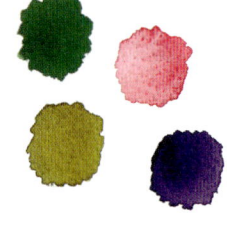

This project is great fun, looks fab, and is very satisfying: what's not to like? Using a lever punch to create uniform circles gives a cool graphic look, which is a nice contrast to the loose organic textures contained within. Punching out the circles is addictive – I love it when the punched circle reveals itself, like a tiny miniature composition!

## MATERIALS

- Winsor & Newton professional watercolors
- Daler Rowney Aquafine Artboard
- Bockingford 300g cold pressed watercolor paper
- Da Vinci Casaneo quill brush - size 2
- Uni-ball Signo pen – white, 1mm (Broad)
- Winsor & Newton Drawing Ink – gold
- Fiskars Lever Punch: Circle – 2.5cm (1 in) or cut circles by hand if you don't have a punch)
- Double-sided adhesive sheets (double-sided tape or glue will work too)

## COLOR CHOICES

Here I've been inspired by gemstones and jewel-like tones of purples, pinks, and greens, with lots of gold thrown in for good measure. As this piece is pure abstract, there's no need to stick to a particular palette – it will look amazing in pretty much any shade – but include darker and lighter areas to ensure some nice contrasts in your piece.

### WINSOR & NEWTON COLOR REFERENCES

- Hooker's Green
- Olive Green
- Permanent Magenta
- Winsor Violet (Dioxazine)

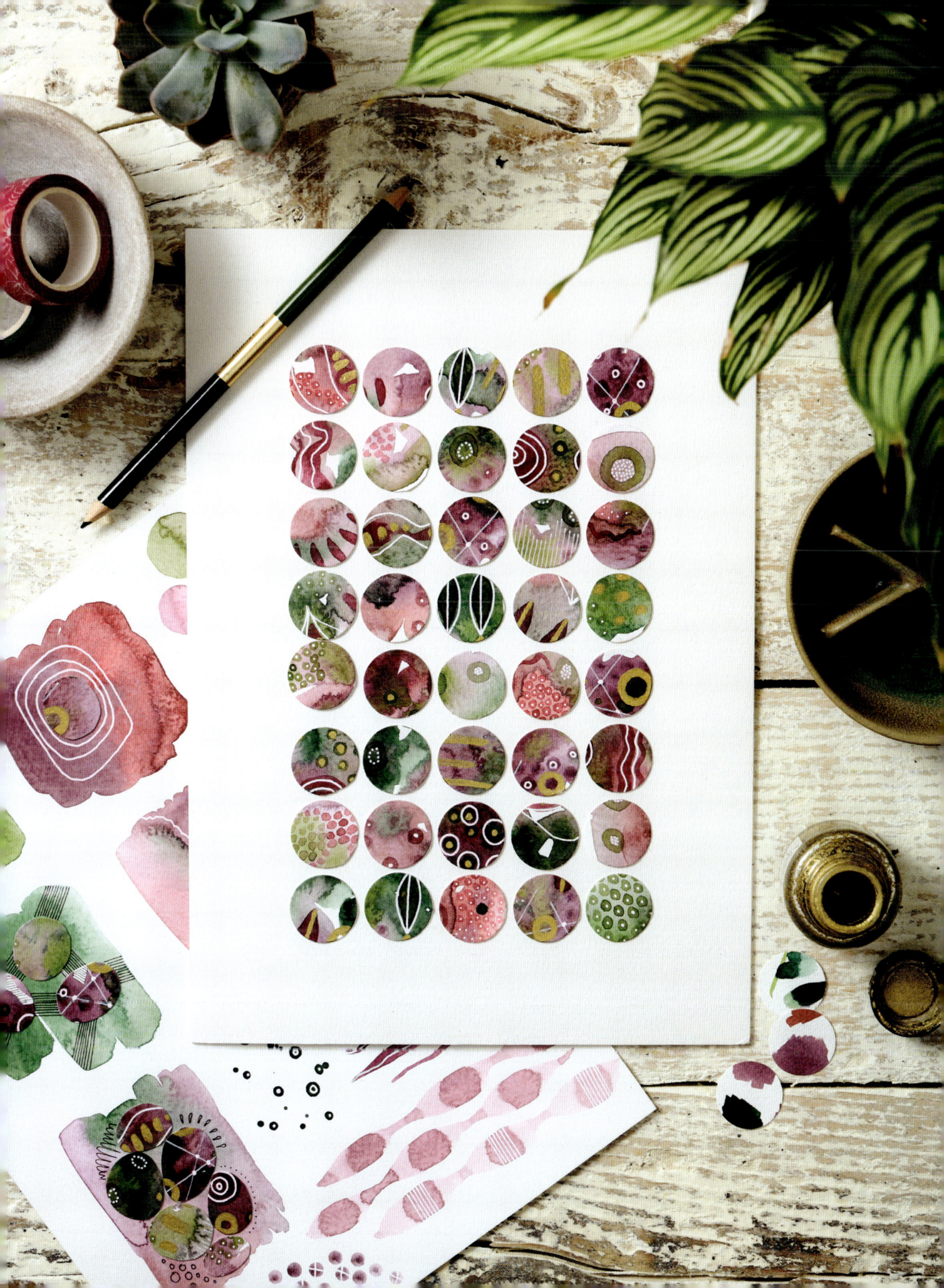

## Step 1: **PAINTING YOUR BACKGROUND**

To start this project, mix up some paint washes of various strengths. I also like to create some extra, softer shades by color mixing. Now, start to apply your mixes randomly to your watercolor paper, letting the colors mix and merge. Keep some colors deep and some soft – you want a real variety of tone and texture here. Make sure you leave some white areas, too – don't cover the whole page. Leave to dry completely.

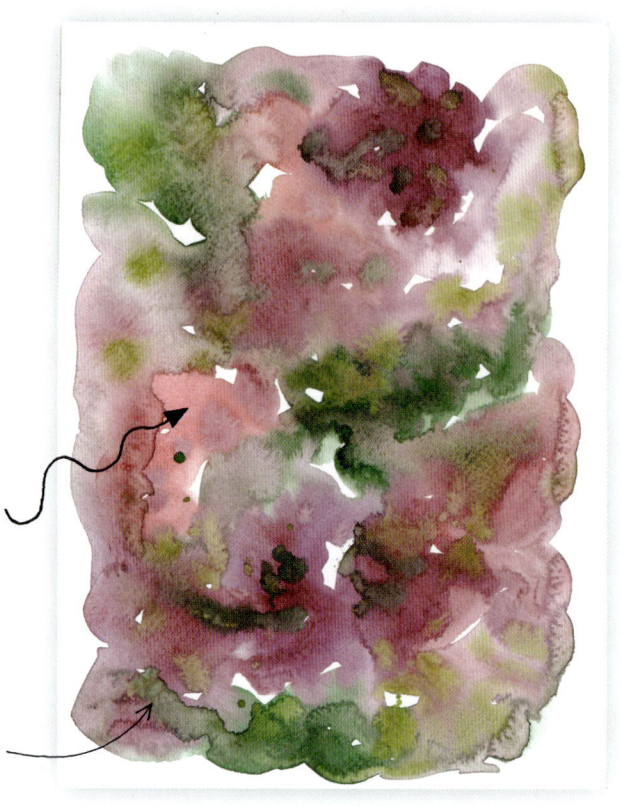

*I've mixed pink and purple together to create a new, softer shade.*

*Working really wet at this stage creates blooms and areas of texture, especially where the paint pools. Lean into the flow and enjoy happy accidents and blends!*

## Step 2: **ADDING DETAILS TO THE BACKGROUND**

Layer two is where I add wet to dry paint (see Core Watercolor Techniques: Wet on Dry) to add nice defined shapes to the soft organic background. I've used my brush as a stamp to make teardrop shapes (see Core Watercolor Techniques: Mark-Making Directory) as well as painting circles and dots, which can help add interest to any areas that feel a bit flat or boring!

*Be sure to vary the size and shapes of your painted details. Adding large bold marks as well as smaller details will add interest to your finished piece.*

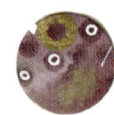
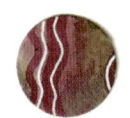

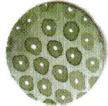
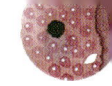

## Step 3: WHITE EMBELLISHMENTS

Very much like the previous step, you want to use this stage to add contrast and interest. White is great for areas that look a little dark, as it will brighten them up – at this stage you coul also use black embellishments if you have areas that are too light or look "wishy washy".

*Once again, variety is key at this stage. Try curved and straight lines, small dots, and large circles – you want to fill the page with exciting marks!*

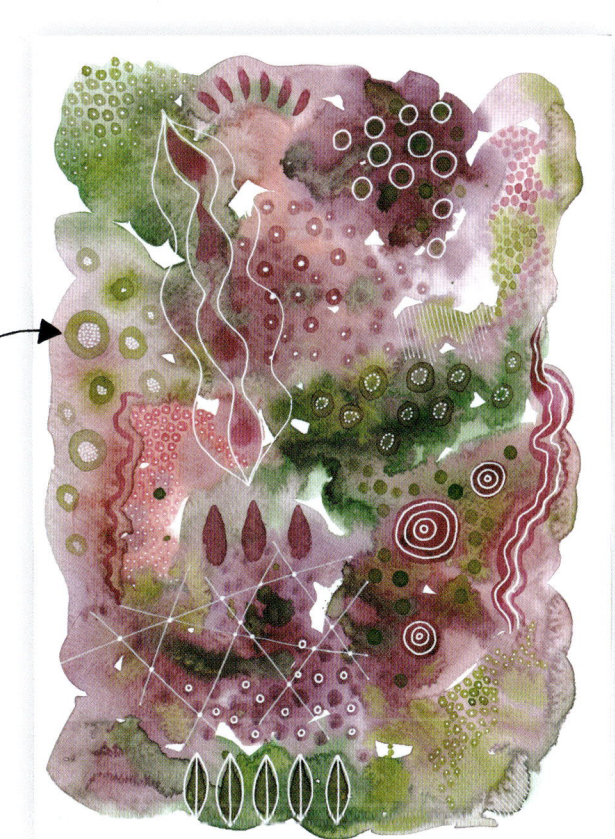

## Step 4: GOLD EMBELLISHMENTS

Once you are happy with the white elements, we want to use gold ink to add shine to key areas of the composition. Add rows of gold spots to areas to which you want to draw attention.

*Add rows or clusters of gold dots and spots for emphasis.*

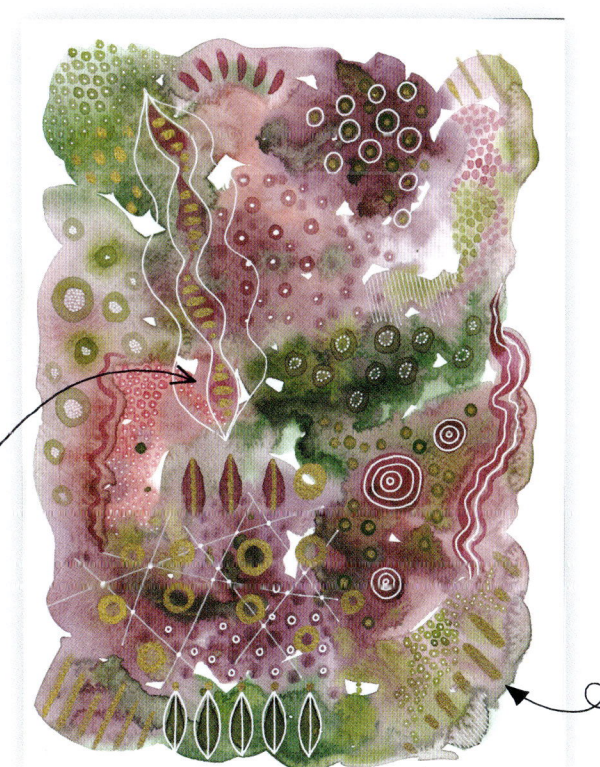

*You can also use gold to cover any areas that feel muddy or that you're not so happy with – as the gold is opaque, it can hide a multitude of sins!*

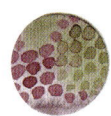
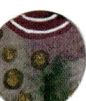

## Step 5: PUNCHING OUT THE CIRCLES

Once your background is fully dry and you're happy with it, add a double-sided adhesive sheet to the back (see Getting Started with Collage). This means that once you have punched out your circles, you can simply peel off the backing paper and stick them straight onto your background.

With the adhesive sheet applied, use the lever punch to create circle cutouts. I like to start from one edge and move along, punching as I go! Keep punching until you've used up the whole background.

*If you have a favorite section of your painting, place the punch carefully to ensure you contain the details within a circle.*

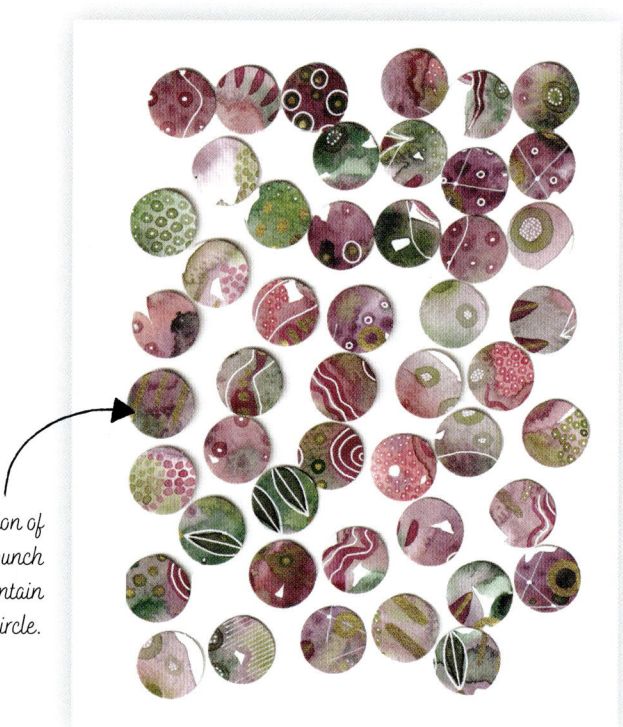

## Step 6: LAYING OUT YOUR FINAL PIECE

Once all the circles are punched out, you're ready to lay them out in a composition. Here I've created a simple grid pattern, working from the top of the sheet to the bottom, but feel free to arrange your circles as you like – in rows, circles, squares... go wild!

*Top Tip:* Any spare circles are great for making greeting cards or gift tags, or simply use them like stickers and attach to your notebook or paint tin. If you have larger areas of paper left, use scissors to cut out random shapes – you name it, the world is your oyster!

# More Inspiration

Here I have taken my Graphic Circles collage piece to the next level by adding cutouts to a block composition. I have also decorated the punched circles with celestial moons and suns, reflecting the stars and clouds that I created in the blocks. It's another way to use your circle punch that gives a totally different look and feel.

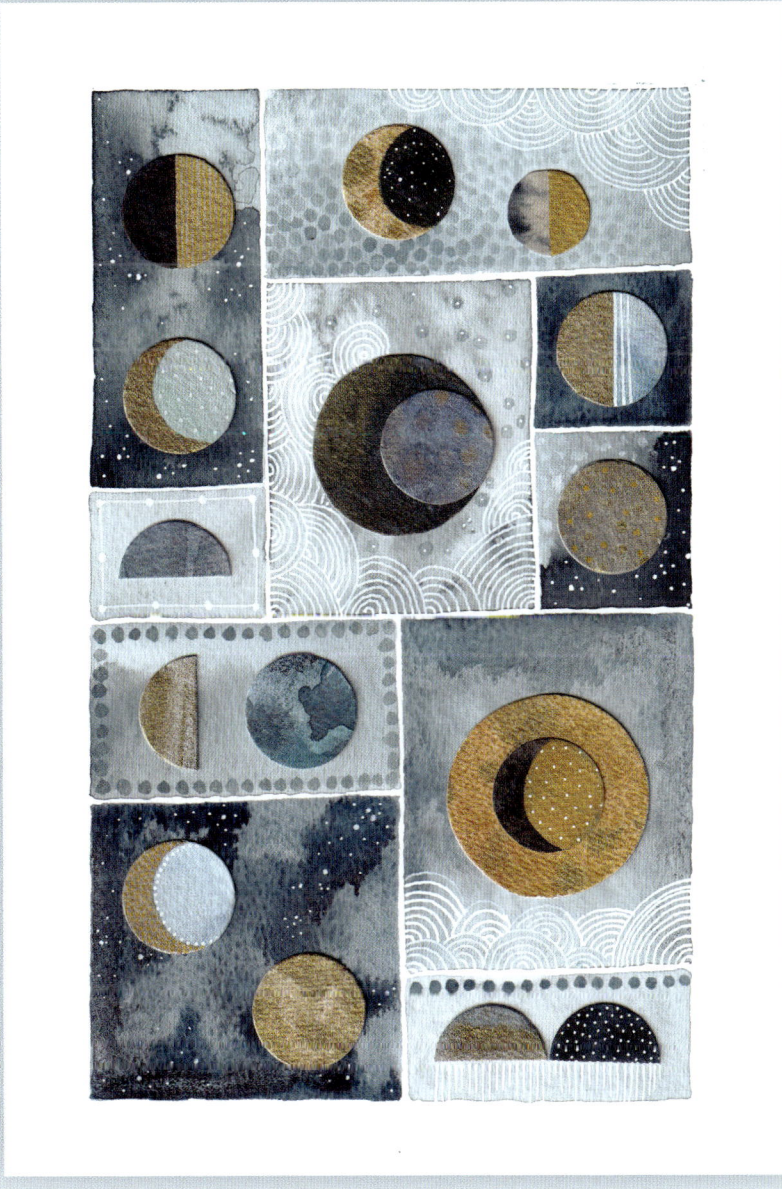

# Perfect Peaches

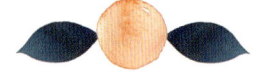

This project is a lovely simple way to play with collage materials. It uses textured paper to add bright vibrant peaches to layers of painted leaves. This helps to create depth and great contrasts in color and texture. I've kept the embellishment pared back to stop it looking too fussy, but feel free to add in extra layers of black, white, and metallic details.

## MATERIALS

- Winsor & Newton professional watercolors
- Daler Rowney Aquafine Artboard
- Bockingford 300g rough watercolor paper (cold press would be fine too)
- Da Vinci Casaneo quill brush – size 2
- Uni-ball Signo pen – white, 1mm (Broad)
- Winsor & Newton Drawing Ink – gold
- Sharp scissors
- Double-sided adhesive sheets (double-sided tape or glue will work too)
- Pencil

## COLOR CHOICES

With this fruity project, you have endless possibilities. Here I've used peaches, but you could try apples, oranges, pears, figs, grapes, and more; just alter the color accordingly! I could have used conventional green leaves here, but I like the contrast between the blue and orange. Feel free to go ahead and use the colors that you're drawn to when you sit down to paint.

### WINSOR & NEWTON COLOR REFERENCES

- Cadmium-Free Red
- Cadmium-Free Yellow
- Chinese White
- Indigo
- Payne's Gray
- Prussian Blue
- Winsor Orange

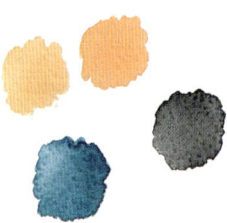

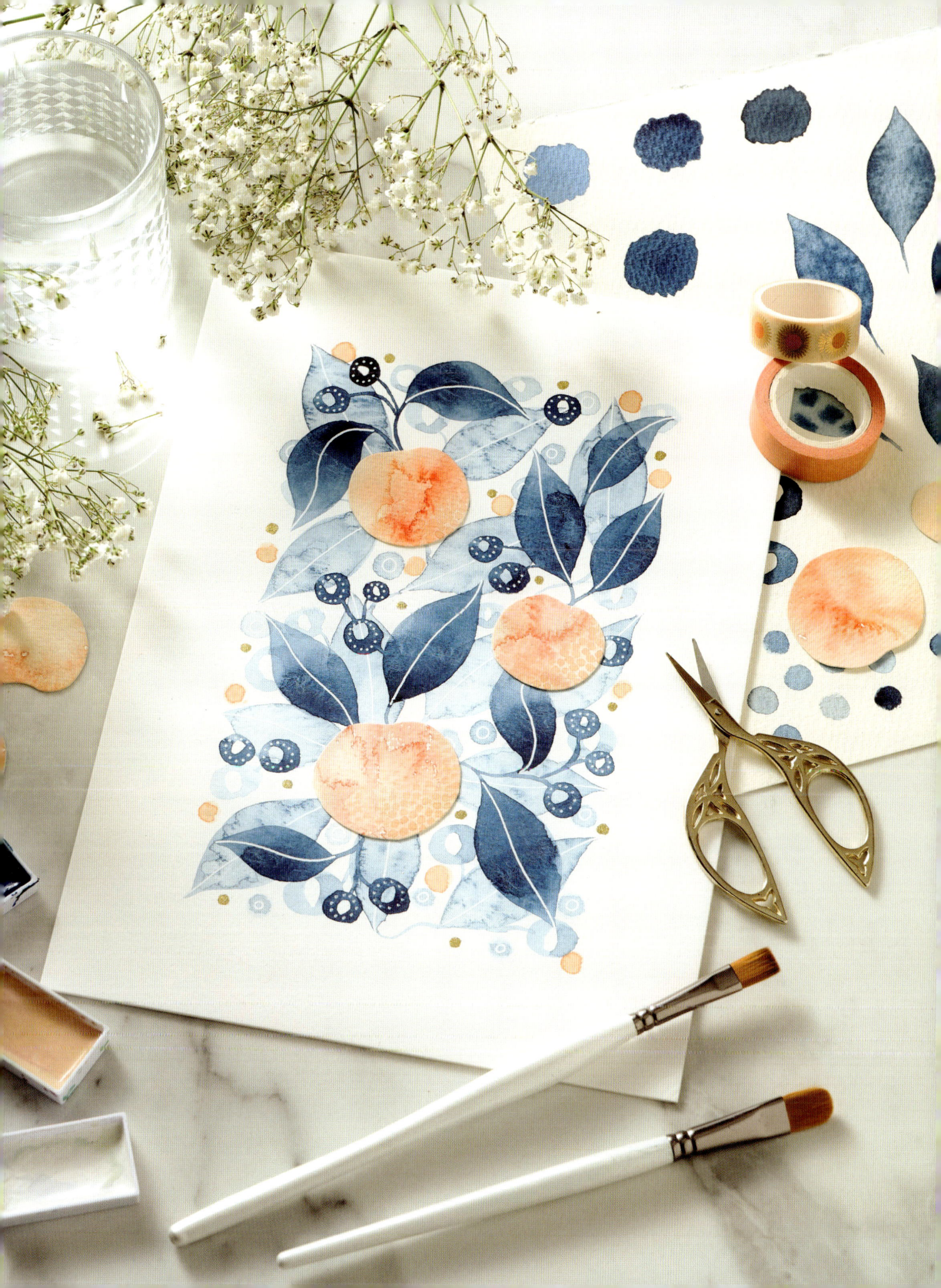

## Step 1: WET PAINT

To begin, mask out your sheet of artboard to create an area for painting (see Core Watercolor Techniques: Masking Borders). Once this is done, you can begin painting your leaves. I didn't draw these out in pencil first as they are just an underlayer – you'll only see fragments of them showing under the main leaves, so they don't have to be perfect! I've added fresh water to the leaves while still wet to create water blooms and texture – this gives a light airy feel that will add contrast to the darker leaves that we'll add later. Leave to dry completely.

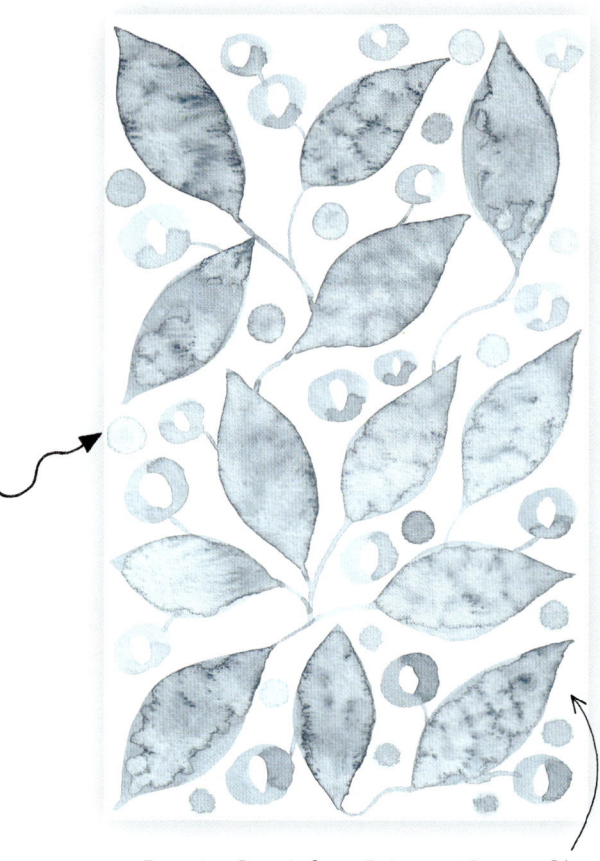

*I've added loose watercolor circles and fingerprint dots to fill blank spaces. This adds detail and interest when I apply the next paint layers in Step 5.*

*I mixed up Payne's Gray, Indigo, and Prussian Blue into soft washes for this first light layer of leaves; mix your colors to find the shade you like best!*

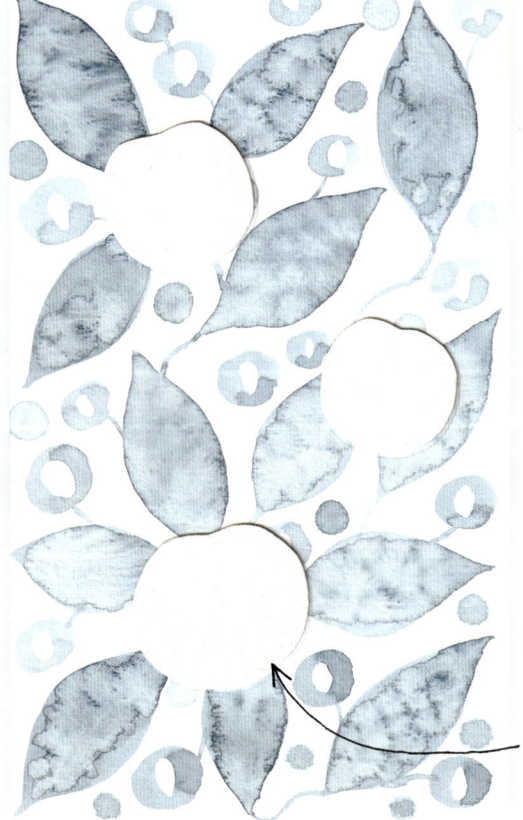

## Step 2: POSITIONING YOUR FRUIT

Now that your first layer of leaves is dry, you can work out where you'd like to place your peaches. I always work in groups of odd numbers – threes or fives would work best here – as this looks more balanced than even numbers in a composition. Here I've cut out some rough peach shapes so that I can work out where my final fruits should sit. I have placed the slightly larger peach at the bottom of my piece to help give a feeling of balance. Lightly draw around your peaches so you have a faint outline that will guide you when you add your next painted layer.

*Cutting out test shapes is a good trick to work out your collage composition. Try moving them around as well as adding and removing pieces until you are happy with the arrangement.*

## Step 3: COLLAGE BACKGROUND

Next up, paint your piece of rough watercolor paper so that it can dry when you move back to the leaves. I've used a palette to mix up yellow, orange, and red, then I added some white to each to create softer pastel shades. Cover the page with the different colors – feel free to be messy with this as it helps give a more natural finish. I then splattered the sheet with drops of clean water to create random blooms and textures.

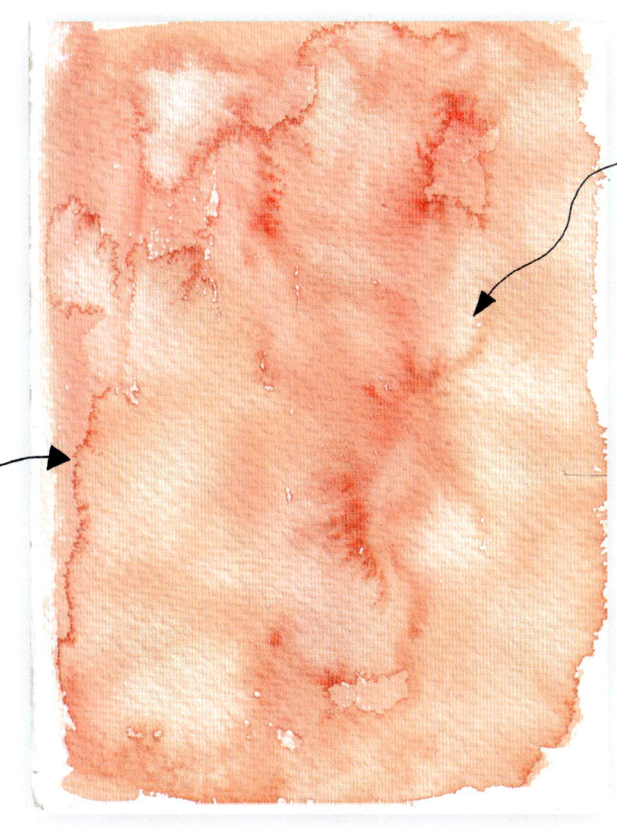

*Try adding dark tones next to lighter parts, and use water to create blooms and textures to break up any harsh areas of solid color.*

*Make sure you add your colors in random patterns; there are no straight lines in nature, so you want your colors to merge and flow into each other.*

## Step 4: COLLAGE SHAPES

Once your collage background is completely dry, back it with a double-sided adhesive sheet (see Getting Started with Collage) to create a sticker sheet ready for cutting up. Sketch out your peach shapes, creating a variety of sizes – you can always trim them down later if they don't fit perfectly onto your piece. Cut out the shapes, ready to use in Step 6.

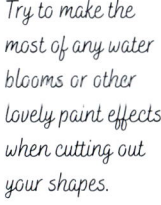

*Try to make the most of any water blooms or other lovely paint effects when cutting out your shapes.*

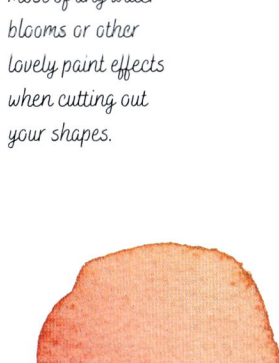

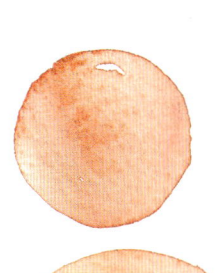

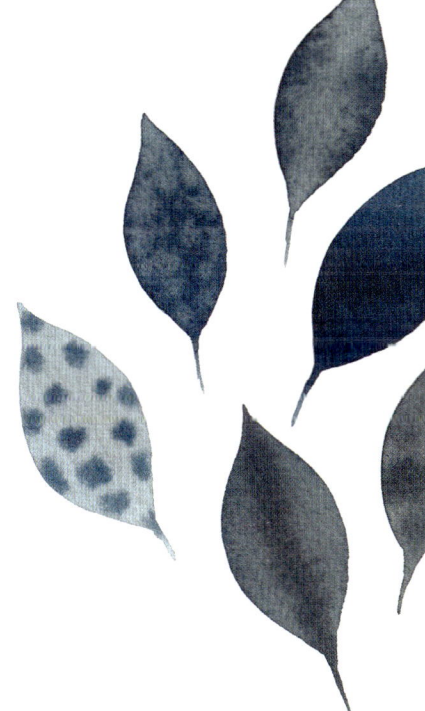

## Step 5: WET ON DRY

At this stage, we're going to add depth and interest by adding another layer of leaves on top of the first layer using a darker blue. I've added some leaves to come out from where the top of the peaches will sit, using the pencil outlines as a guide. This will give the feeling that they're growing on a tree. I also filled any spaces with loose circles (see Core Watercolor Techniques: Mark-Making Directory).

*I've used a stronger mix of color to ensure that these leaves are darker than the first layer.*

*I made some little fingerprint dots to add more hints of peach around the composition. There's nothing wrong with getting near the end and deciding the piece needs something extra!*

*Flooding more color into the bottom of each leaf gives a nice two-tone effect.*

## Step 6: ADDING THE PEACHES AND EMBELLISHMENTS

Now the background composition is finalized, stick on the peaches using the faint pencil outlines as a guide for placement. Then it's time to look at where you'd like to embellish. I've added some simple white lines along the center of each leaf and a ring of dots inside each circle using my white pen. I've also added some gold spots using a paintbrush to add a little shine!

*Looking at the embellished piece, I wanted to add a little more of the peachy color, so I added small raindrop spots to the edge of each fruit.*

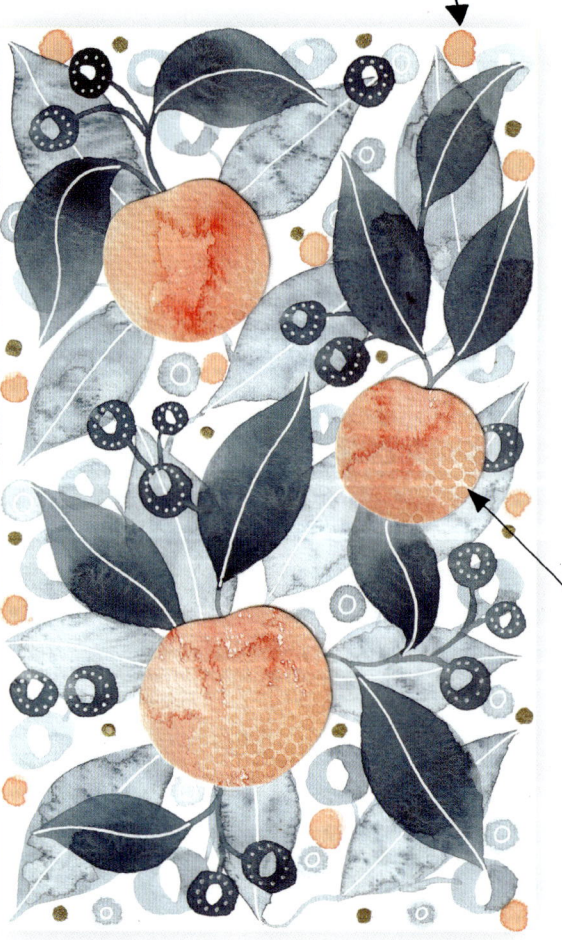

# More Inspiration

Once you have mastered the techniques, the whole fruit bowl is ripe for the picking. Here, I've used lemons to give a fresh vibrant look against leafy green foliage, but you could try plums, apples, pears... you name it!

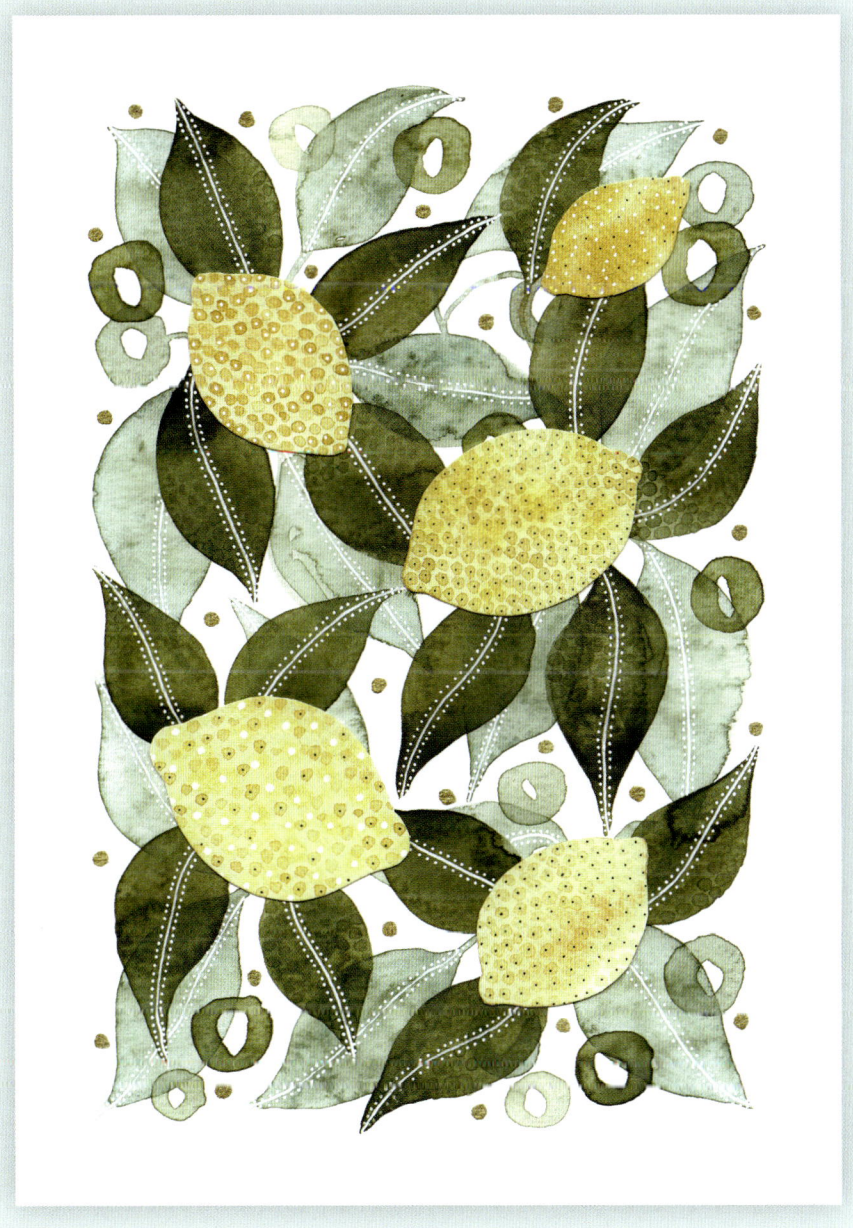

# Botanical Blocks

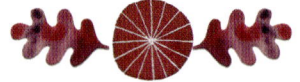

For this project, we're going to collage simple botanical shapes onto a background of textured watercolor blocks. The size and shape of the blocks will guide the composition, and the harmonious palette creates depth. We'll create contrast by collaging in a range of colors. This piece starts to pop when the white embellishment is added to the watercolor shapes.

## MATERIALS

- Winsor & Newton professional watercolors
- Daler Rowney Aquafine Artboard
- Da Vinci Casaneo quill brush - size 2
- Uni-ball Signo pen – white, 1mm (Broad)
- Posca paint pen – white, 0.7mm (Ultra Fine)
- Sharp scissors
- Double-sided adhesive sheets (double-sided tape or glue will work too)
- Ruler and pencil

## COLOR CHOICES

I've used a rich autumnal palette for this piece as that's what I saw from my studio window as I painted, but you could use different seasonal shades. I've selected colors that reflect nature, but feel free to go wild – as with all color selection, it's a personal choice. So go for it, and enjoy using whatever colors you are drawn to on the day!

### WINSOR & NEWTON COLOR REFERENCES

- Alizarin Crimson
- Permanent Magenta
- Winsor Orange
- Yellow Ochre

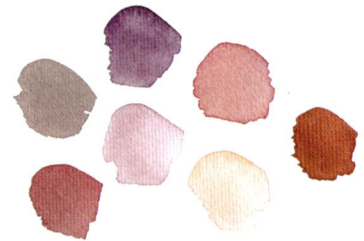

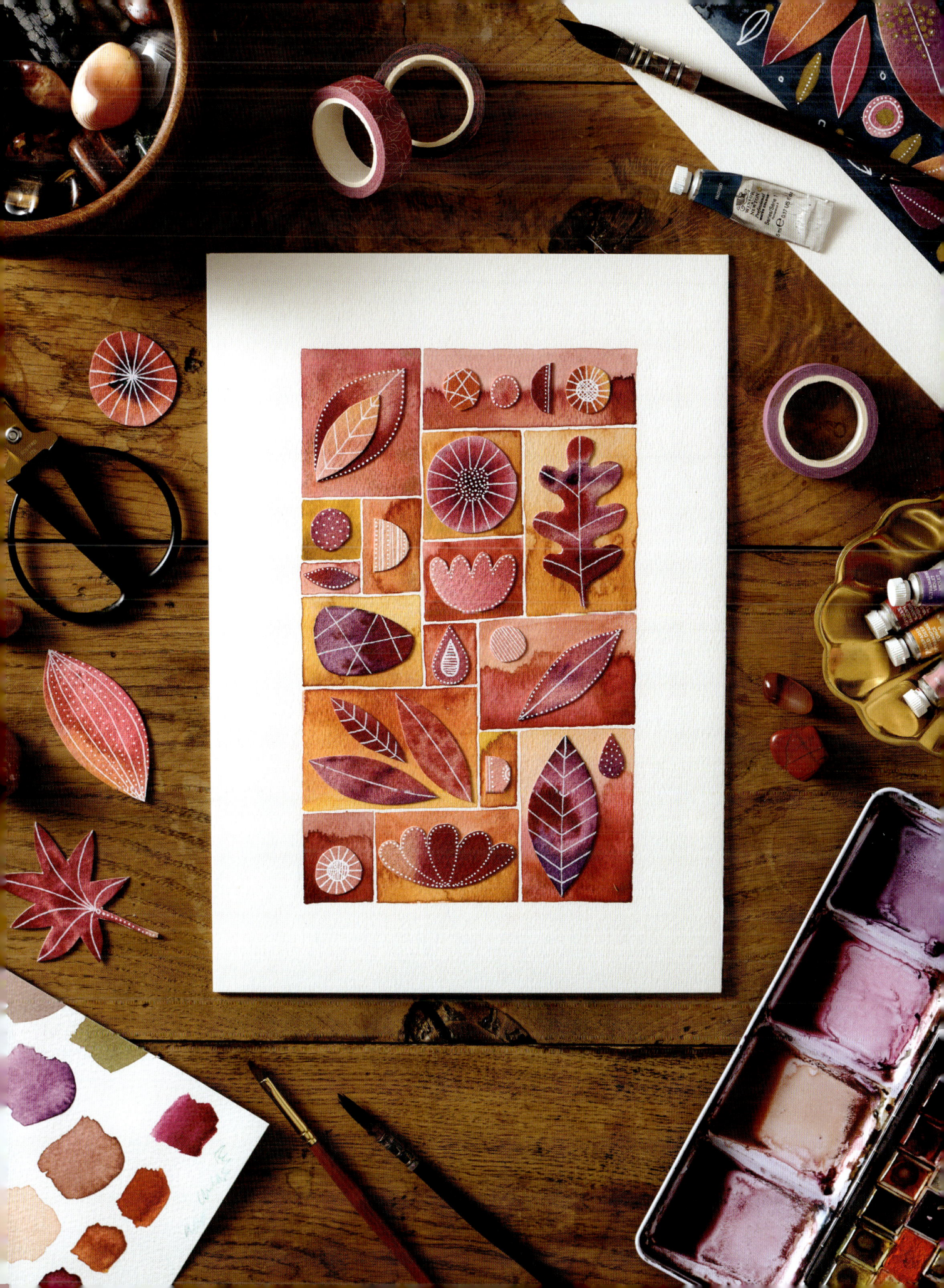

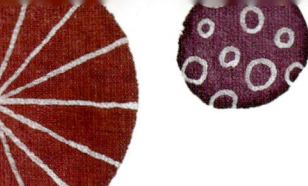

## Step 1: WET PAINT

To begin, mask out your sheet of artboard (see Core Watercolor Techniques: Masking Borders), then you can sketch out your blocks in pencil. I used a ruler to mark out a grid to help me keep my lines straight. Now you're ready to paint! Start by filling in the blocks, leaving a thin white strip of dry paper in between them – this helps define the shapes and will stop your wet paints from merging together. I painted some areas of my blocks with a thin layer, and others I've flooded at one end for darker tones. You can also drop in fresh water to create interesting watercolor blooms. Leave to dry completely.

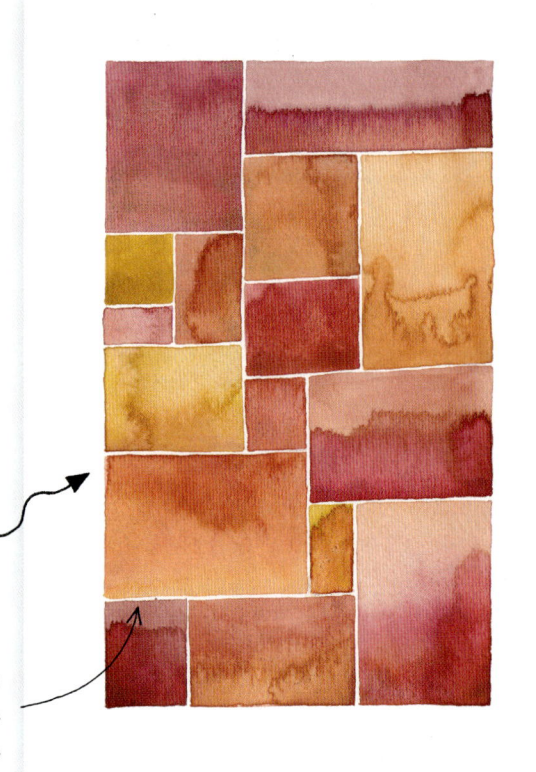

*Sketch out a mix of squares and rectangles in a range of sizes as these will contain your collage elements.*

*Don't worry if your white strips aren't perfect (mine can be a little wobbly!), you can straighten them later with a white pen.*

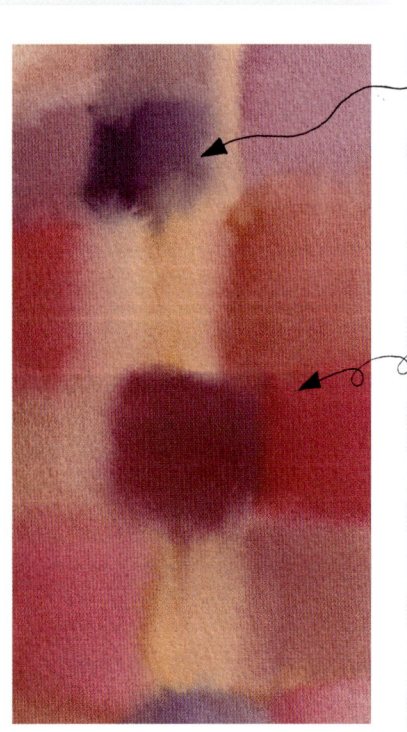

*Be really relaxed at this stage, filling the sheet with a mix of your colors. Try using darker colors next to lighter ones to add contrast.*

*I've used square blocks of color here but stripes and circles work, too. A lot of the edges will be lost when this is cut up, so feel free to stay loose.*

## Step 2: COLLAGE BACKGROUND

I like to select my paints and then mix them to create lots of different harmonious shades. Use these shades to cover a full sheet of paper – this is what we'll be cutting our botanical shapes from in the next steps. Leave to dry completely, then back your painted background with a double-sided sheet (see Getting Started with Collage). If you plan to use glue instead, skip this part of the step and move on to making your collage shapes.

*Top Tip* Make sure you don't have too many straight lines running through your collage background. Try to overlap blocks and keep them random in size and shape to keep things looking soft and organic.

## Step 3: COLLAGE SHAPES

Now that you have your "sticker sheet" prepared, sketch out your botanical shapes. Remember that you can do this either on the painted front or the back of the sheet. Play with the shapes you use, and have fun! Cut carefully around the shapes, and your stickers are ready to use.

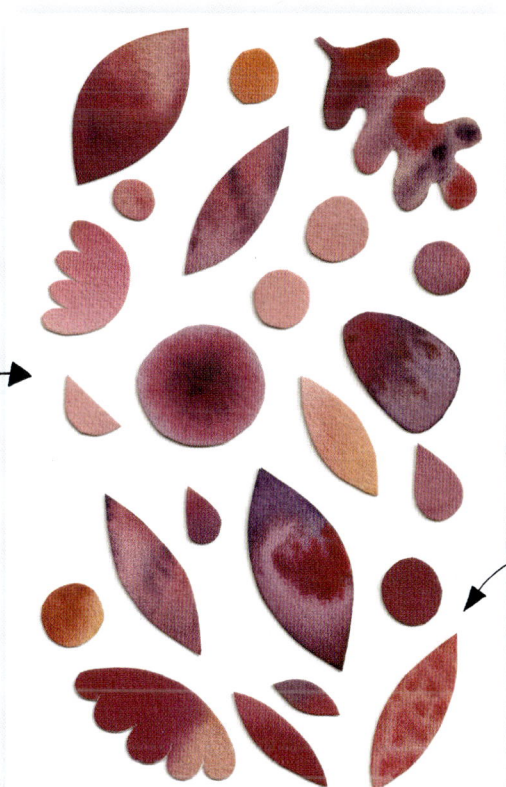

*Make your shapes in a range of sizes to fit the blocks you painted in Step 1.*

*I've used basic leaf shapes as well as circles and floral motifs, but you could try any shape you like.*

## Step 4: ADDING THE SHAPES

Once you've cut out a selection of shapes, have fun laying the botanical elements onto the blocks painted in Step 1. Play around and try different compositions. Once you're happy with the layout, carefully remove the backing paper of the adhesive sheet and stick down (or use glue at this stage if you prefer).

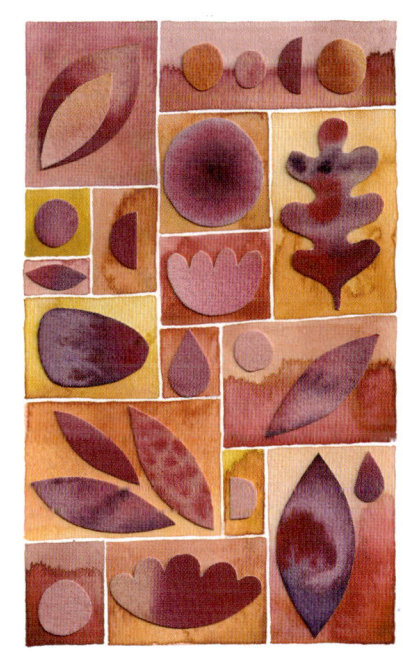

*If any of your collage pieces don't fit well into the blocks, simply cut them down to size.*

*Create contrast by adding light colors onto dark and vice versa — a purple leaf on a purple background won't stand out!*

## *Step 5:* **WHITE EMBELLISHMENTS**

Once the composition is finalized, I look at the blocks, collage shapes, and overall composition and decide what/where I'd like to embellish. For this project, I've used a white paint pen to add highlights to help the piece pop and give contrast where needed. Add as little or as much as you'd like.

Allow all your details to dry before carefully removing the masking-tape border. Do this slowly to ensure the paper underneath does not rip. Once this is removed, stand back and admire your finished piece! You'll find that a brightly colored pieced like this really benefits from the breathing space a white border provides.

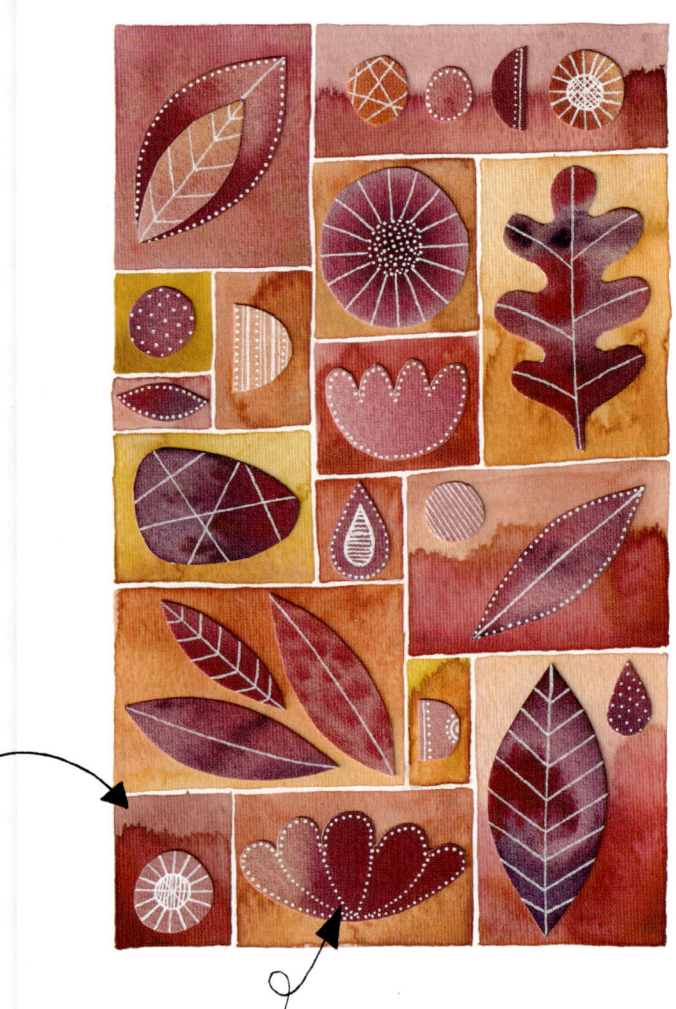

*I used white to add highlights and contrast against the strong color palette. Black or gold could also work!*

*If any of your collage pieces are too similar to the background color, a dotted or solid outline will help them stand out.*

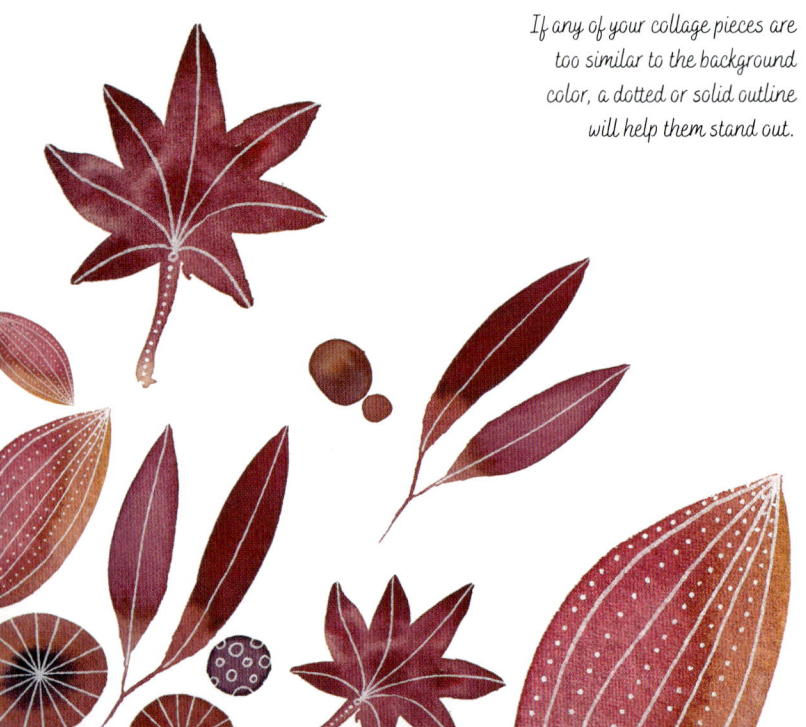

*Top Tip*

Less is more! Sometimes I can overwork a piece by adding too much embellishment. It's good to take a step back, take a breath, or even go and grab a drink – it's always worth looking at your work with fresh eyes on your return!

# More Inspiration

To experiment further, I created this new piece without the background blocks. It gives a sense of natural elements collected on a nature walk. The random positioning on the page, as well as the darker background, give this a totally different feel even though the colors and patterns of the botanical shapes are very similar.

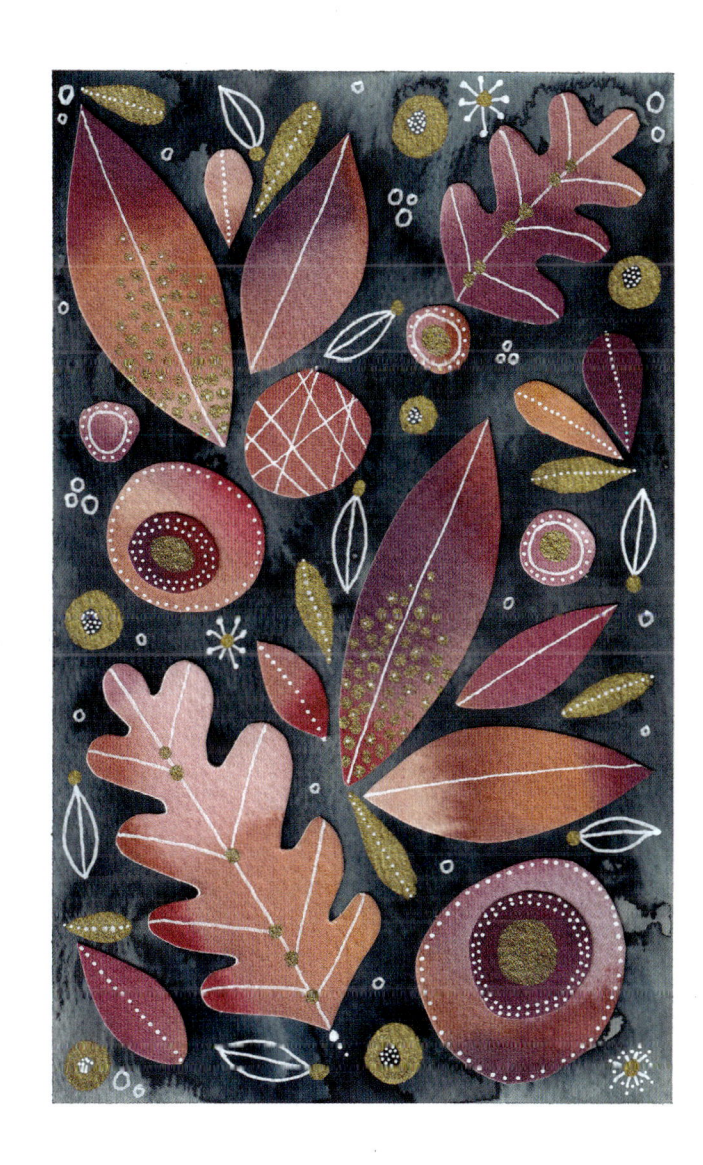

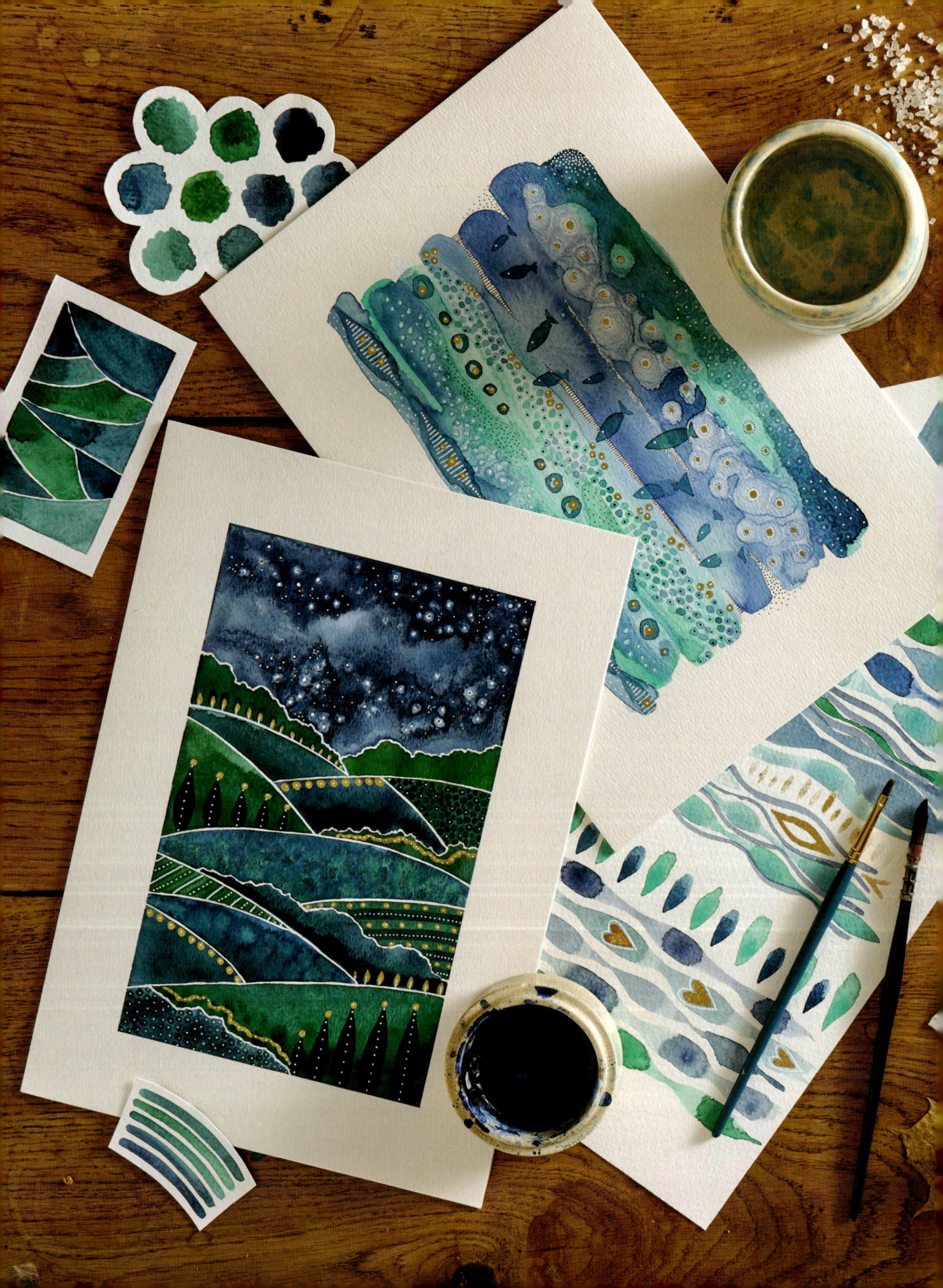

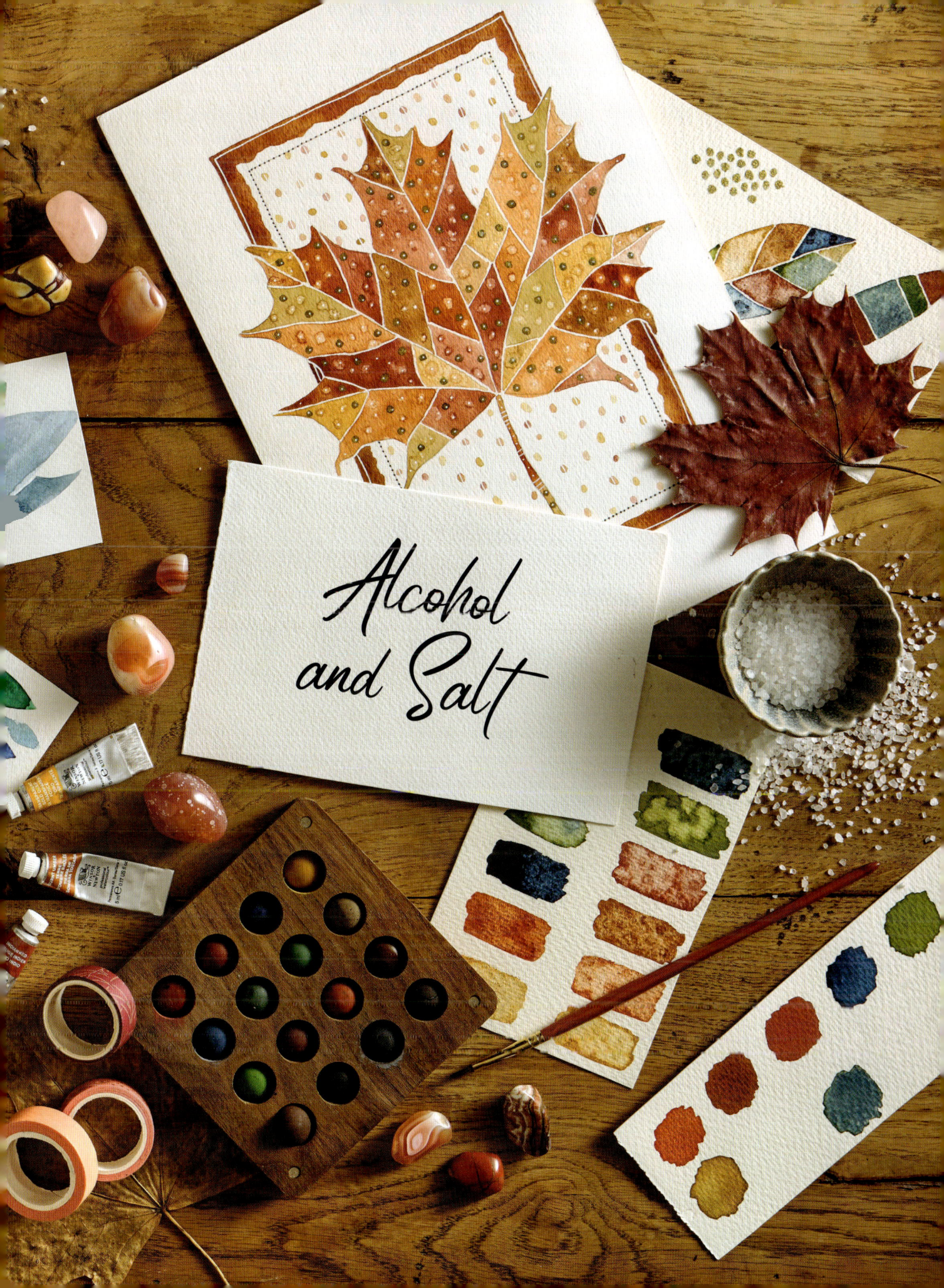

Alcohol
and Salt

# Alcohol and Salt Techniques

Once of the things I love about watercolor is the myriad textures that can be achieved, whether using wet-on-wet techniques like water blooms or by adding 'extras' into my painting to add different effects. Two of my favorite additions are alcohol and salt. Both give fantastic texture and can add real visual interest to a piece. They are particularly good with dark colors as they leech out the color from the paint, leaving areas of lighter highlights.

## GETTING STARTED WITH ALCOHOL

Many artists use alcohol to create textural effects by adding it to wet watercolor paint. It causes the pigment to repel and creates interesting patterns or white areas on the painted surface. Essentially, it acts as a resist due to its inability to mix fully with water-based paints.

### MATERIALS

- Painted watercolor paper, still wet
- Pure alcohol such as isopropyl/rubbing alcohol (this won't work with spirits like gin or vodka)
- Applicator of choice (this could be a brush, cotton bud (Q-Tip), stick, spray... have fun and experiment!)

### METHOD

1. This technique gives the best results when the paint is wet, so aim to work quickly.

2. Apply the alcohol to the page, leaving space in between your marks if you don't want them to merge. Here I've used a small brush to give defined shapes.

3. Leave to dry completely. The alcohol will spread and develop as the paint dries – I like the organic and random effect achieved here where some of the shapes have bled into each other.

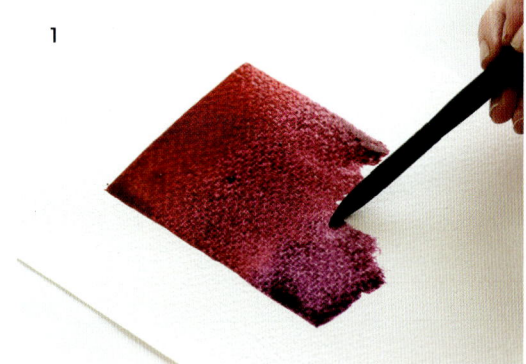

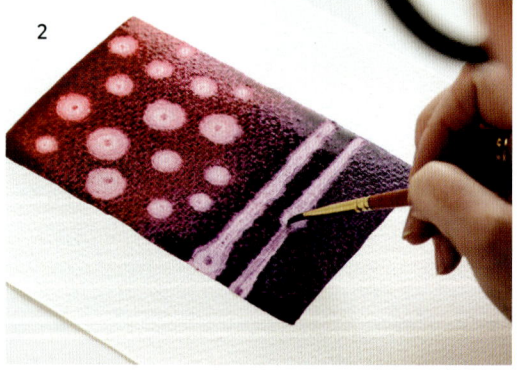

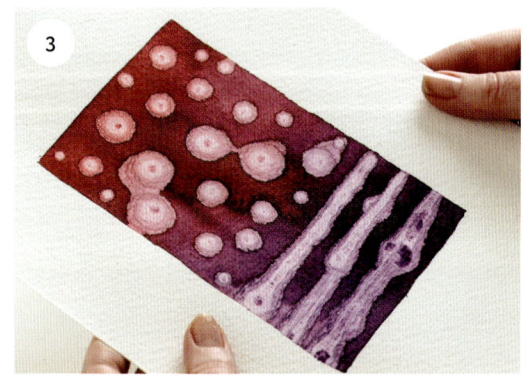

# GETTING STARTED WITH SALT

Salt is a super inexpensive and widely available tool for watercolor painting. It creates textured and abstract patterns by absorbing water and pigment from the paint, leaving you with organic natural texture. Salt is hygroscopic, meaning it attracts the water and pigment molecules in watercolor paint. When sprinkled on wet paint, the salt absorbs water and pigment, creating a star-like shape with a textured center. This process creates a sparkly effect, and can be used to achieve a variety of results.

*Top Tip:* If your paint is too wet, the salt won't have much effect, and if the paper is too dry, the salt won't absorb enough moisture. Try experimenting on scrap paper to ensure you get the right result before starting your piece.

## MATERIALS

- Painted watercolor paper, still damp
- Sea salt or rock salt – coarser salts will generally create larger, more defined patterns

### METHOD

1. The salt technique works best when the paint is damp but not too wet, and the paper isn't too dry (see Tip, above right).

2. Add a liberal sprinkling of fine sea salt in the desired area to create a subtle all-over texture like small pinpricks of light – perfect for stars in a night sky.

3. Leave your painting to dry completely. Once dry, brush away any remaining salt. If you discover any sections of paint that are still wet beneath the salt, simply dab them with a tissue or cloth to help them dry out.

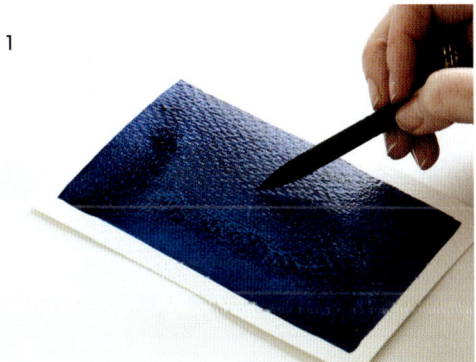

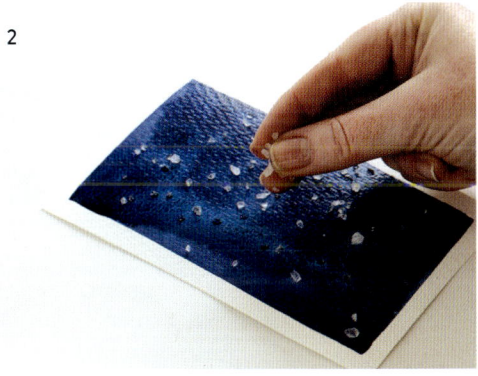

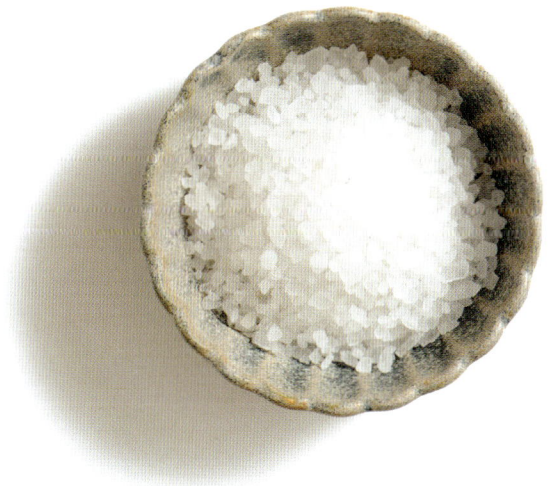

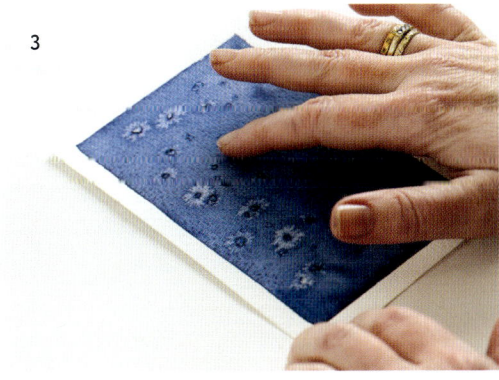

# Underwater Bubbles

This project is super relaxed and organic. The composition is led by the shapes made by the alcohol when it is dropped into wet paint and by the texture of the watercolor once it has dried. Lean into the happy accidents and merges – I think this all adds to the underwater vibes: loose, fluid, and layered!

## MATERIALS

- Winsor & Newton professional watercolors
- Daler Rowney Aquafine Artboard
- Da Vinci Casaneo quill brush - size 2, plus old brushes for applying the alcohol
- Winsor & Newton filbert brush – size 2
- Uni-ball Signo pen – white, 1mm (Broad)
- Black fineliners –sizes 0.1 and 0.4
- Winsor & Newton Drawing Ink – gold
- Pure isopropyl alcohol

## COLOR CHOICES

Here I've indulged my urge to use my favorite watercolor palette of blues, aquas, and greens, and I've included fish-shaped marks to suggest an underwater scene. In reality, this is pretty much an abstract, so take out the fish shapes and you could create this piece in any number of different color palettes – see More Inspiration for how stunning it looks in reds and golds!

### WINSOR & NEWTON COLOR REFERENCES

- Cobalt Turquoise Light
- Hooker's Green
- Indanthrene Blue
- Indigo
- Prussian Blue

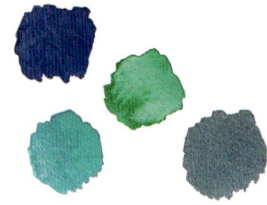

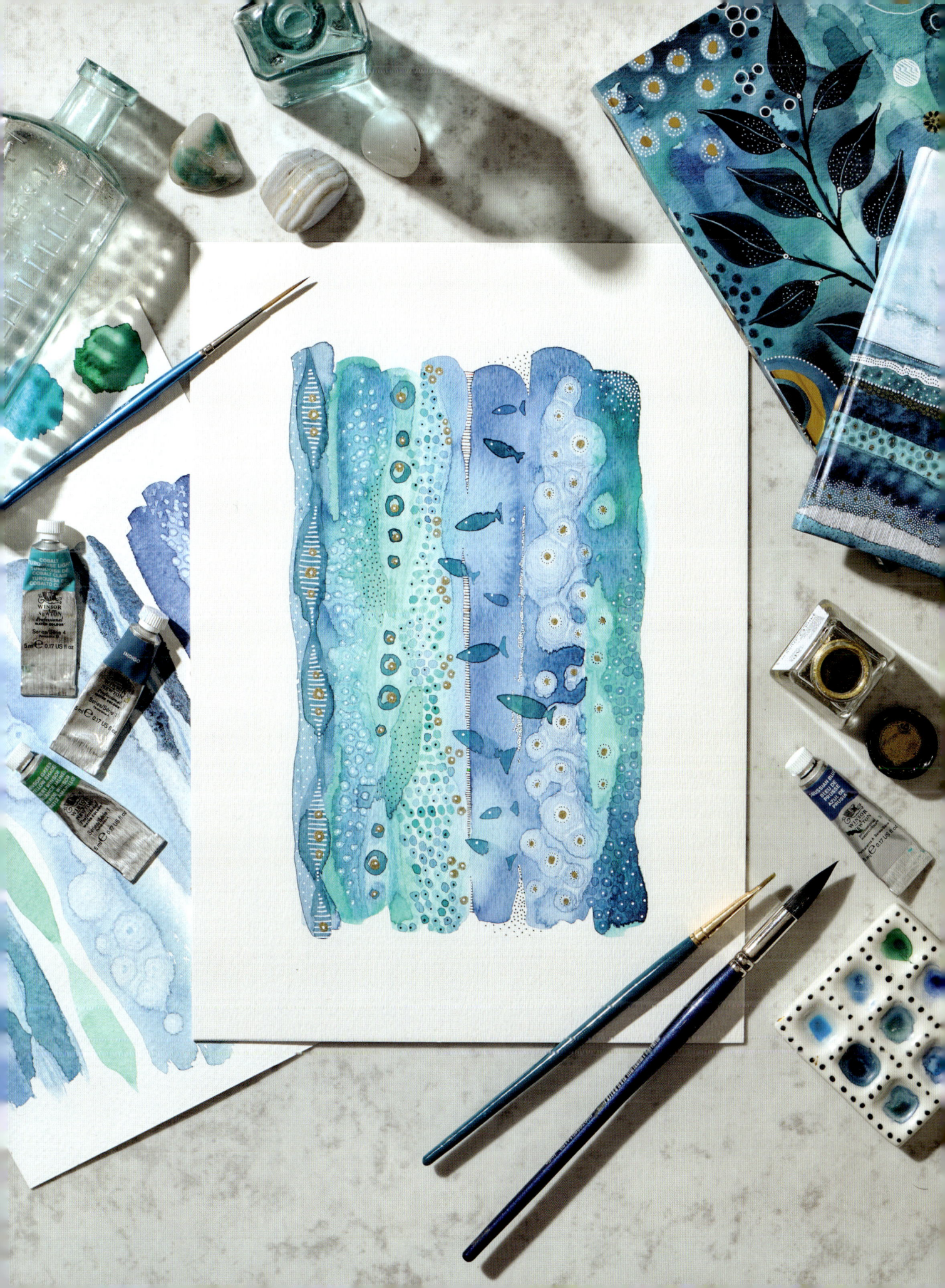

## Step 1: WET PAINT AND ALCOHOL

Start by masking off your page (see Core Watercolor Techniques: Masking Borders). Although this isn't truly necessary as you won't be painting over the edge, I like to keep my borders crisp and white, and it keeps things clean. Mix up some loose washes of each color and run vertical lines of paint down the page with your quill brush. Keep the lines soft, avoiding any hard edges – it should feel watery and organic. Fill across the page with your different colors.

Now, while the paint is still wet, dip an old brush into neat alcohol and add large dots of it onto the paint. Make sure your brush is well loaded for some and less so for others to create different size "bubbles". Working in a different area of the painted stripes (I like to space these textures out), load a smaller old brush and add lots of dots of alcohol. Continue to add lighter space and texture into the background by painting a couple of loose wavy lines with the alcohol.

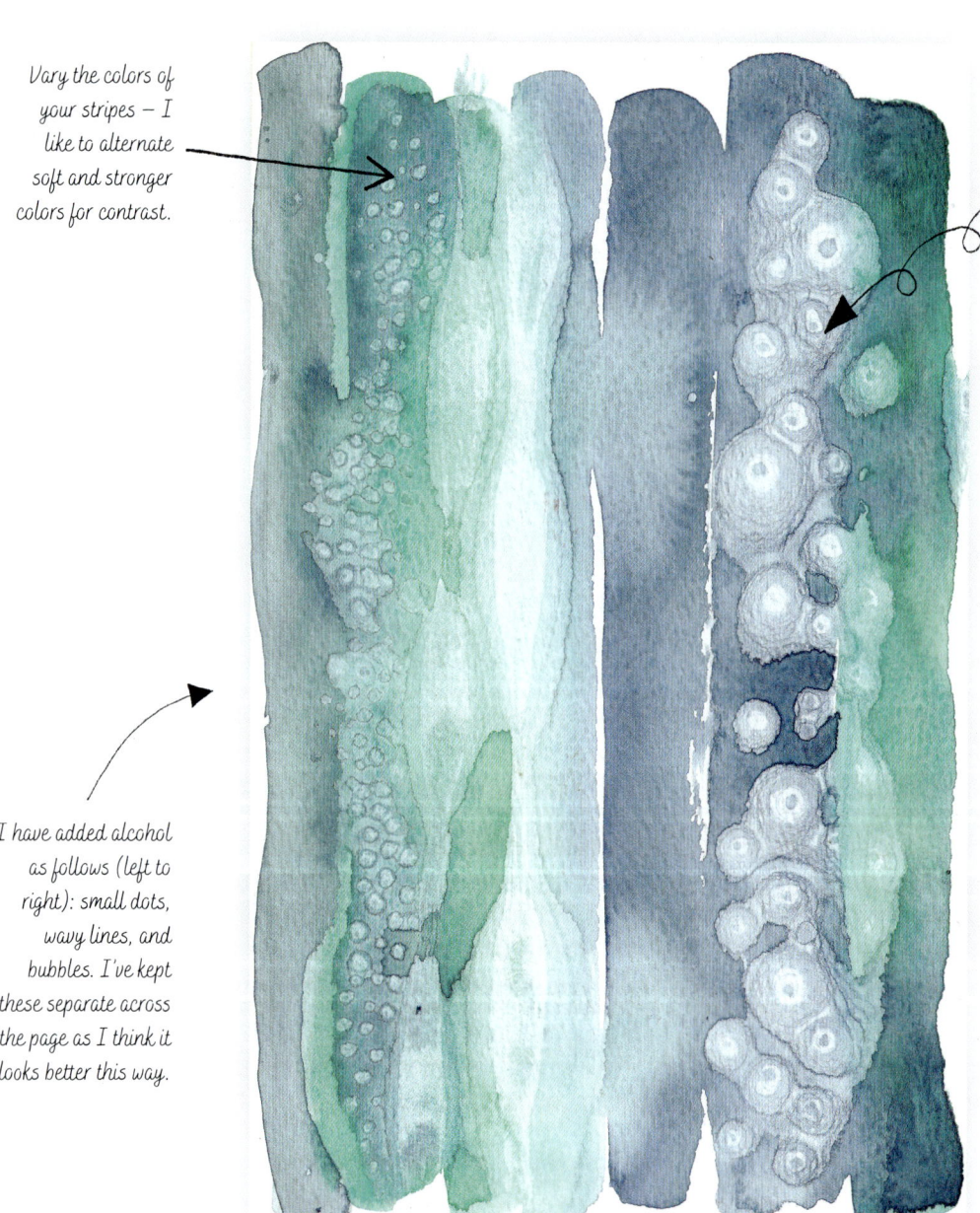

*Vary the colors of your stripes – I like to alternate soft and stronger colors for contrast.*

*Carefully choose where to add your alcohol. When dropped into wet watercolor, it looks white and cloudy, which shows up best against a dark background.*

*I have added alcohol as follows (left to right): small dots, wavy lines, and bubbles. I've kept these separate across the page as I think it looks better this way.*

## Step 2: WET ON DRY

Once your initial layer is dry, it's time to add the next layer. The first layer was all wet on wet, producing shapes that are soft and flowing. This is now your opportunity to add defined marks into the piece. Try adding raindrop spots, loose circles, wavy lines, and brush stamps (see Core Watercolor Techniques: Mark-Making Directory). I've added a small triangle to the end of each brush stamp to look like a fish tail.

*To avoid the painting looking too crammed with details, I've limited the fish shapes to one area.*

*I aim to add as much texture and contrast to my piece as possible. Here, I've added mark making in different sizes, from the small spots through to the loose circles and wavy lines.*

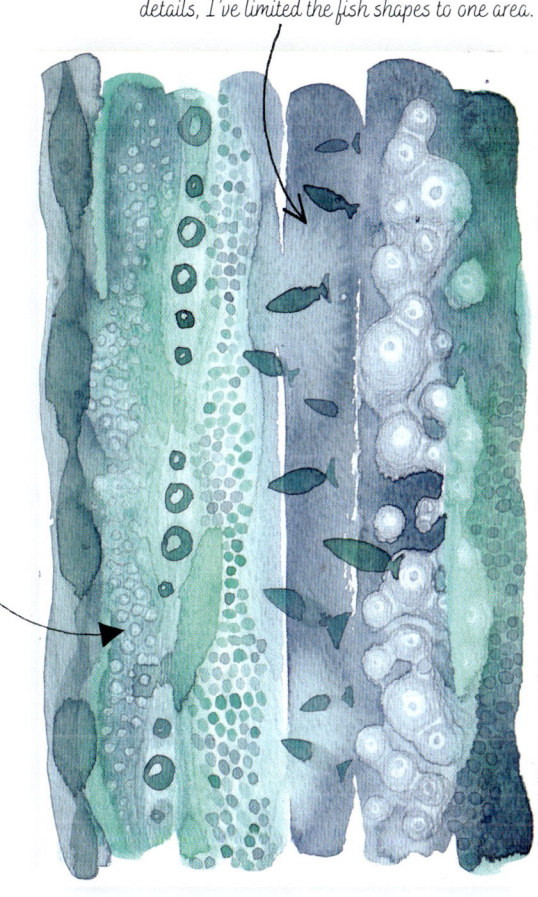

## Step 3: BLACK EMBELLISHMENTS

Next up, take a good look at your piece: what does it need? My piece was looking very soft and pale, so I decided to add details in black to add interest and give contrast. Using a black fineliner, add some rows of small lines as well as dots across the piece, ensuring that you use the embellishment to accentuate textures and marks that you like.

*I've added tiny black lines to areas of white between the stripes of color. This adds texture but keeps the stripes looking separate.*

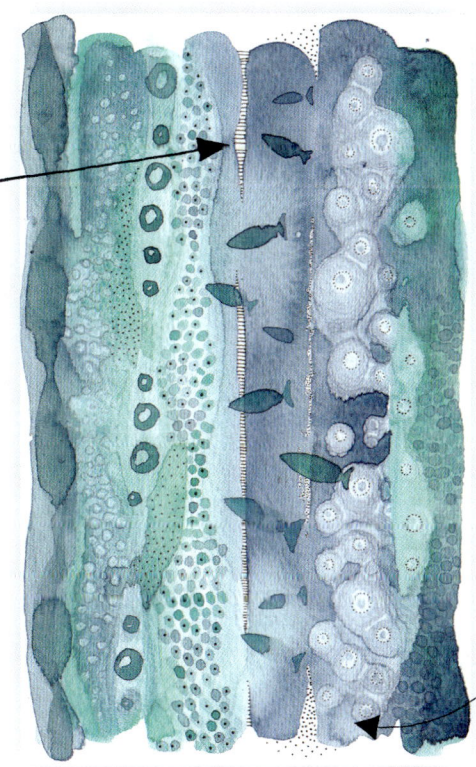

*I've added small and larger dots using two fineliners. In some areas, I wanted the black to be subtle, whereas in others I wanted it to pack more of a punch.*

## Step 4: WHITE EMBELLISHMENTS

Once you're happy with the black, add some white decoration. I think of this as the reverse effect of the black, using it to add freshness and highlights. Use the white pen to add dots and lines to help light up areas that may look too dark or plain.

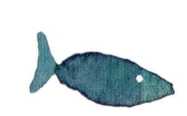

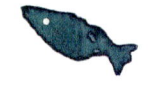

*I love the lightness that white embellishments add to the piece. Use white to lift dark areas, or simply layer more texture onto lighter tones.*

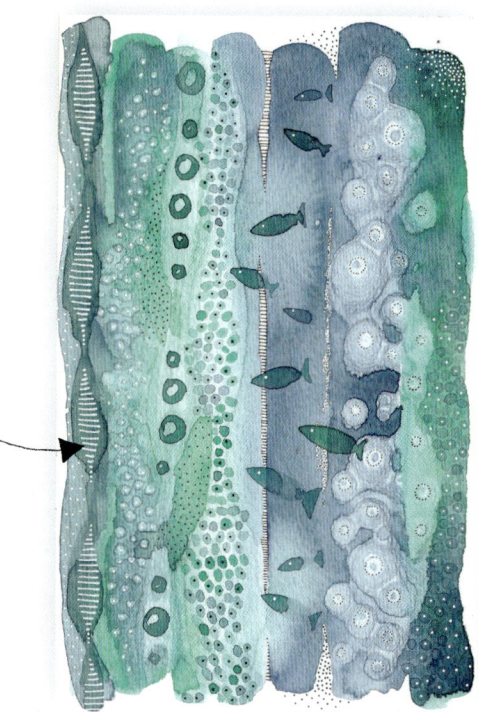

## Step 5: GOLD EMBELLISHMENTS

Now that you've added black and white embellishments, decide whether you'd like to add some metallic details. Here, I've used gold to add warmth and richness – you could try silver to give a cooler look. I've used it sparingly (occasionally, less is more!), highlighting only key areas of the piece. I applied my gold with a small filbert brush to create dots similar in size to my raindrop spots.

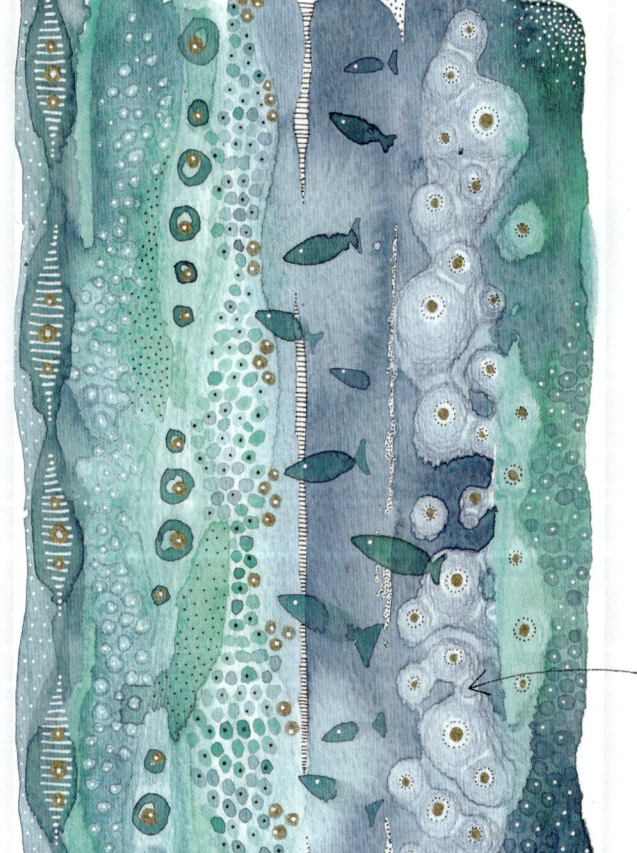

*Don't go too heavy on the gold – a small pop of sparkle can be enough! If in doubt, add a little, then step back and have a good look. You can always add more, but it's hard to remove if you've overdone it.*

# More Inspiration

These stripe designs are so versatile! Painted in the blue palette, the design feels very watery; this example has the opposite effect, with the vivid reds and oranges giving a fiery feel. It was inspired by the intense colors of a vine in my garden in autumn.

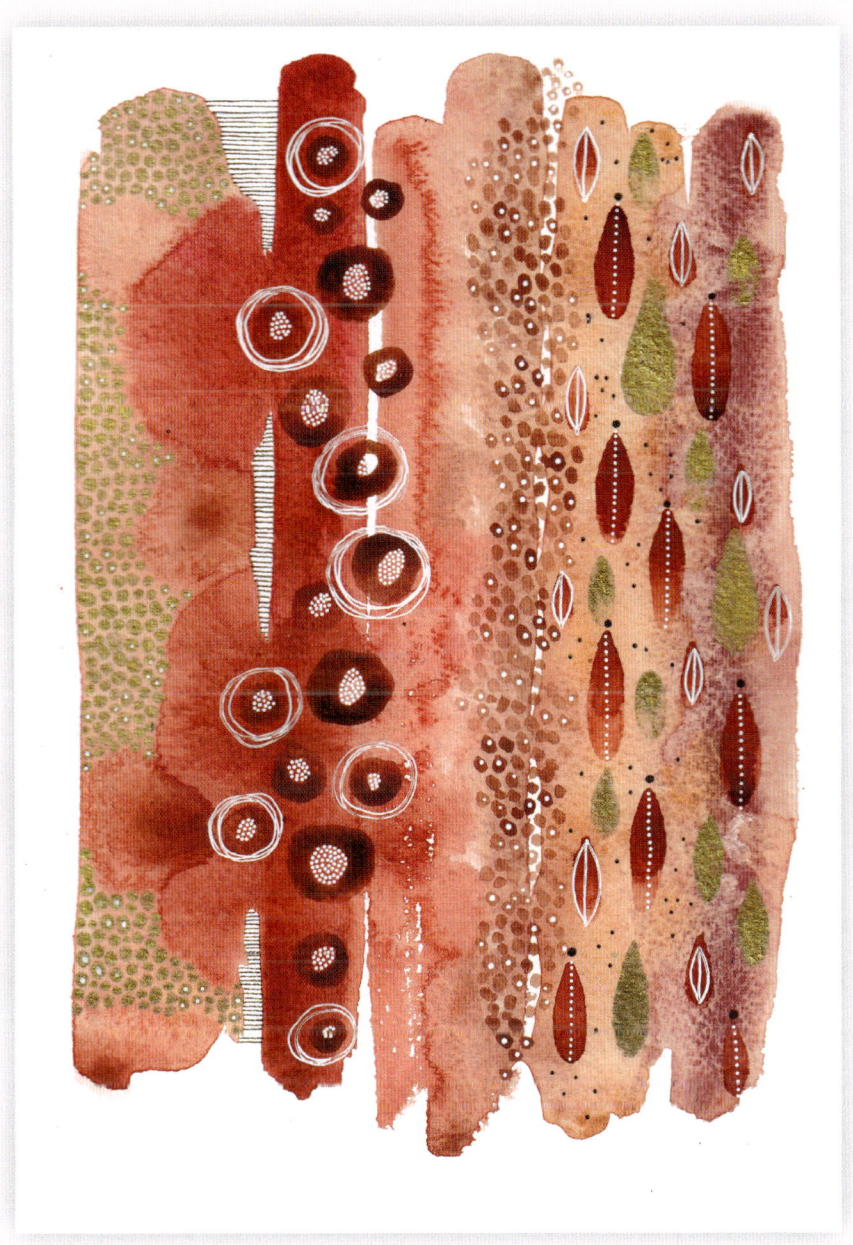

# Patchwork Leaf

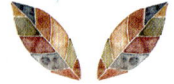

Leaves are a constant inspiration to me, from the lush green shoots of spring, through to falling leaves in autumnal shades! For this project, pick any leaf you like – the same principle applies whether it's from a tree, bush, or flower. You can even try this with smaller leaves, creating a piece that has multiple leaf motifs rather than one large one as I have here.

## MATERIALS

- Winsor & Newton professional watercolors
- Daler Rowney Aquafine Artboard
- Da Vinci Casaneo quill brush - size 2
- Filbert and round brushes
- Posca paint pen – white, 0.7mm (Ultra Fine)
- Black fineliner 0.8mm
- Winsor & Newton Drawing Ink – gold
- Coarse rock salt
- Pencil

## COLOR CHOICES

For this project, I have celebrated the fall season with a rich palette of deep hues. I've used the colors straight from the tube as well as mixed together to create some additional shades. Use natural colors and evoke your favorite season, or go psychedelic and opt for a wild rainbow of colors and pattern. See More Inspiration for a very unnatural palette of aquas and ocean inspired blues!

### WINSOR & NEWTON COLOR REFERENCES

- Burnt Sienna
- Burnt Umber
- Indian Red
- Yellow Ochre

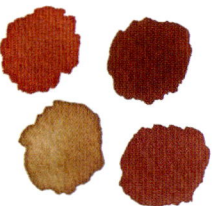

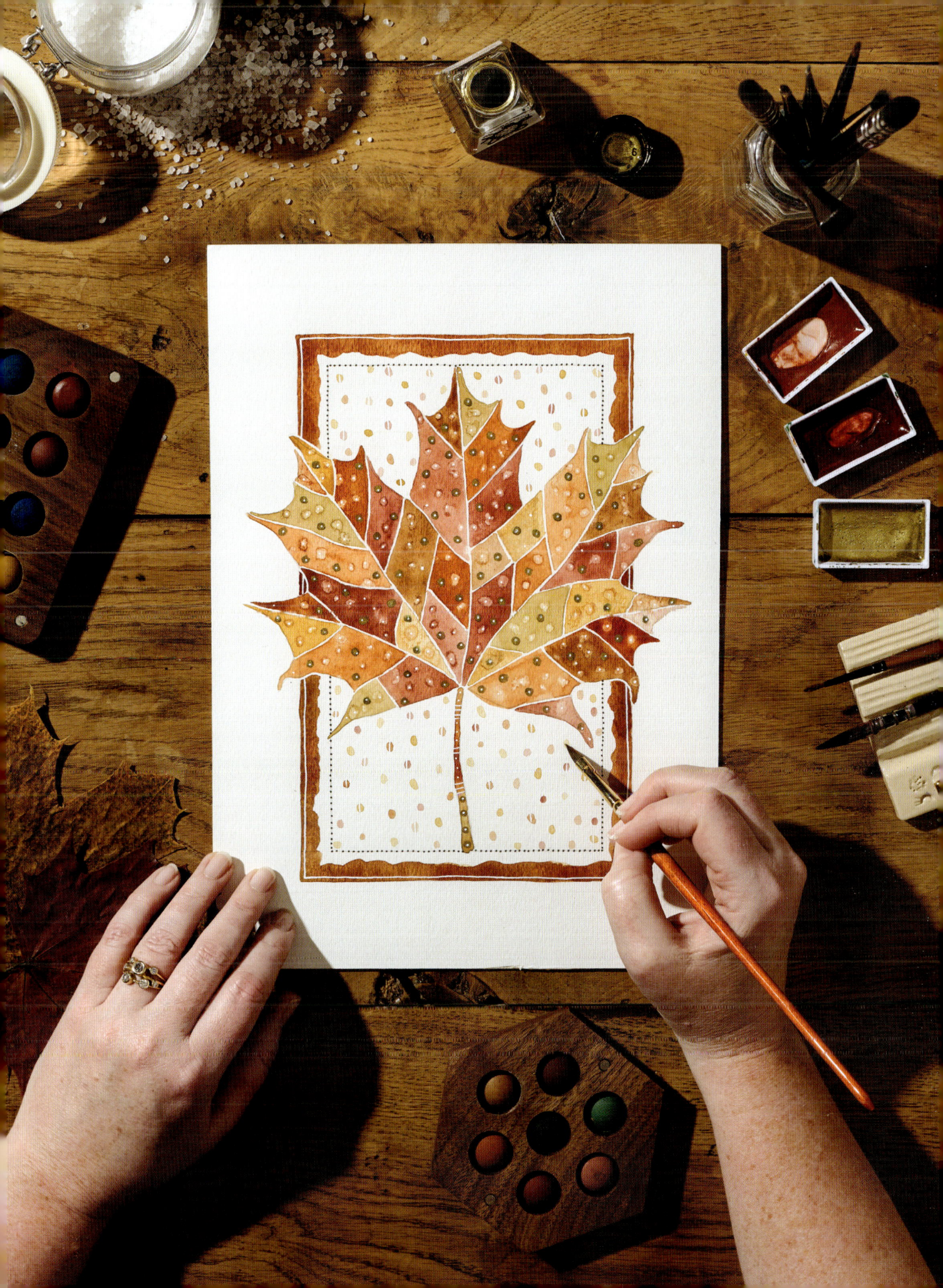

## Step 1: PENCIL SKETCH

To begin, use a pencil to draw an even line around the edge of your page to make a border that's roughly the same width as masking tape would be. Now you can sketch out your leaf shape. For this project, I made life easy and drew around a leaf from the garden (cheating, I know, but it takes the pressure off the composition!). Once you have your outline, sketch in the main veins of the leaf, which sub divides the sections to give lots of lovely areas to paint. Don't worry if your leaf is bigger than your painting area and breaks through your border – I think this looks quite cool!

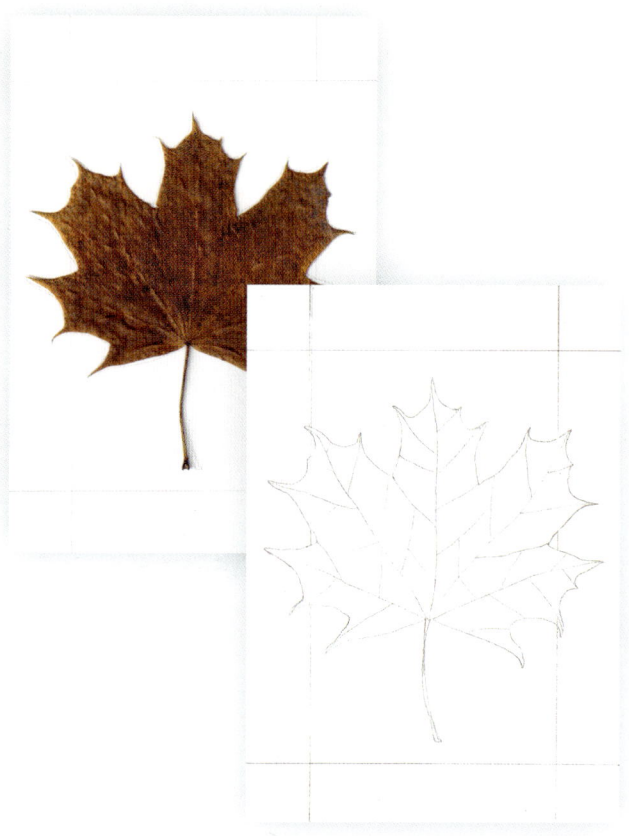

## Step 2: WET PAINT AND SALT

Now that you have the border marked out and your shapes sketched out, you can start to paint. Create a light wash of each of the colors in your palette. Start to paint in the separate sections of your leaf, leaving a thin white line of dry paper in between each for the veins – I tend to paint one color at a time to ensure I have an even spread of each. While the paint is still wet, choose a few larger crystals of rock salt and drop some into each painted section (you'll see the salt start to soak up the paint). Repeat for each color until your whole leaf is painted in. Leave to dry completely.

*I created a wider palette by mixing some of the listed paint colors together, creating extra shades and hues.*

*Top Tip:* If any of your sections touch and run together, this is easily fixed. Just add the white line back in with a white pen once the piece has dried – no one will know the difference!

## Step 3: GOLD EMBELLISHMENTS

Once your piece is completely dry, remove the rock salt (see Getting Started with Salt). You should now have some interesting paler marks on your leaf. Once I can see the natural textures made by the salt, I like to embellish each section of the leaf with small dots of gold ink, using a small filbert or round brush to apply it.

*The gold really works well as it's warm against this soft autumnal color palette. You could try silver embellishment with a cooler palette.*

*I like to make sure I have dots in every section to ensure a nicely balancd piece.*

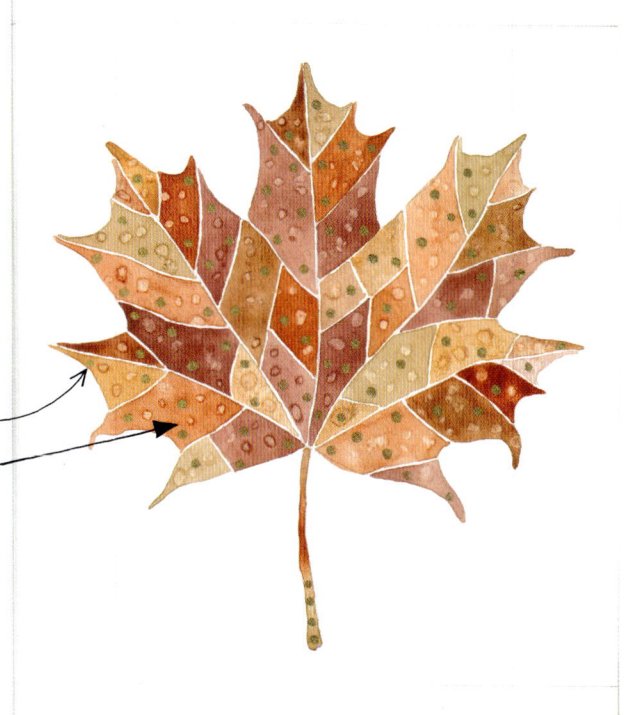

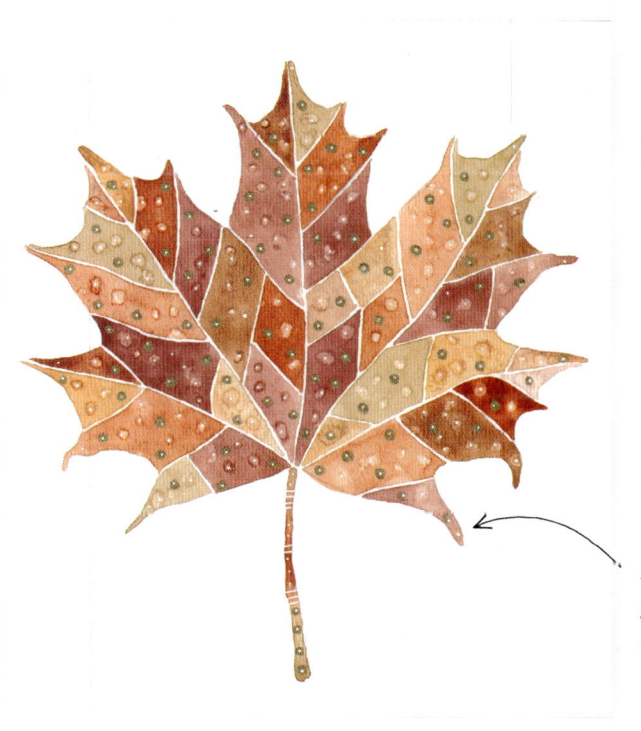

## Step 4: WHITE EMBELLISHMENTS

Now that I have my salt marks and gold spots of ink, I like to use a white paint pen to add a single dot to the center of each. This softens the marks and spots and adds visual interest.

*I've used white for this piece, but you could use a single dot of black if you'd like greater contrast.*

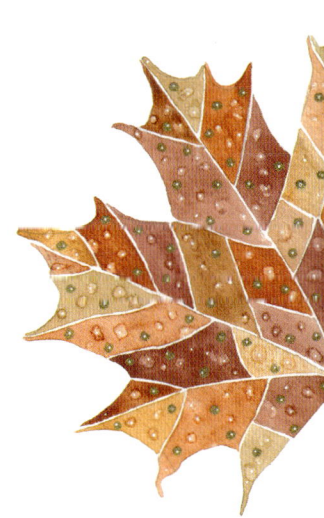

## Step 5: BORDER AND BACKGROUND

Now, you could just leave (pun intended!) the leaf there, but I like to add a decorative border to make this feel more like a finished piece. Add a second pencil line about 15mm (½in) inside the pencil borderline from Step 1 to create a narrow inner border (although feel free to make this as thick or as thin as you'd like!). Working very carefully, use some of your leftover paints to add the inner border between the pencil lines, painting a straight line on the outer edge and a soft organic line on the inside. I chose not to paint right up to my inner pencil line.

To ensure that the leaf doesn't look like it's floating in midair inside the border, I have used more leftover paint to add small spots to the background. These are very watery, so they look nice and soft.

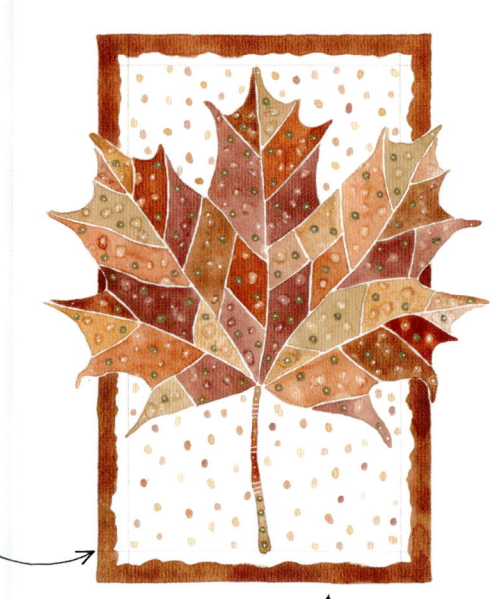

*Add drops of water into your border to create blooms, which will give a lovely texture.*

*At this point in the project you can let your creativity run wild, so try different colors and textures for your border if you prefer.*

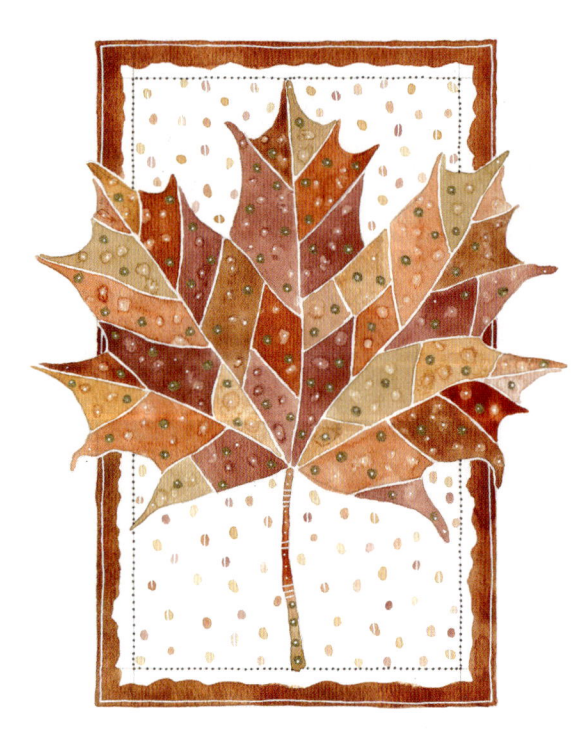

## Step 6: FINAL TOUCHES

Once the painted border and background spots are dry, step back and look at the piece to decide if it needs any extra embellishments. I added a line of small black dots along the pencil line inside the painted border to add definition, and drew a single white line in pen around the border's outside edge. I also added a tiny white line through about half of the background dots to make them look even more subtle.

> *Top Tip:* Don't forget to stand back and look at your piece. The viewer won't always be as close as you are when you paint, so assess it from a distance to see whether you need more contrast or bolder embellishments.

# More Inspiration

Here, I've used the same method as for the main project but omitted the salt and extra embellishments to give a cool, stylized, graphic look. As you know, I cannot resist some added decoration and sparkle, but I've restricted this to the border, which is a fun mix of watercolor and gold raindrop spots, all encased within a sharp border of black fineliner dots.

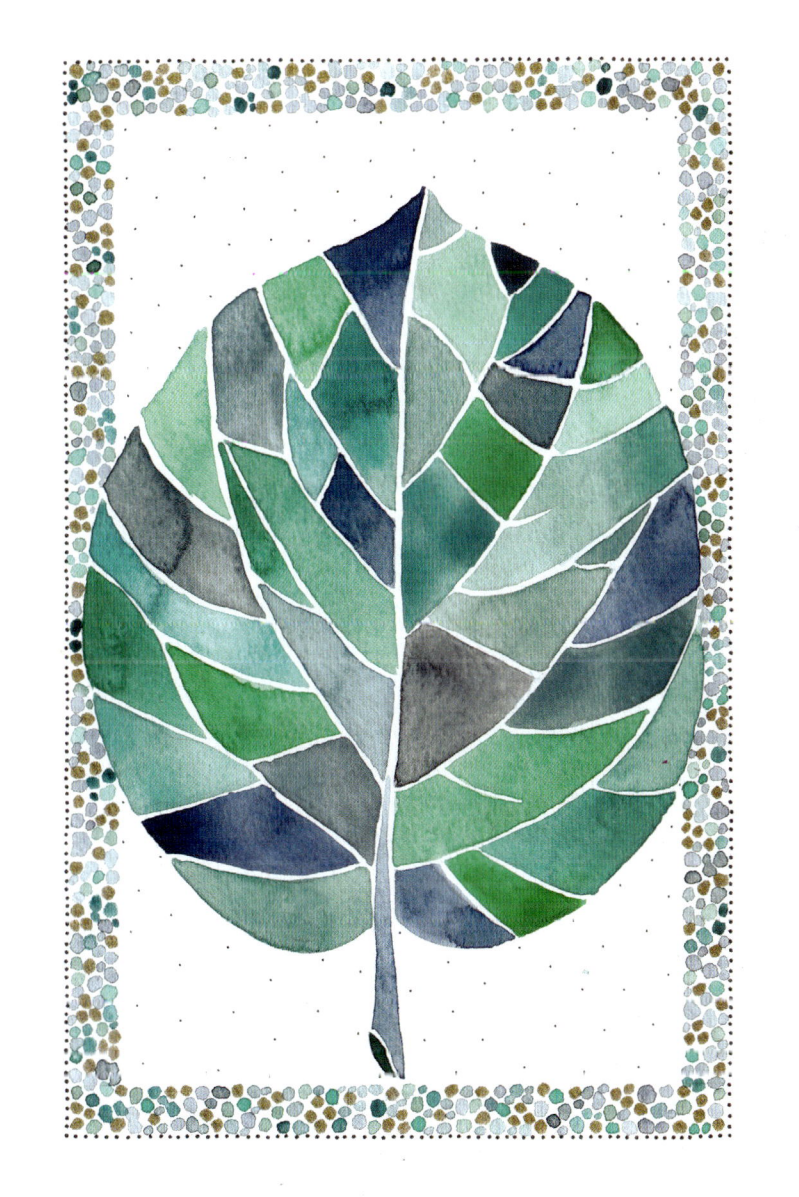

# Starry Landscape

To create a moody night-time feel, I've used a rich dark palette to show how an imagined countryside scene might look under starlight. The stars themselves are created using individual grains of coarse sea salt. I have embellished these twinkles with gold and white for extra highlights. This project is simple, but so effective – and you can embellish it as little or as much as you like. I say go for it!

## MATERIALS

- Winsor & Newton professional watercolors
- Daler Rowney Aquafine Artboard
- Da Vinci Casaneo quill brush - size 2
- Posca paint pen – white, 0.7mm (Ultra Fine)
- Winsor & Newton Drawing Ink – gold
- Coarse rock salt
- Pencil

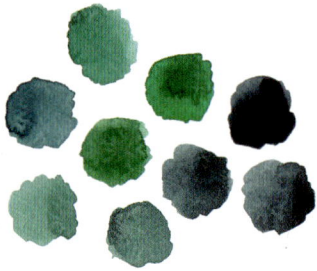

## COLOR CHOICES

For this project I was thinking about an abstract landscape at night, with the dark sky and stars creating a soft blue-green glow over the fields and trees. I've used accents of gold, as I love the richness it adds, but silver moonlight could work just as well if that's more your thing. If you want your painting to feel really different, you could try a multicolored palette to add a surreal wow factor!

### WINSOR & NEWTON COLOR REFERENCES

- Hooker's Green
- Indanthrene Blue
- Indigo
- Prussian Blue
- Winsor Green (Yellow Shade)

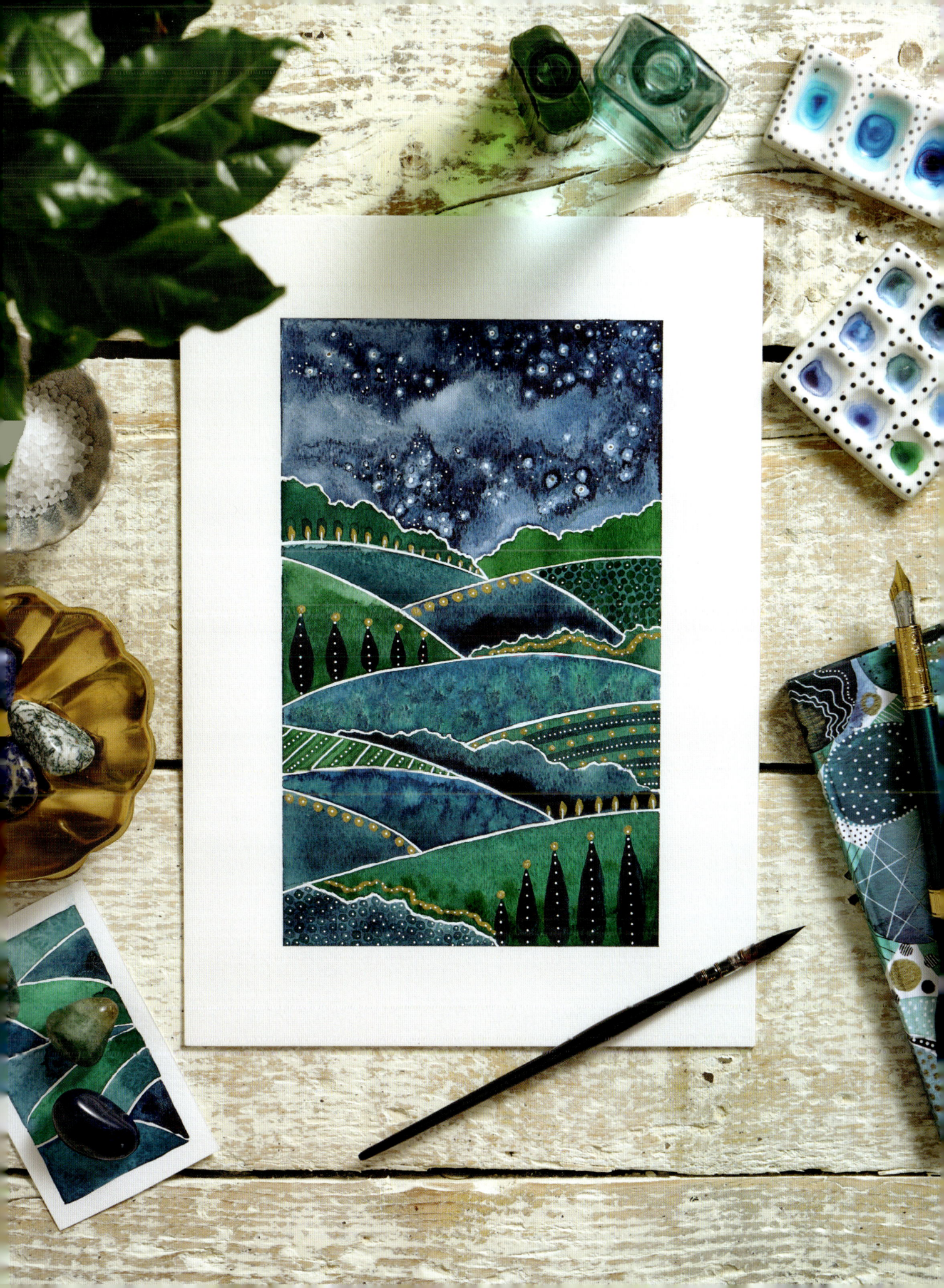

## Step 1: PENCIL SKETCH

To begin, mask out your sheet of artboard to create an area for painting (see Core Watercolor Techniques: Masking Borders). Once this is done, you can start to sketch out your landscape in pencil. I like to give roughly two-thirds of my page to landscape and one third to sky, as this helps the piece look nice and balanced. When sketching in your hills, have some lines that run right across the page and some short lines that section up a large shape (think of the "patchwork" of hills and fields you see in the countryside).

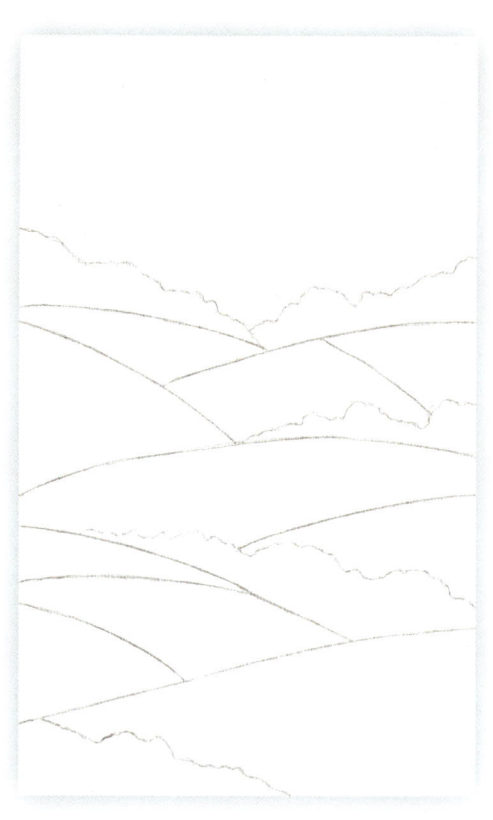

*Top Tip:* Remember to keep the sections nice and large. If they're too small, it will be very fiddly and difficult to paint in the sections while keeping the border crisp and white.

## Step 2: WET PAINT – LANDSCAPE

Now that you have your page masked out and the shapes sketched, you can start to paint! Start filling each of the sections with color, remembering to keep a thin white line of dry paper between each to stop the colors running together. I've tried to use a nice mix of blues and greens randomly across the page, painting some flat and some using the wet-on-wet technique (see Core Watercolor Techniques: Wet on Wet) to add extra color and water blooms. Once you have completed this step, let the piece dry completely.

*Top Tip:* If any of your sections do touch and run together, simply add in a new line once dry, using a white paint pen.

*Be sure to get contrast by keeping your "cloud" and deep sky sections separate; you don't want the whole sky to be just one color.*

## Step 3: **WET PAINT AND SALT – SKY**

For the next step, I mixed up two batches of Indigo, one as a more watery wash and the other with a stronger pigment. Turning your page upside down for ease, start by painting the tree line at the horizon, and then fill in the whole sky with the lighter wash. Next, working quickly before anything dries, take your darker mix and add it in random places across the sky. The lighter sections will start to look like clouds, with the darker areas representing the night sky behind them. With the paint still wet, add single grains of salt to the darker areas – these will become your stars. Leave everything to dry completely.

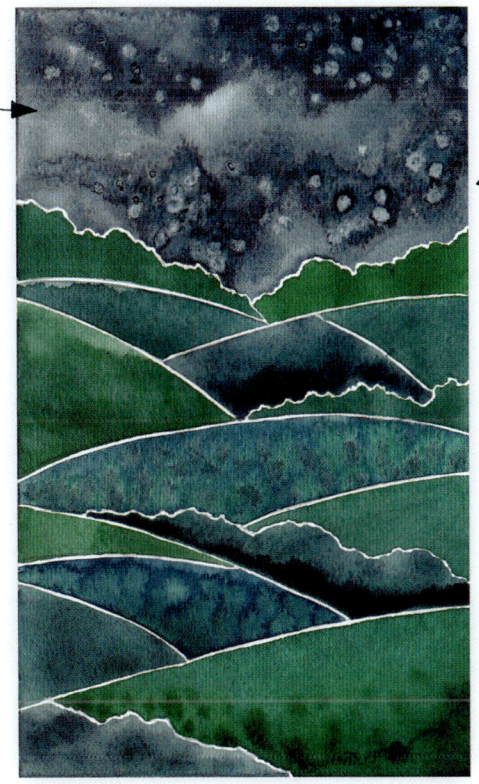

*Try adding salt to the very darkest patches of paint. This will look like stars in the clear areas of sky (you wouldn't see stars in the cloudy areas).*

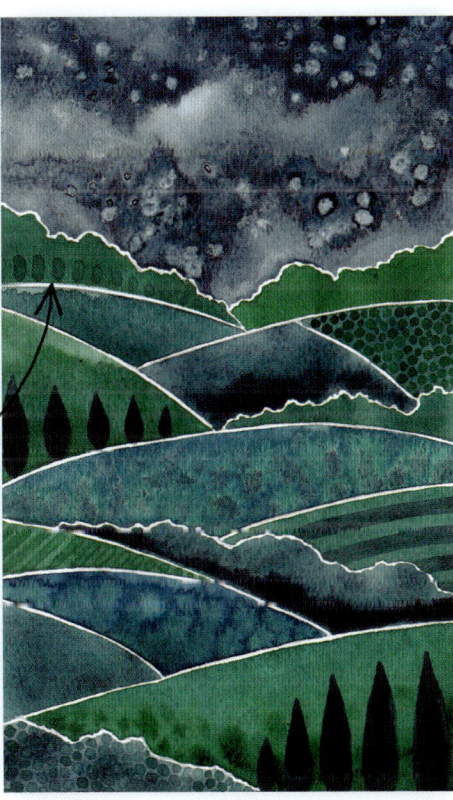

*Use wet-on-dry details to add interest to your landscape, especially on areas where the paint has dried flat with little texture.*

*Once dried, remove the salt carefully as some areas of paint may still be damp underneath.*

*Use the side of your quill brush like a stamp to form teardrop shapes for the trees.*

## Step 4: **WET ON DRY**

Once your piece is completely dry, gently remove the salt (see Getting Started with Salt). Now we can paint in details before moving on to embellishment. For this stage you can do as little or as much as you like – I've added some simple brush stamps to look like trees and added raindrop spots to add texture to some of the painted sections (see Core Watercolor Techniques: Mark-Making Directory).

## Step 5: WHITE EMBELLISHMENTS

Now the fun begins: embellishments! I've used a white pen to add smaller details to the hills in the form of rows of lines and dots for extra dimension. I've also added an extra twinkle to the stars.

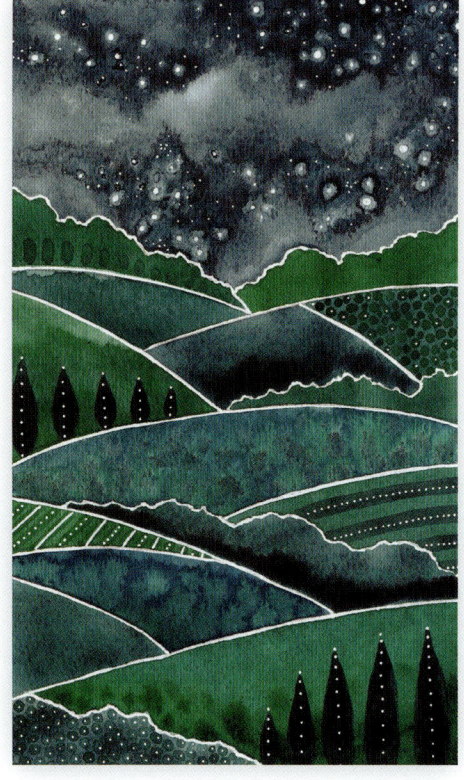

*Where you've used the salt, you'll have little pale areas of paint. Add a single white dot to turn these into your stars.*

*Use white details to help add contrast to any areas that look a little flat or don't stand out against their neighboring colors.*

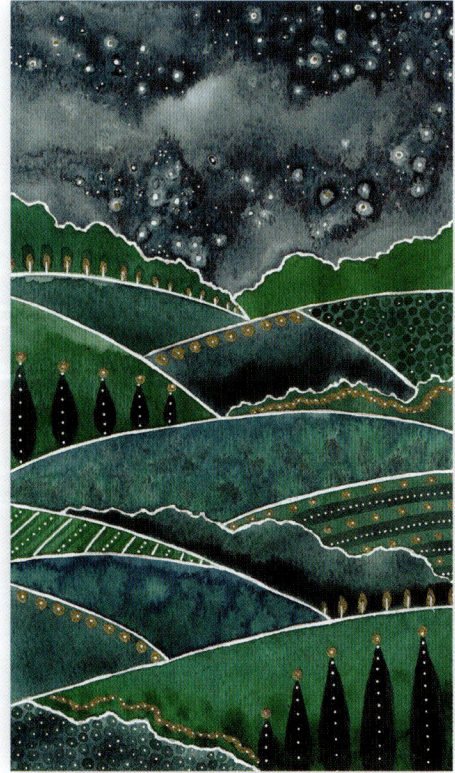

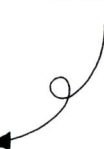

*Add gold to areas you love and want to highlight, but be sure to have an even spread of metallic embellishments across the page.*

## Step 6: GOLD EMBELLISHMENTS

As this is quite a dark piece, I used metallic ink to add some real pop and sparkle. I've concentrated on key areas to create focal points. If you add gold everywhere, it ends up looking flat and lacking in contrast.

Allow all of your details to dry before carefully removing the masking-tape border. Do this slowly so that the paper underneath doesn't rip. Once this is removed, stand back and admire your finished piece!

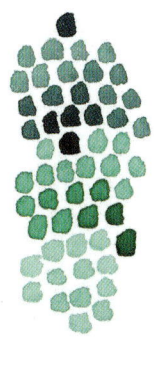
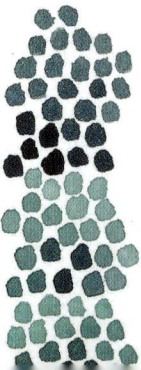

# More Inspiration

This piece was painted at an art retreat in Italy, where I was inspired by the landscape and gray stormy skies. I decided to recreate my original composition in a new color palette, while sticking with deep saturated colors. The gold embellishment takes the piece from stylized realism to something a little more magical!

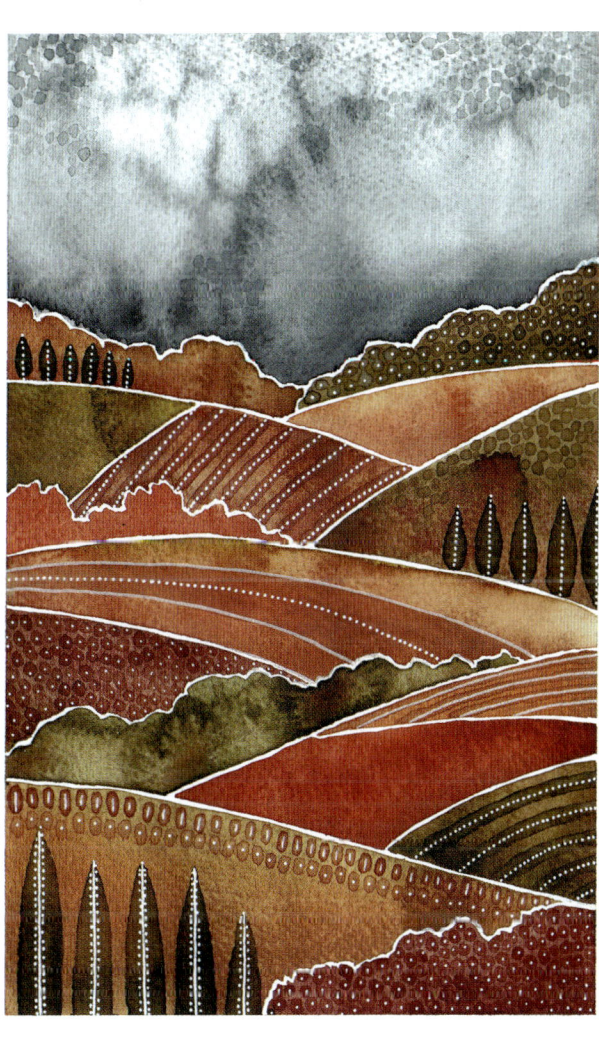

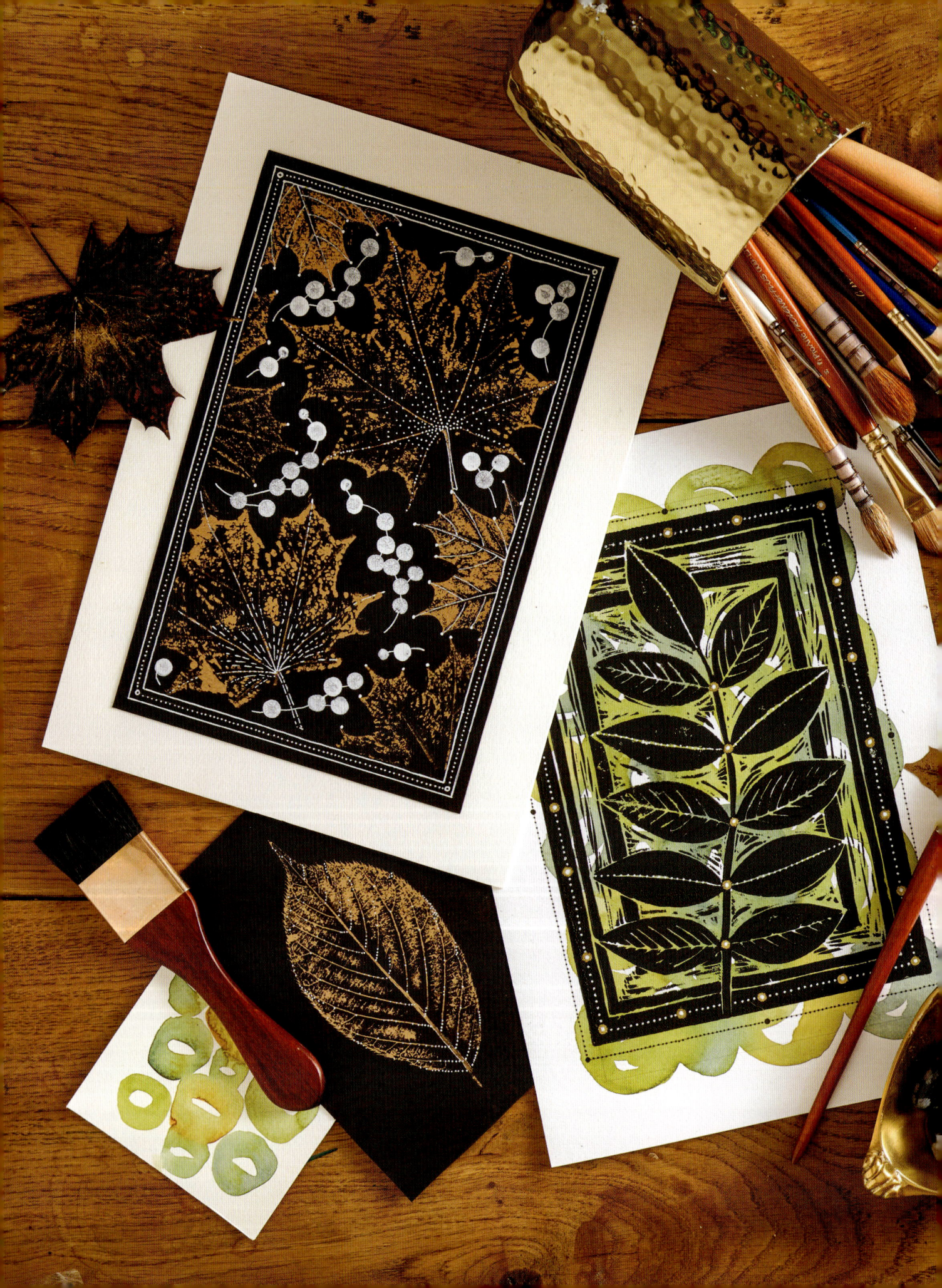

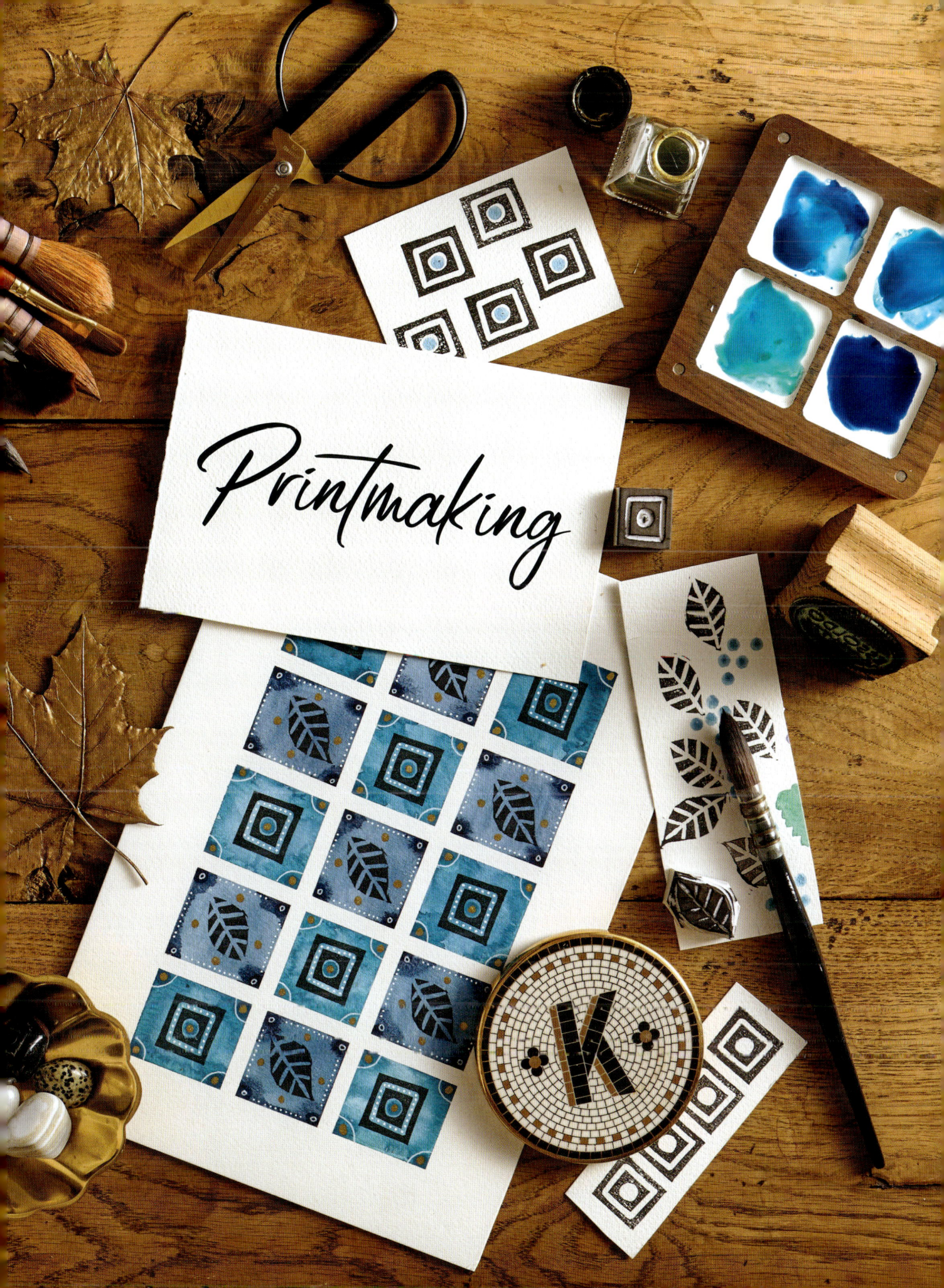

Printmaking

# Printmaking Techniques

Definition: *Printmaking – the activity or occupation of making pictures or designs by printing them from specially prepared plates, blocks, or found materials.*

As my father spent his entire career in the print industry, it's little wonder that the process has always fascinated me. From an early age I loved printing: making potato prints at school, experimenting with screen printing at college, and progressing into techniques like etching when a family friend bought a press. I loved the idea of being able to create multiple prints from a single block or plate – the opportunities felt endless! Fast forward to my current work, and as my watercolor practice grew and developed it seemed natural to start looking at printmaking again. Now in a home studio without the space or equipment for complex processes, I've played with a few techniques to find something that works for me. I hope they work for you, too!

## GETTING STARTED WITH PRINTMAKING

I have neither the knowledge or the space in this chapter to cover off the vast and varied forms of printmaking available to you, so I will instead focus on the three techniques that I have used in this book. These are all examples of 'relief' printing, where you remove the parts of the block that you don't want to transfer to your paper, rather than 'intaglio' printing, which is the reverse (the recessed areas are printed).

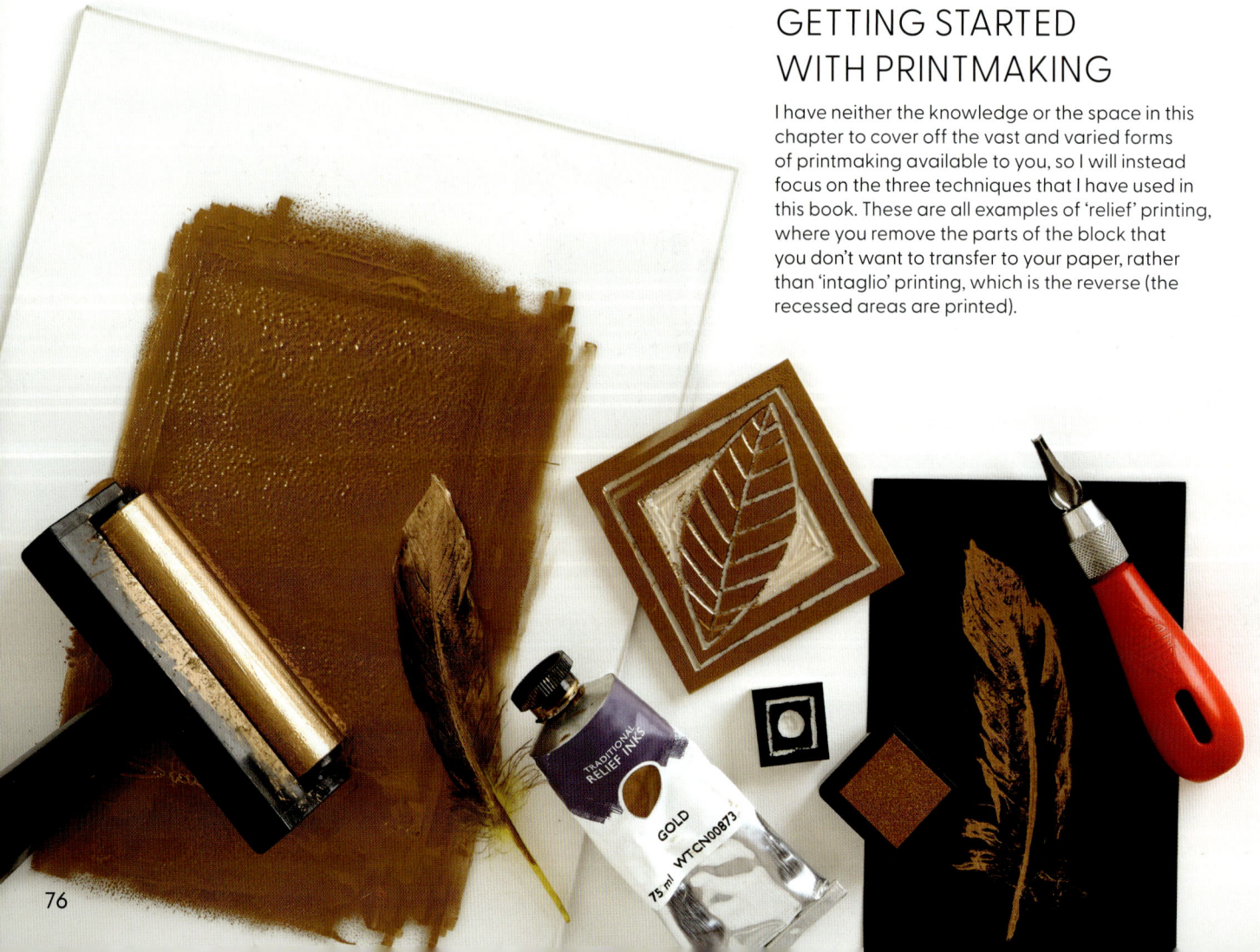

## CREATING YOUR OWN RUBBER STAMPS

Using school-style erasers is a cheap and easy way to create your own rubber stamps that can be used time and again to create patterns, embellish your artwork, and even to stamp your own gift wrap and stationery! Now this probably feels daunting, but it really isn't – it's a super simple technique. To try it out, you'll need the following:

### MATERIALS

- A selection of differently sized erasers
- Pencil to draw out your designs
- Craft knife or scalpel to cut the edges of your stamp
- Lino carving tool
- Scrap paper
- Ink pad – color of your choice but I recommend starting with black as it's such a useful color

### METHOD

1. First select an eraser that's the right size and shape to make your stamp, or cut a larger eraser down to size – I will often use rectangular erasers and cut them down into squares with a craft knife.

2. Next, take a pencil and draw a very simple design onto the eraser stamps – these can get more complex as you practice and your skills grow!

3. Working carefully, use a lino tool to carve out your design. The areas you carve away will be negative space – here, I am carving out a central dot with a square outline around it that will not transfer any ink to the paper.

4. Now open your ink pad and apply it to the top of your stamp, or press the stamp onto the pad – try both ways and see which you prefer. Firmly press the inked rubber stamp onto a piece of scrap paper, and lift it off to reveal your print. If you aren't happy with your print, you can always a carve a little more away to tweak your design.

*Top Tip:* When creating your stamps, remember that the area you carve out transfers no color, and the area left behind will show in black.

**1**

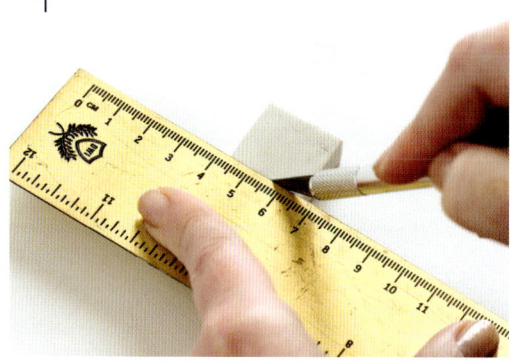

**2**

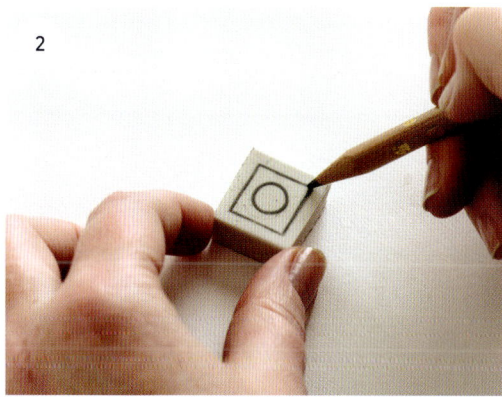

**3**

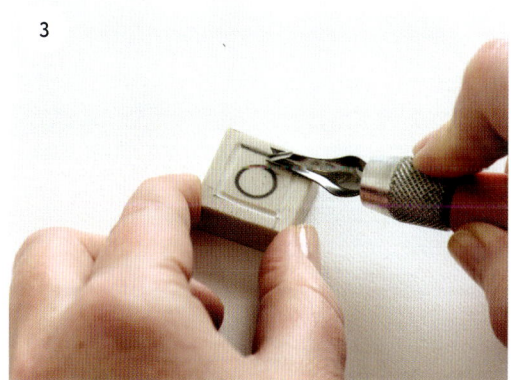

**4**

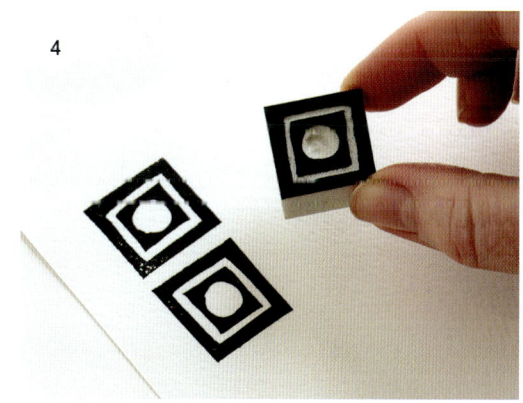

## SIMPLE PRINTING WITH FOUND OBJECTS

Printing can be as easy as inking up an object and pressing it against paper to make a simple impression. Leaves and flowers are my favorites for this technique. As organic objects, you don't need to worry about making a perfect print – if there's a lack of symmetry or any imperfections, it doesn't matter; use this as an opportunity to add embellishment – I like to use white or gold pens. To try this type of printmaking, you'll need the following:

### MATERIALS

- Printing ink and a sheet of glass, Perspex or cardboard
- A small roller (also called a brayer)
- Scrap paper and paper for your piece – thinner paper works best for this
- Something to print – feathers, leaves, lace, fabric, textured card... anything with texture, really!

### METHOD

1. First take your printing ink and roll out a small amount – about an inch – on a non-porous surface (a sheet of glass or Perspex is ideal, but a rigid sheet of cardboard will do). Use your roller to spread the ink out, ensuring that your roller is well coated with a thin layer of ink. If it looks too thick, keep rolling out until you get to the desired thickness.

2. Now lay out your found object on a sheet of scrap paper and use the roller to carefully coat one side with ink. You may have to roll over it several times to ensure good coverage.

3. Lay your object ink-side down on your project paper. Once you have placed it, don't move it or the print will smudge. Now lay a piece of clean scrap paper over the whole thing and gently but firmly press down on the back to transfer the ink to the paper below.

4. Remove your scrap paper and slowly peel away your object, which should reveal the print. Leave to dry overnight, as printing ink has a slower drying time to some other inks.

*Top Tip:* To prevent found leaves from curling up as they dry out, pat them dry with kitchen paper and place inside an old book or between sheets of paper with a heavy weight on top. Leave for a few days. This will press the leaves, helping them stay flat.

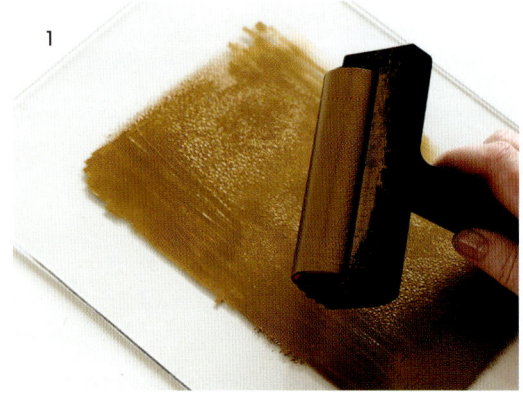

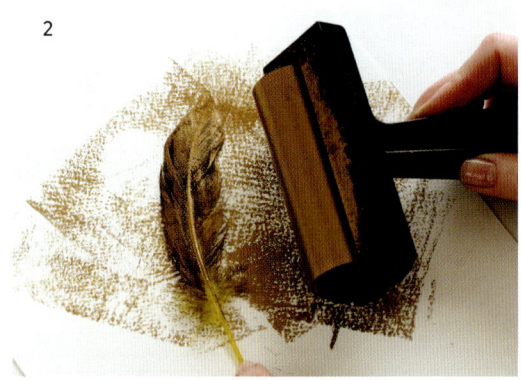

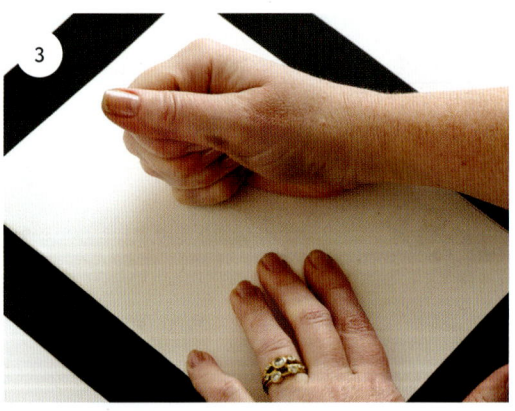

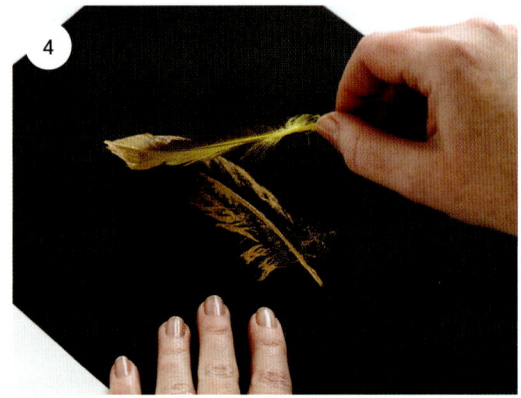

## LINO PRINTING

Lino printing, also known as linocut printing, is a technique that involves carving a design into a block of linoleum (or sometimes rubber or vinyl) and then inking up and printing the remaining areas with ink.

### MATERIALS

- Pencil
- Lino block
- Permanent pen (optional)
- Lino carving tool
- Roller
- Printing ink and sheet of glass/Perspex/cardboard
- Scrap paper

### METHOD

1. First, come up with your design. Carving can be tricky to start with, so begin with simple designs that don't have too many tight circular shapes, which can be awkward to carve out. Straight lines and soft curves work best to help you gain confidence. Draw your design onto your lino block in pencil. For a stronger guide, you can draw over the lines with a permanent pen, or color in the areas you want to keep.

2. Now use your lino tool to carve away the areas you don't want to transfer to your page – remember, you are carving away the negative space; the areas you leave will get inked up and create your final print. Aim to apply an even pressure as you carve, and move the blade away from you in case you slip with the sharp cutting tool.

3. Ink up your roller as you did for Simple Printing with Found Objects, coating it with a smooth, thin, even layer of color. Now roll over the design on your lino block – the ink will only adhere to the raised layer of lino that was left uncarved – the carved area will remain clear.

4. With the ink side up, place the block onto some scrap paper. Take your project paper and lay it over the inked surface of the block – I suggest you practice printing on plain scrap paper for the first few prints to get the hang of it. Press down firmly using the back of your hand, then rub the paper to ensure an even transfer of ink – make sure all areas of the inked block are in contact with the paper. Once you're happy this has happened, slowly lift the paper from one edge to reveal your print!

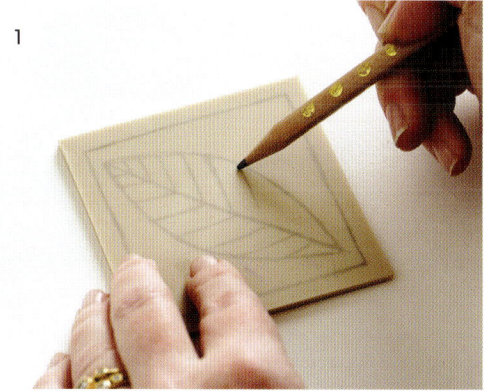

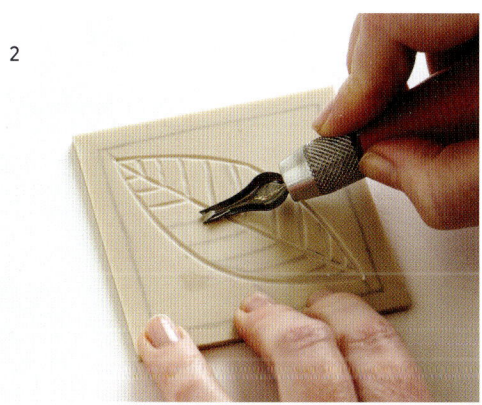

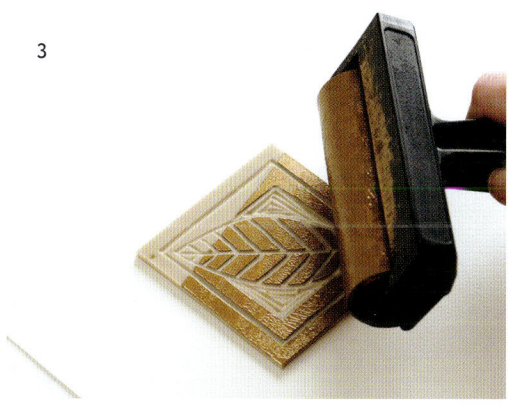

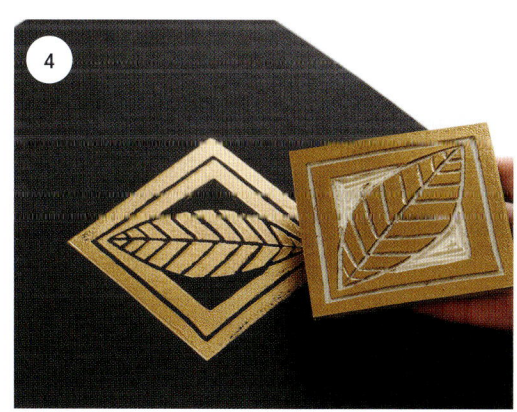

# Tile Mosaic

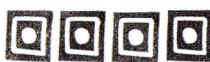

If you're nervous about printmaking, this is a lovely easy introduction that uses a simple carved eraser to make striking graphic prints on a tile-style design. I love creating these repeat patterns. They are fun and relaxing as there's no pressure to form a composition; simply create your grid, paint, stamp, and then decorate – the design options are endless!

## MATERIALS

- Winsor & Newton professional watercolors
- Daler Rowney Aquafine Artboard
- Da Vinci Casaneo quill brush – size 2
- Posca paint pen – white, 0.7mm (Ultra Fine)
- A firm square or rectangular eraser
- Lino carving tool – thin tip
- Black ink pad
- Winsor & Newton Drawing Ink – gold
- Cotton bud (Q-tip)
- Thin washi tape
- Scissors, pencil and ruler

## COLOR CHOICES

I first created these pieces after a holiday to Portugal, where I was so inspired by the beautiful decorative ceramics. Portuguese tiles are often in classic shades of blue and white; here I've added in some aqua and teal (and of course gold!) to give my own twist to the look. As with many of my projects, the color options are endless, so play and explore – why not try this design in your own favorite colors?

### WINSOR & NEWTON COLOR REFERENCES

- Aqua
- Indigo
- Turquoise

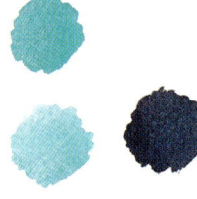

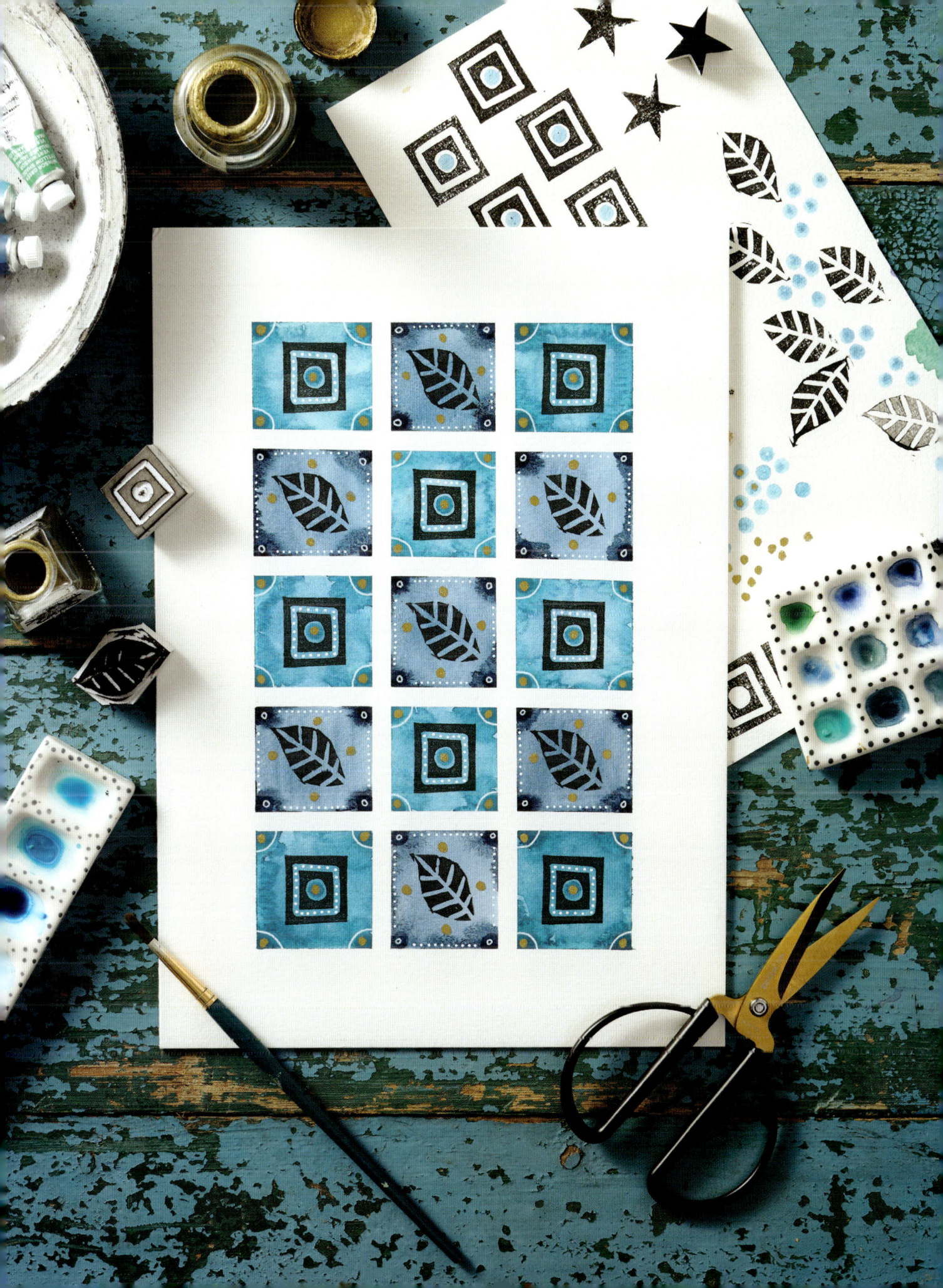

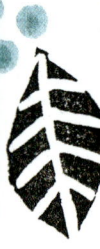

## Step 1: PENCIL GRIDLINES

To begin, mask out your sheet of artboard (see Core Watercolor Techniques: Masking Borders), then use a pencil and ruler to mark out your grid of squares. For this A4 sheet, I've created a 15-square grid – that is, five rows of three columns.

*I've stuck to a grid of square shapes rather than rectangles as they give the feel of a classic ceramic tile.*

*I've kept my squares large on the page. Rows of three look good, and the squares won't be too small and fiddly to decorate.*

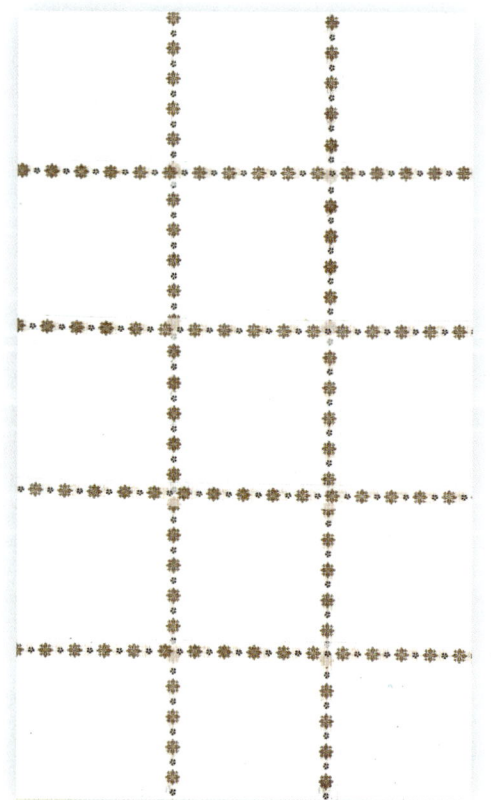

## Step 2: ADDING THE WASHI TAPE

Now that you have your pencil grid, it's time to add your washi tape. I use a thin variety, which I buy cheaply online. The pattern or color doesn't matter for this, as we'll be removing it at the end. Make sure to apply the tape as evenly as possible over your pencil lines to create a nice straight and even grid.

*Press the washi tape down firmly, as we'll be painting over it in the next step.*

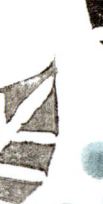
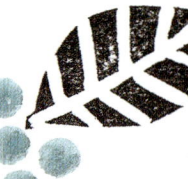

## Step 2: FIRST LAYER OF PAINT

With our masked-out page divided with washi gridlines, we can now start to add color! First mix a nice loose wash of aqua/turquoise, and brush it over alternate squares of the grid. With the paint still wet, add some more pigmented paint to each corner to give a stronger color – this adds a nice effect to the tiles when dry. Once this set of squares is complete, do exactly the same with the remaining squares, but this time using indigo. These colors give a subtle checkerboard effect.

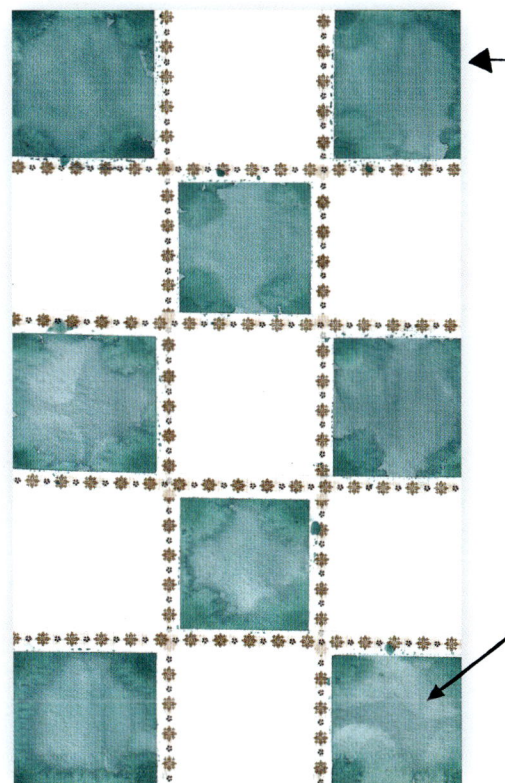

*As this is a repeat design, make sure that what you do on one tile, you do on all the tiles in that color.*

*Don't worry if your tiles dry slightly differently, as this will give them a unique, hand-painted look.*

*If you want to emphasize the checkerboard design, make one of the colors much darker for greater contrast. Here I wanted used aqua and indigo.*

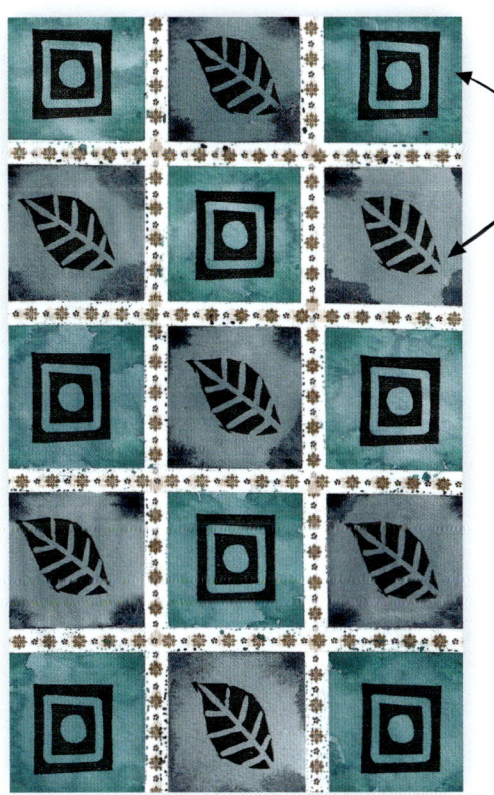

*For my alternating designs, I like the contrast of the hard lines of the square and the softer curves of the leaf shape.*

## Step 4: CREATING YOUR STAMP

Referring to Getting Started with Printmaking, take your eraser and cut it into two small squares to create rubber stamps – each stamp will need to fit into your grid squares. Sketch and carve out your designs (I've chosen a square and circle on one, and a leaf on the other). Ink up and press a stamp into the center of each square (you can always test your stamps on a piece of scrap paper first!), alternating the designs as shown.

*Top Tip: I find it easier to use my stamps one at a time, so stamp all your leaves out first, and then fill in the gaps with the square design.*

## Step 5: WHITE EMBELLISHMENTS

Now that we have our alternative grid of aqua squares and indigo leaves, we can get to embellishing! As this piece has quite strong blocky colors, I find accents of white work particularly well to add some freshness and detailed highlights. I've added rows of dots, circles, and lines to accentuate key areas of each tile, such as in the centers and at the corners.

*The part circles on the aqua squares balance the darker corners of the indigo tiles.*

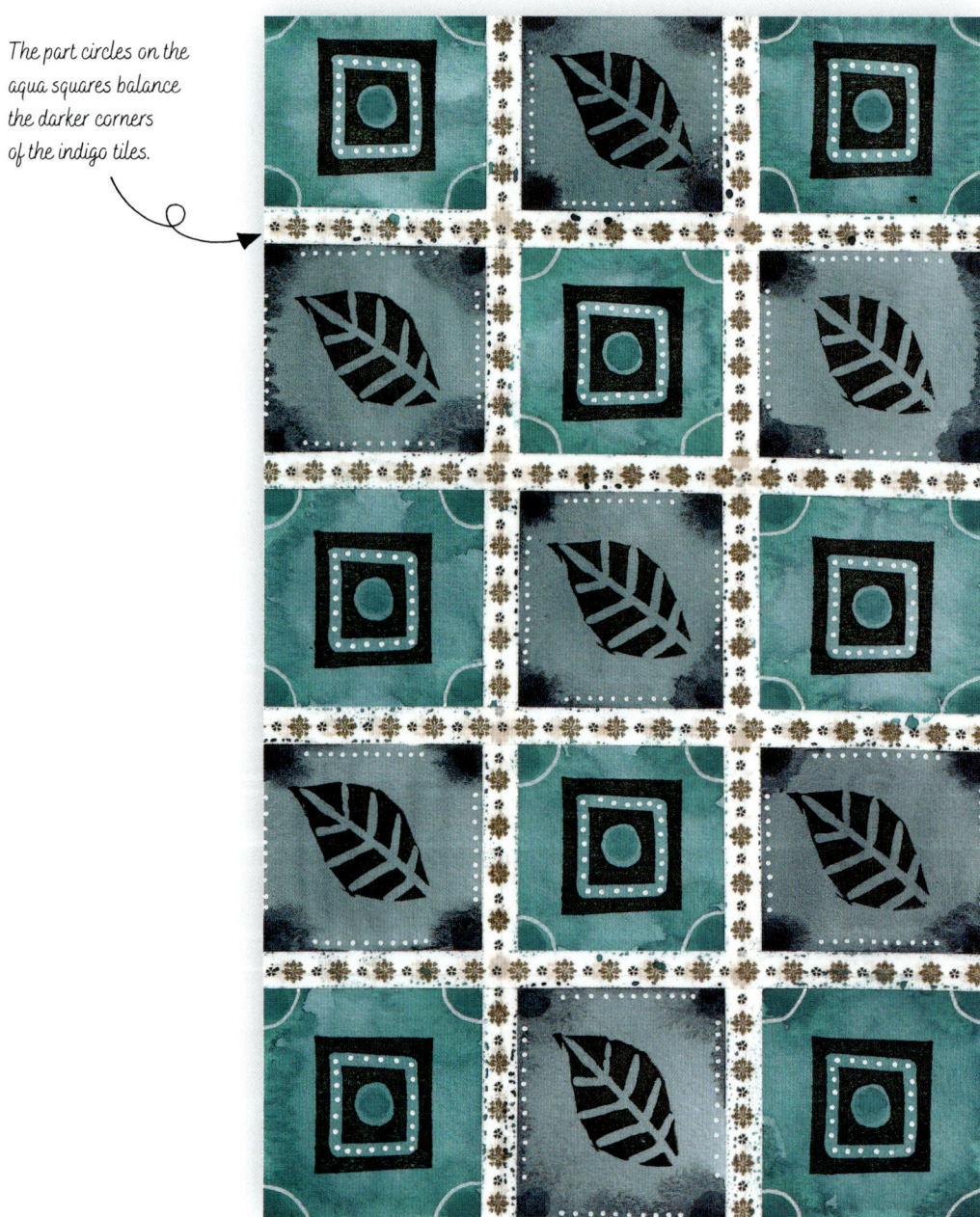

## Step 6: GOLD EMBELLISHMENTS

At this stage, take a really good look at the piece and work out what it needs. More white? Any black details? I decided I needed a couple of extra white details in the corners of my indigo squares, but most of all I saw that some metallic embellishments would really lift the piece, elevating it to something special! I used my favorite gold ink to add small dots for some sparkle and drama.

*I used a cotton bud (Q-tip) to stamp out my gold details – see Core Techniques: Mark-Making Directory for more ideas.*

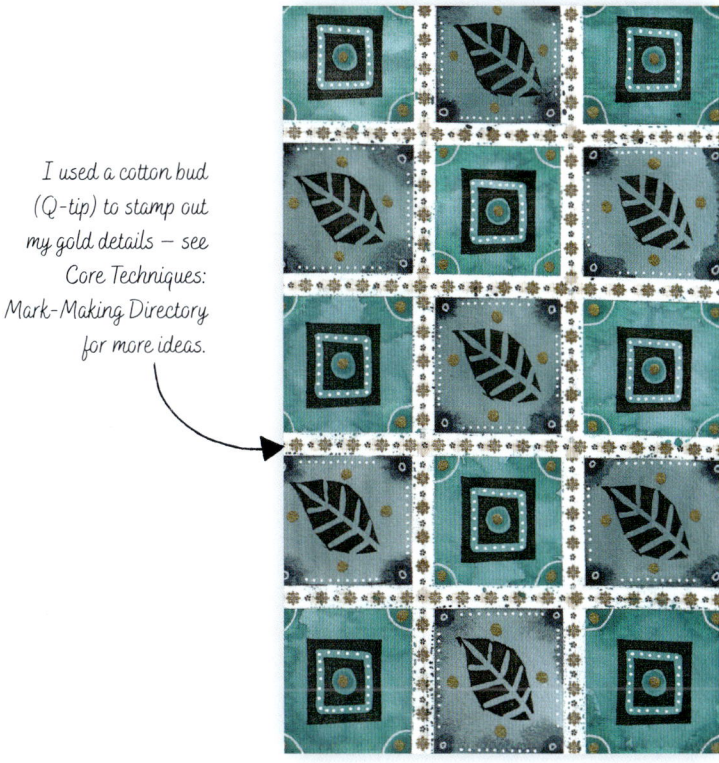

## Step 7: REMOVING THE GRID LINES

Now that everything is dry and you're happy with your design, it's time to remove your washi tape to reveal the crisp white lines underneath. This should look like the grout of your tiling. Once the grid is removed, carefully peel away your outer masking-tape border and sit back and admire your handiwork!

*Use a soft earaser to remove your pencil lines to give a nice crisp finish.*

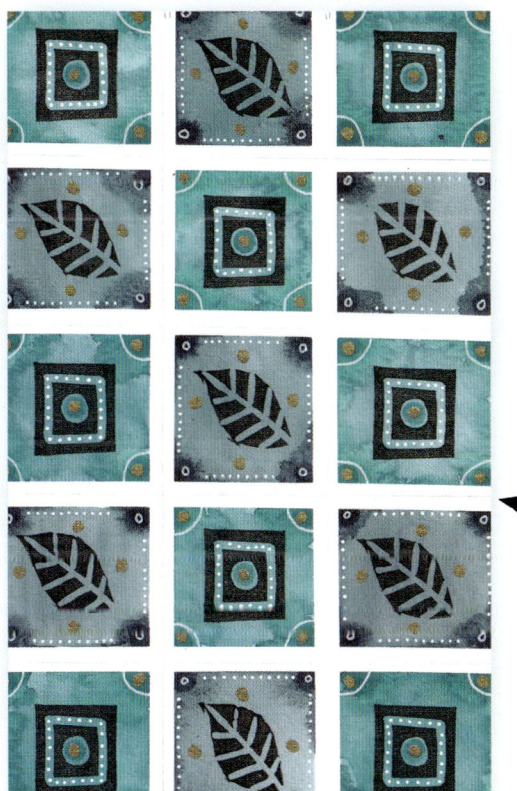

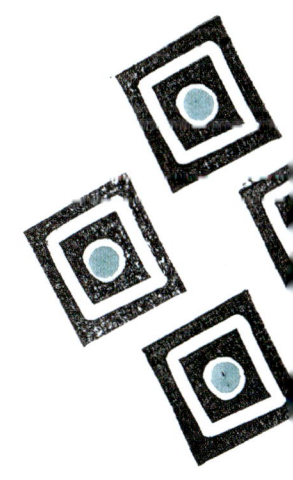

# Botanical Print

I loved creating this project! You don't have to worry too much about composition as the leaf print does most of the hard work, allowing you the freedom to embellish as much (or as little) as you'd like. You can use any kinds of leaves, so go wild with different shapes and sizes. It would be lovely to create a set of three matching prints that showcase different leaves – possibly from your garden or a local park!

## MATERIALS

- Black watercolor paper
- Scrap paper/cardboard
- Posca paint pen – white, 0.7mm (Ultra Fine)
- Uni-ball Signo pen – white, 1mm (Broad)
- Winsor & Newton Drawing Ink – white
- Gold traditional relief ink (you could also try this will gold acrylic paint)
- Fallen leaves (I've pressed mine to make them easier to print with, see Top Tip)
- A small roller
- Foam stamp or cotton bud (Q-tip), or your finger!
- Pencil and ruler

## COLOR CHOICES

As I write, it's the end of autumn here in the UK, so there is an abundance of leaves to choose from. We're just on the cusp of winter, so I've decided to ring the changes by printing on black watercolor paper with gold ink, using accents of white to give this a cool and wintery feel that I love. Depending on what time of year you're trying this (and where in the world you are!) you can use any color of paper, or why not try painting a watercolor background and then printing onto that?

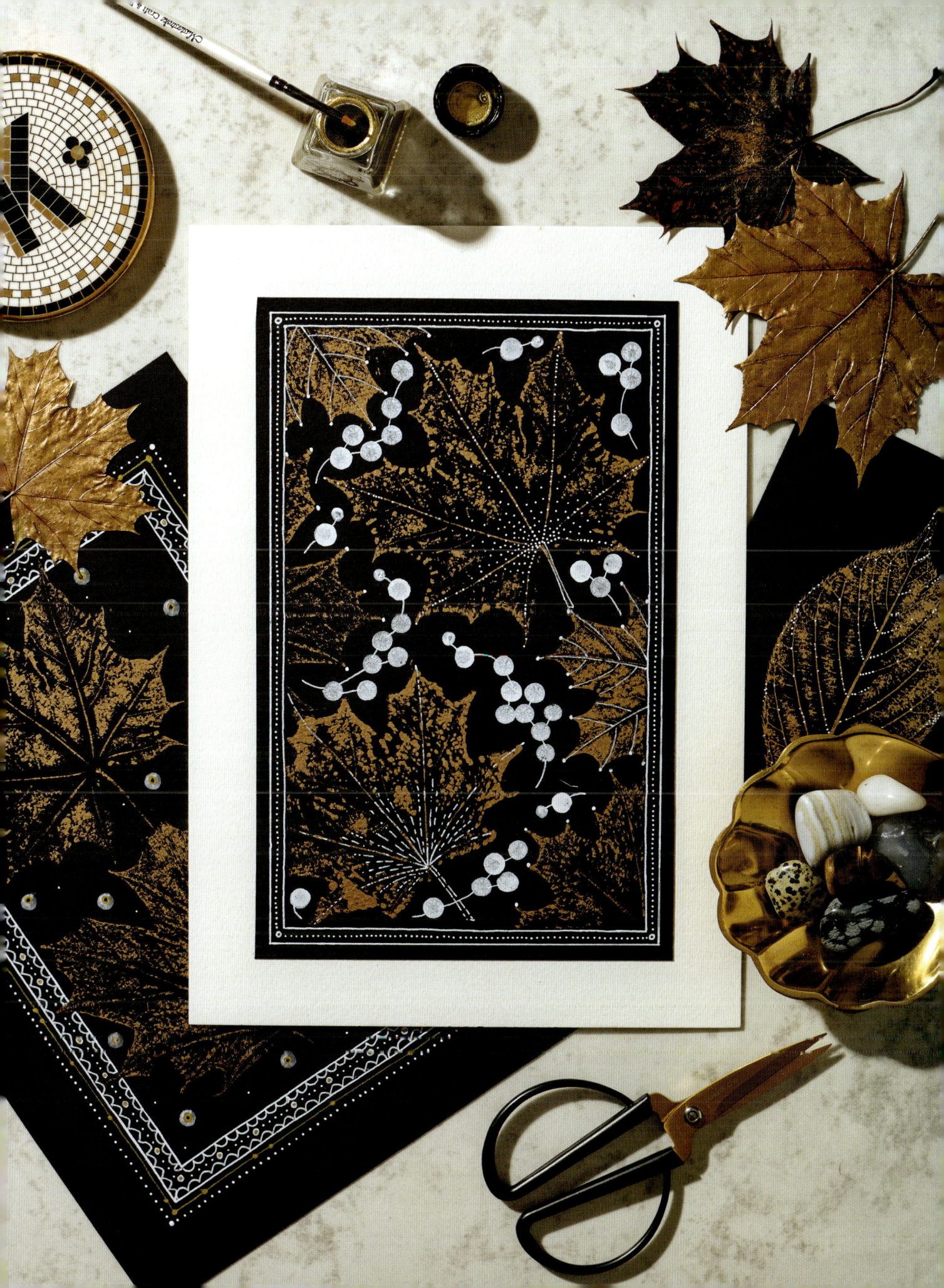

## Step 1: PRINTING YOUR LEAF SHAPES

Mask your page to give you a defined area in which to print (see Core Watercolor Techniques: Masking Borders). Now you're ready to start making your leaf prints. First, coat your roller with a thin layer of ink (see Getting Started with Printmaking). Lay out your first leaf and use the roller to coat one side with a fine, even layer of gold ink. If you're doing multiple leaves, prep them all now so that you're ready to move on to create your design. Take your piece of masked up paper and lay the leaves down in your chosen arrangement, gold-side down. Using clean scrap paper as a barrier, rub over the back of the leaves to create the print. Make sure to do this right across the page for an even transfer. Remove the scrap paper and slowly peel each leaf off the page to reveal your print. Leave to dry at least overnight.

*Top Tip* I used very low tack masking tape as black watercolor paper rips easily. As we're not painting over the tape, you don't need to smooth it down too much; this will help you remove it cleanly with no tearing.

*For my composition I laid out two larger leaves first as the main focus, and then added smaller leaves around them to fill the space.*

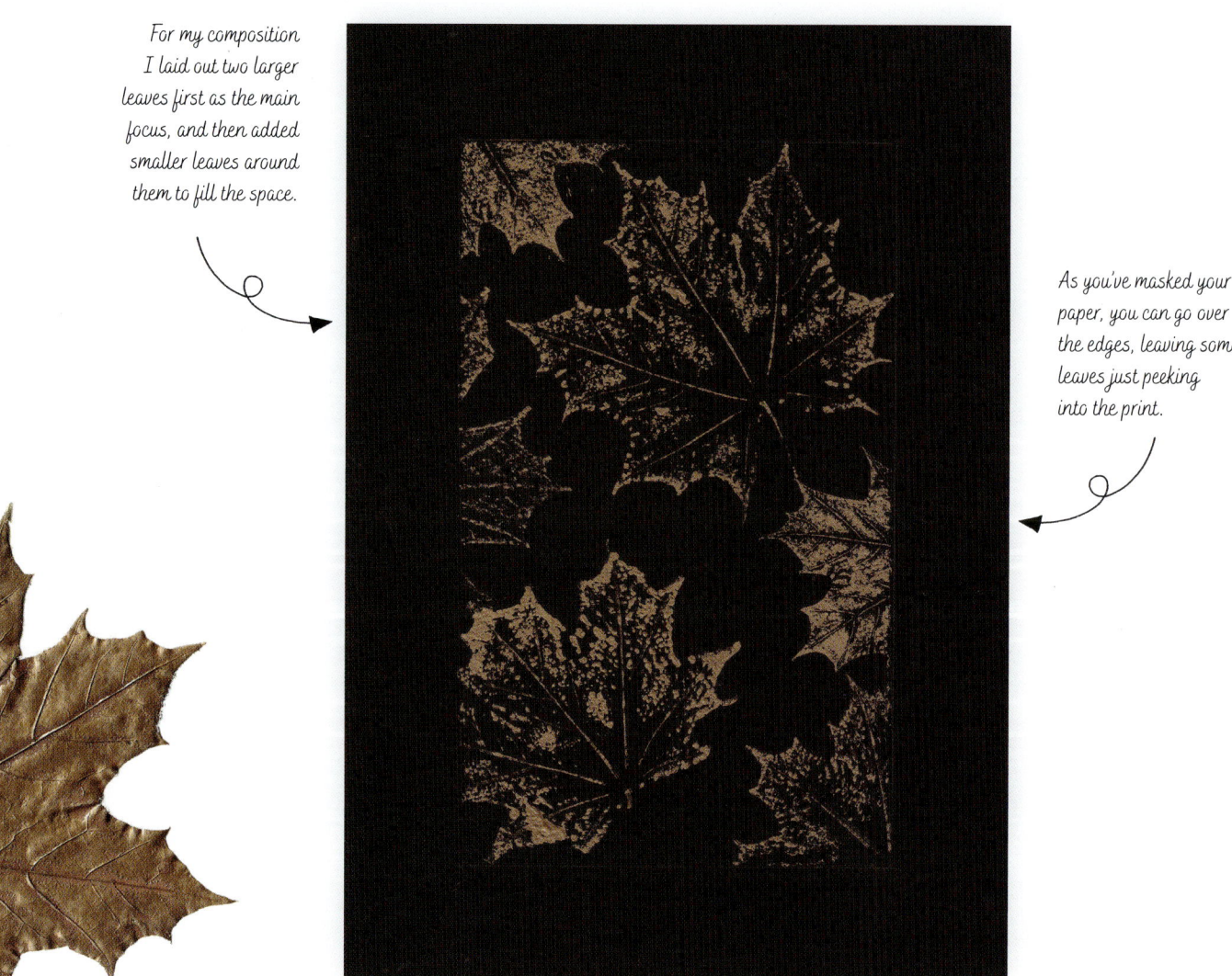

*As you've masked your paper, you can go over the edges, leaving some leaves just peeking into the print.*

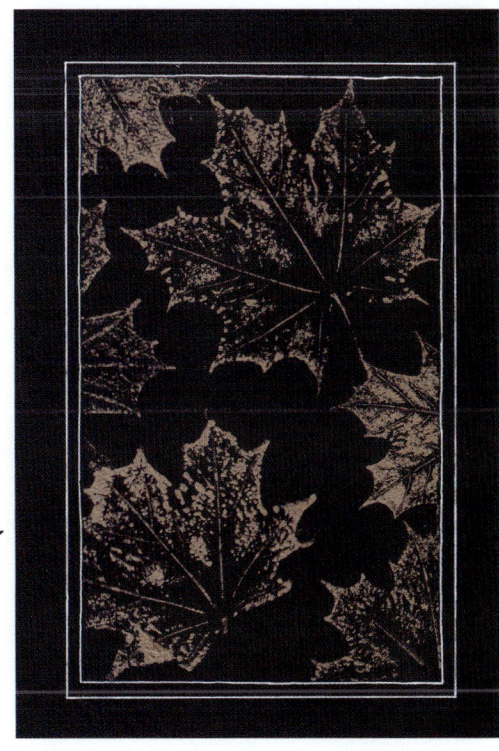

## Step 2: WHITE BORDER OUTLINE

Once your print is fully dried, very carefully remove your tape and start to add the white details. First, use a pencil and ruler to create a border around the edge of your design, starting where the masking tape would have been. Now add a second pencil border around it (my lines are about 6mm/¼in) apart). Use a white pen to go over the pencil guidelines to create your border outline.

*Use a ruler to keep straight when you draw over the pencil guidelines in white, or if you have a steady hand you can try it freehand!*

*I've added a small border here, around 6mm (¼in), but feel free to create a wider border if you'd like.*

## Step 3: EMBELLISHING THE BORDER AND LEAVES

Now that you have your border outline, you can fill it in with extra detail. I've used a thin line of dots down the center, with a small circle at each of the corners. Feel free to experiment and use dots, dashes, rows of lines... whatever you fancy! To embellish the leaves, I've added elements of white in small dots and dashes to highlight the leaf shape, following the veins in the centers of the leaves and adding dots to the edge of each leaf tip. Again, decorate as you see fit – there's so many opportunities to play and experiment! Leave to dry completely.

*If there are sections of your leaf missing, don't view this as a problem – simply draw the missing parts in white to make them into a feature.*

## *Step 4:* **ADDING BERRIES**

Some bolder white marks will add an interesting contrast to the intricate leaf shapes. I've added berries by using some white ink applied with a small foam stamp and a cotton bud (Q-Tip). Once these have dried, use the white pen to add stalks to the berries and connect them up so that they look like sprigs.

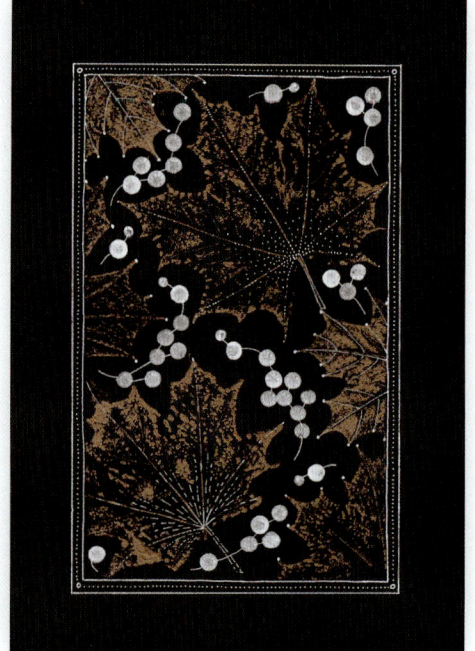

*The lid of the ink bottle acts as a perfect tray to hold your ink for dipping into to make the berries.*

*Top Tip:* If you don't have anything to print with, try using your fingertip to create the round berry shape. Simply coat the very tip of your finger in white ink and press down gently. Practice on some scrap paper until you master the process!

## *Step 5:* **CUTTING OUT AND MOUNTING**

You can skip this stage if you like, but I love the contrast of the deep dark black paper and gold ink with a fresh white border. I cut out my piece, leaving a border of around 5mm (¼in) from the white border outline. I then mounted it on a fresh white piece of paper (or use board). I used double-sided tape to attach it, but you could use glue or spray mount if preferred. Now sit back and admire your work!

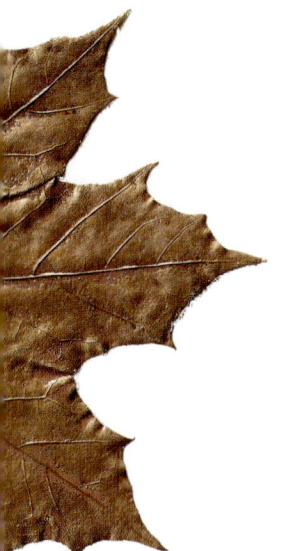

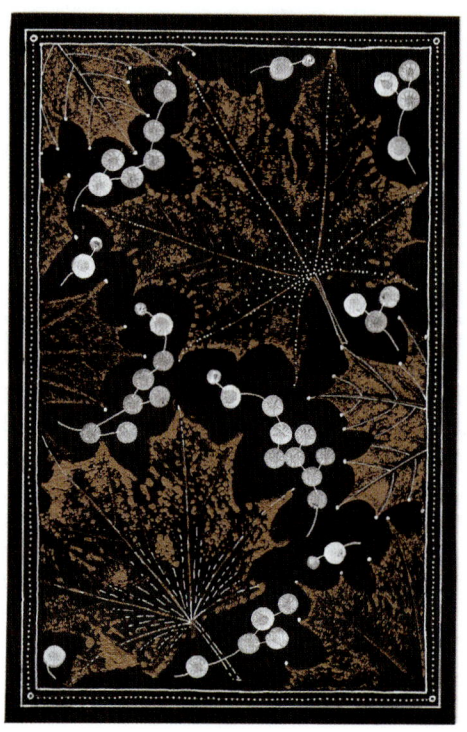

*Cutting out your work is a great idea if you have any rips from your tape or smudges of ink or pen. Happy accidents often help us try new things and create an exciting end result – this is what happened to me the first time I tried this project!*

# More Inspiration

For this piece, I've used the same techniques as shown for the main project but varied the composition. I've focused on a pair of leaves, and amped up the decorative border. I like the interplay between the organic leaves and the delicate lacy lines.

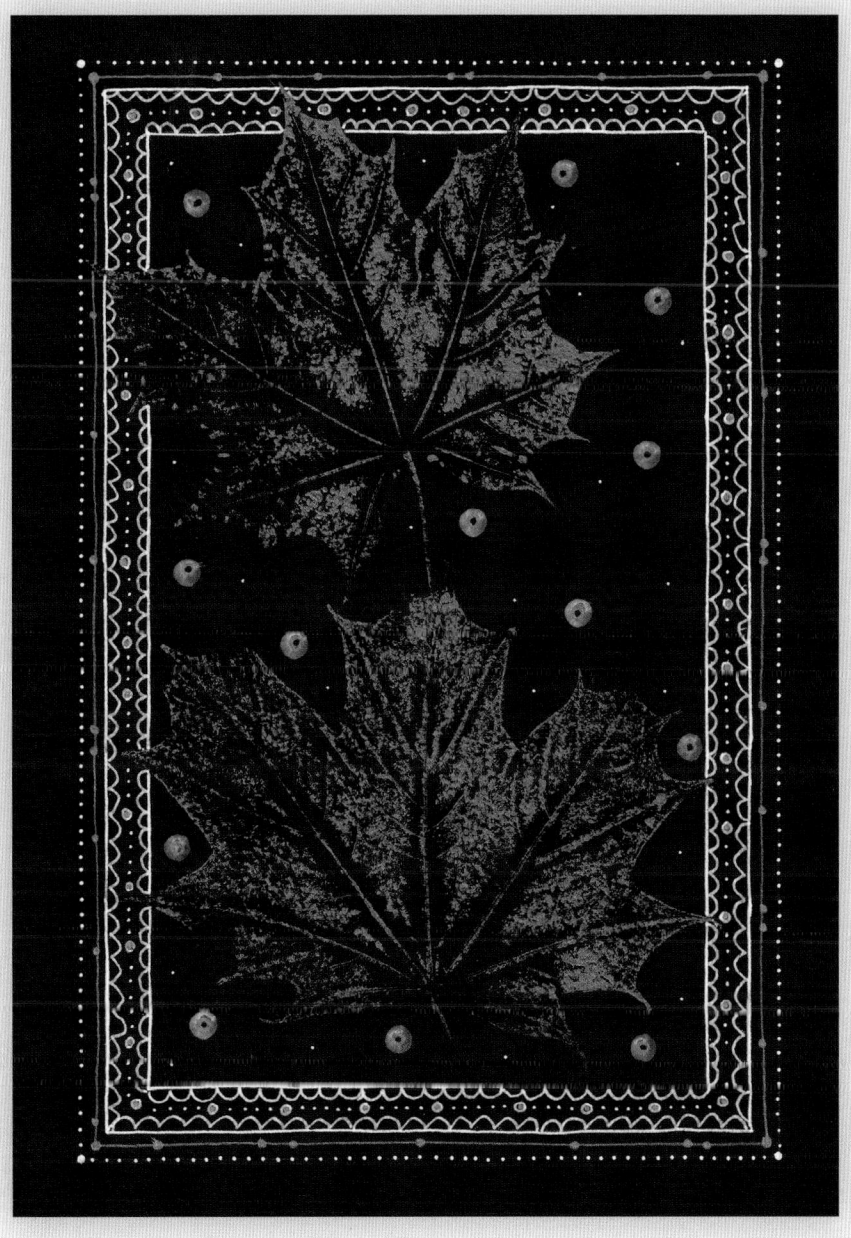

# Leaf-Sprig Linocut

As we progress through the printing projects, I want to offer a project that stretches you a little! It took me a while to get the hang of lino printing (and I'm still by no means an expert), but I love the joy of revealing a new print. The great thing with this technique is that once you have made the block, you can print it again and again in different color inks or with different backgrounds!

## MATERIALS

- Winsor & Newton professional watercolors
- Lightweight watercolor paper (not heavy textured)
- Da Vinci Casaneo quill brush – size 2
- Uni-ball Signo pen – white, 1mm (Broad)
- Tracing paper and soft pencil
- Printing ink
- A small roller
- Lino block or sheet (mine was A5 size)
- Lino carving tool – thin tip

## COLOR CHOICES

Here, I've printed with black ink as I know this will work with so many different backgrounds, papers, and colors. Feel free to experiment and print with other ink colors – white or gold ink would look fab on a deep dark background, giving excellent contrast in your piece. As I'm using black ink, I've made my colors soft yet vibrant to ensure the design shows up well once printed.

### WINSOR & NEWTON COLOR REFERENCES

- Green Gold
- Indigo
- Olive Green
- Transparent Gold Deep

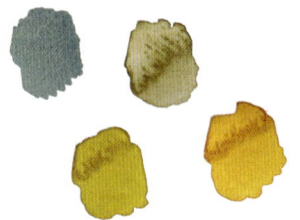

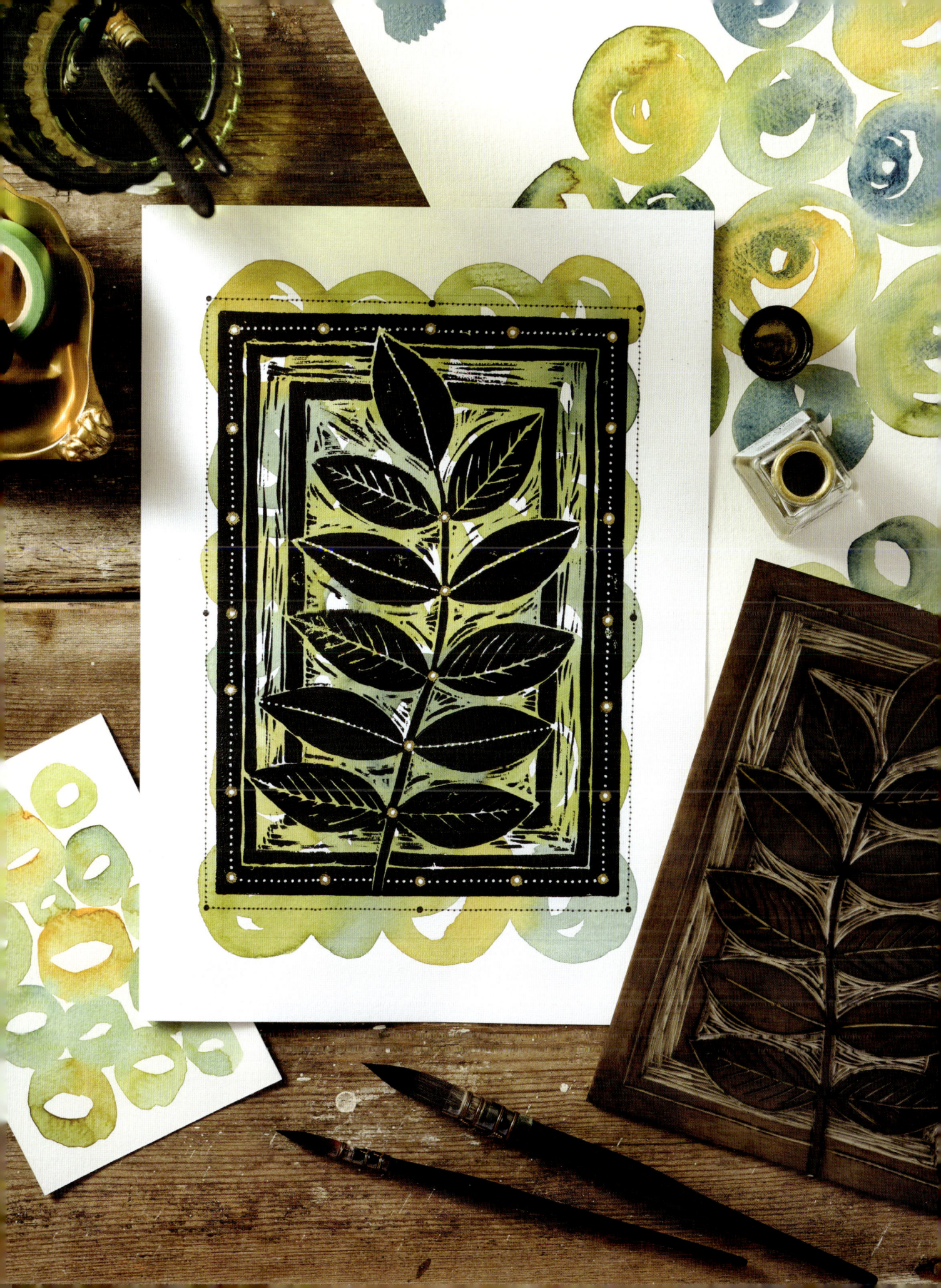

## Step 1: PENCIL SKETCH

The very first thing to think about is what design you'd like to cut into your lino block. Stick with straight lines and soft curves if you're new to lino cutting. I like using natural subjects such as flowers or leaves – organic forms are very forgiving, so you can make adjustments if you slip with your carving tool. I began by sketching out my design on tracing paper, using a soft pencil.

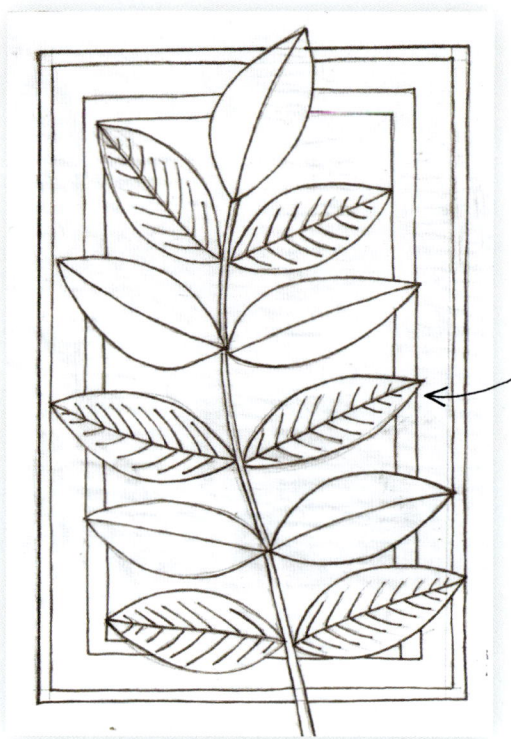

*Mother Nature doesn't mind if your leaves aren't perfectly symmetrical or uniform in size!*

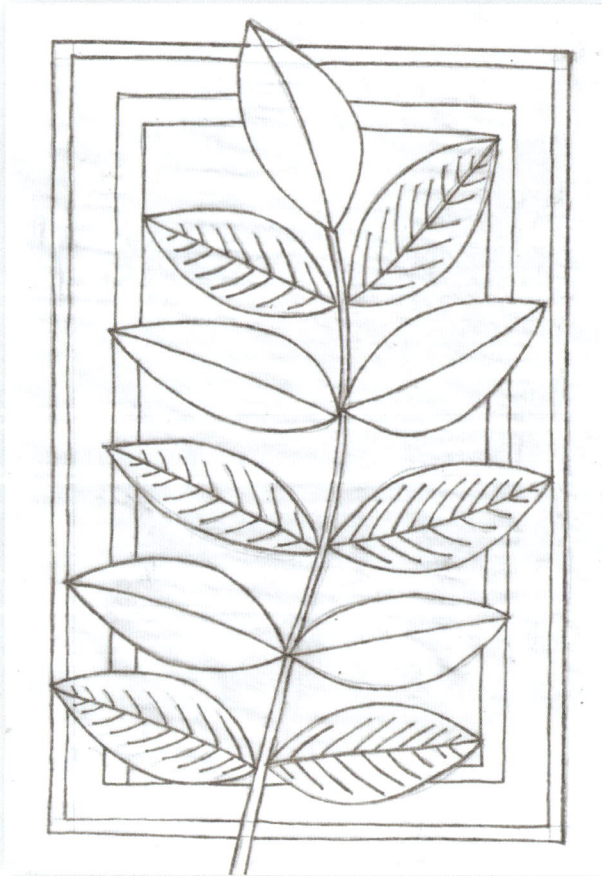

## Step 2: TRACING ONTO THE LINO BLOCK

Now flip your tracing paper over so that your pencil sketch is face down. Place this onto your lino block and use the pencil to cover the back of the lines to transfer them onto your block. This will guide you on where to carve in the next step.

*Top Tip:* If you need a stronger guide for carving, remember that you can use a permanent pen to color in the design on the block. This will help you remember which areas you want to carve away and which you need to keep!

## Step 3: CARVING THE LINO BLOCK

Now that you have your design marked out on the lino block, you can start carving (See Getting Started with Printmaking). Gently slice away the areas that you don't want to see in print, leaving the leaves and border. Also carve out any details that you don't want to transfer in ink, such as the veins of the leaves, so they will stand out as white on the paper.

*Don't worry if little pieces of the background lino still show after carving – this is a signature look for a lino print and adds nice textures to the piece.*

*Top Tip:* Go slowly and carve with an even pressure, moving the cutter away from you.

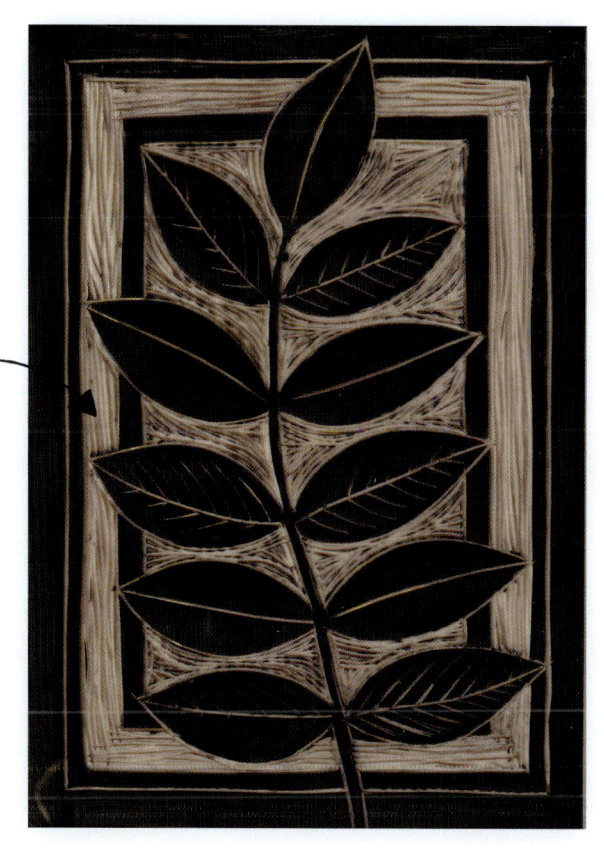

*I've added a pencil border here to ensure I have some white space around the edge of the piece. For a different look, paint your whole page and you will see more of the background beneath the print.*

*I've used soft organic circular shapes for this project, but feel free to create any background design you like. Random mark making or soft watercolor stripes would also work really well!*

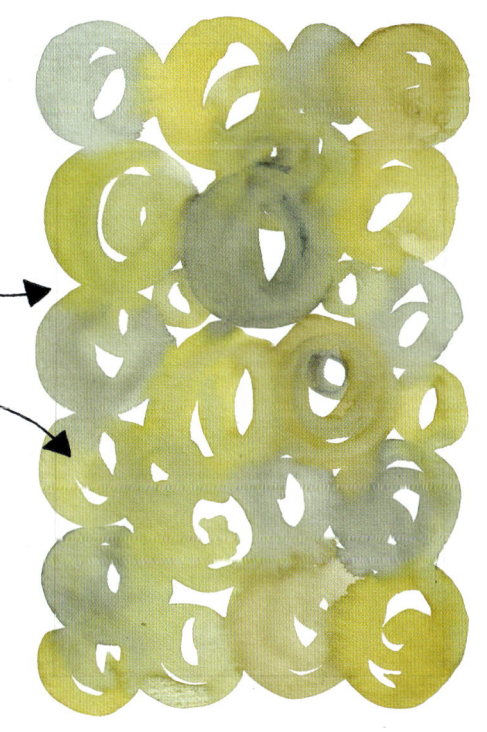

## Step 4: PAINTING YOUR BACKGROUND

Now that you've prepped your lino block, you'll need something to print it onto. You can print directly onto plain paper first to help build your confidence and test that the inking is right. For the final project, though, we'll print onto painted paper. Draw a soft pencil border around your watercolor paper as a guide for where to paint. Using a quill brush, mix up soft washes of your chosen colors, then load your brush. Start to paint large circles inside your guidelines. These don't have to be too pretty or perfect, they just need to fill the inner area with some interesting colors and texture. Once you're happy, leave to dry thoroughly.

## Step 5: **PRINTING**

It's time to make our first print! Coat your roller evenly with a thin layer of ink, then transfer the ink to the carved-out design on your lino block (see Getting Started with Printmaking). If there isn't enough ink on your roller to cover the design completely, just re-roll it in the ink and apply more. Once you're happy with the coverage, place your block ink-up on some clean scrap paper, then gently lay your background painting face down on top. Press down firmly and rub over the back of the paper until the design has been transferred, then peel it away to reveal your print! Leave to dry completely.

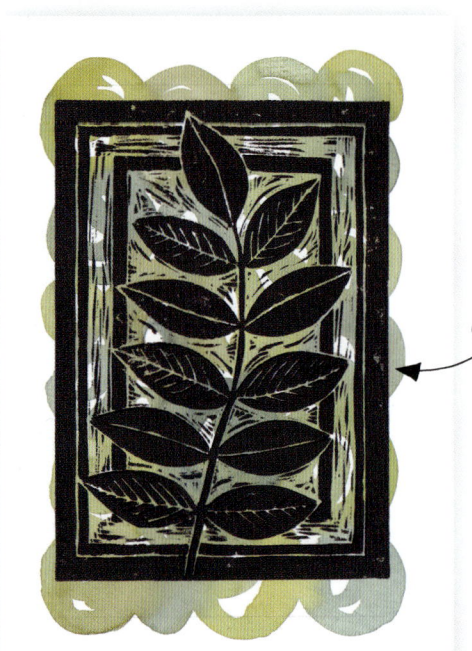

*A flatter, smooth paper will give a crisper print. Using textured paper will give a softer, more organic look as the ink doesn't print so neatly, allowing you to see more texture.*

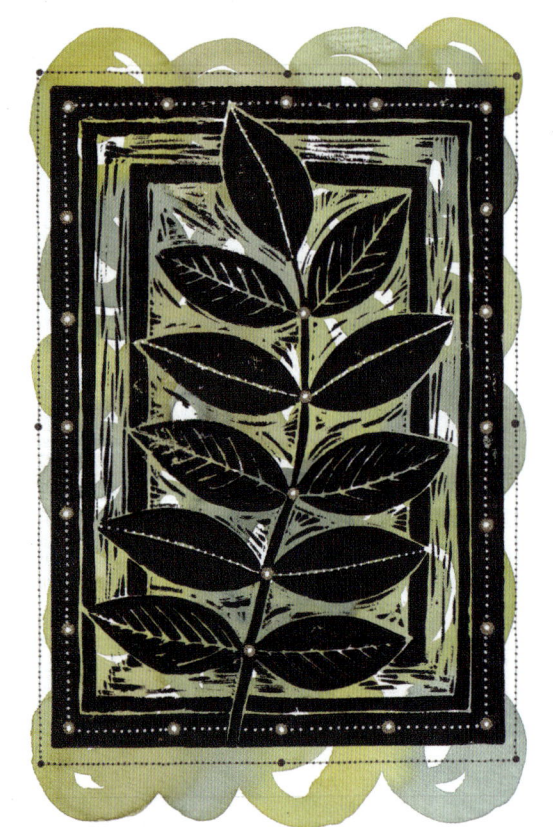

## Step 6: **EMBELLISHMENTS**

Once the ink is totally dry (you may need to leave this for up to 48 hours, depending on your local conditions), your print is finished! While you may like to leave it there, we all know that I can't help but add some extra embellishment... You can add white details to areas of darkness to lift them, or add gold to add highlights and shine. I've done both here to add a little extra pizazz to the piece.

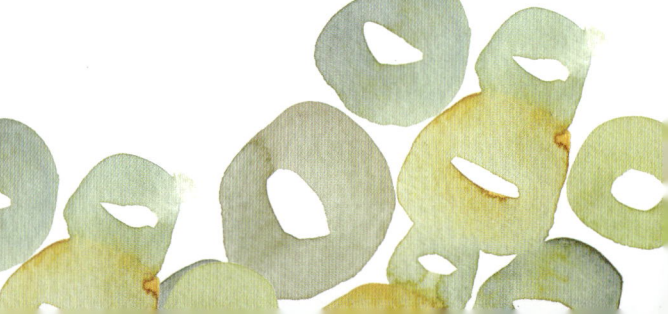

# More Inspiration

Here I've used the same lino block, but a change of color palette in the background takes us from springlike greens to rich, autumnal reds and oranges. Lino is fab as it takes on a whole different look depending on what it's printed on, so try different painted backgrounds and even different papers.

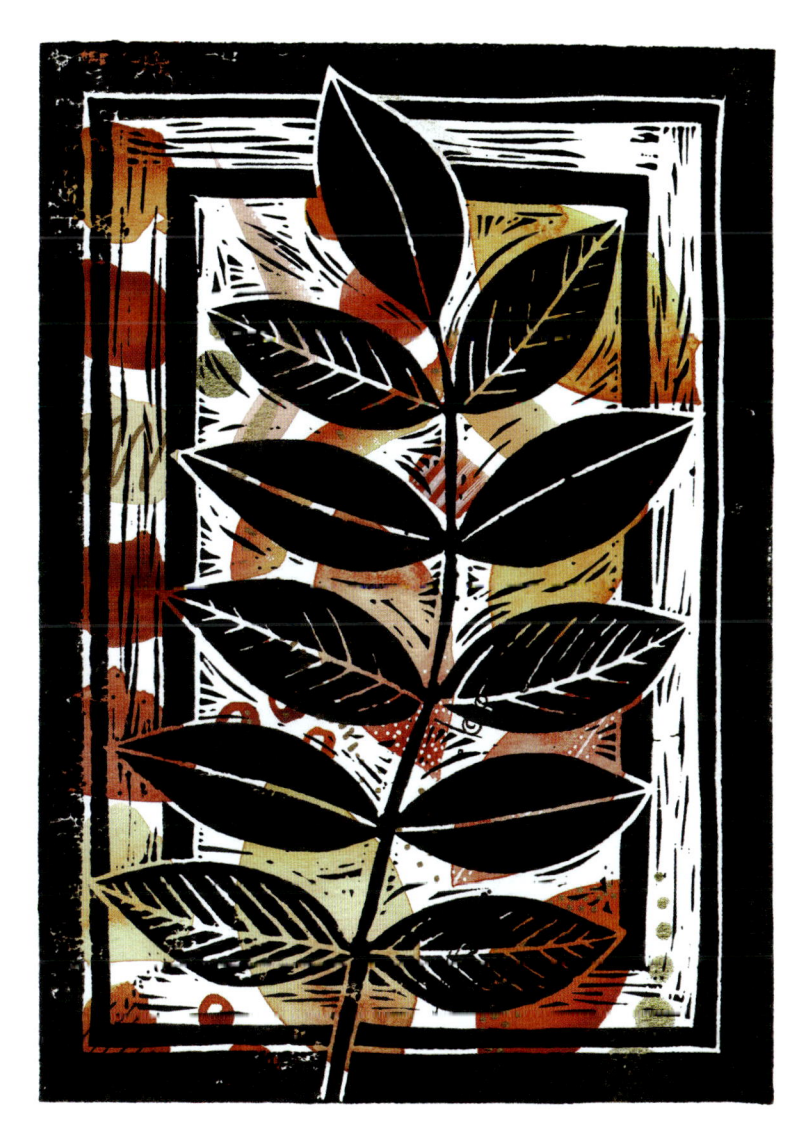

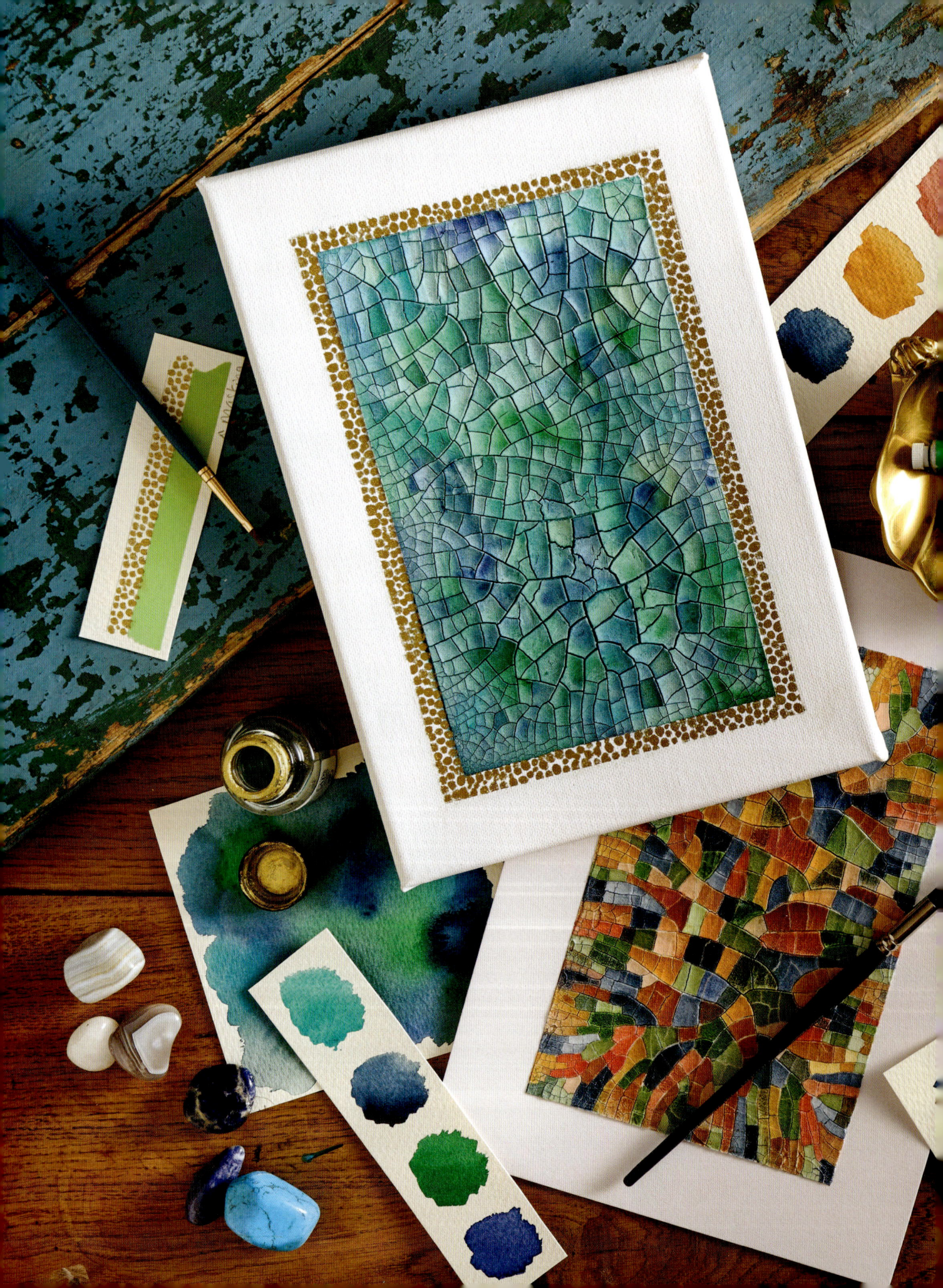

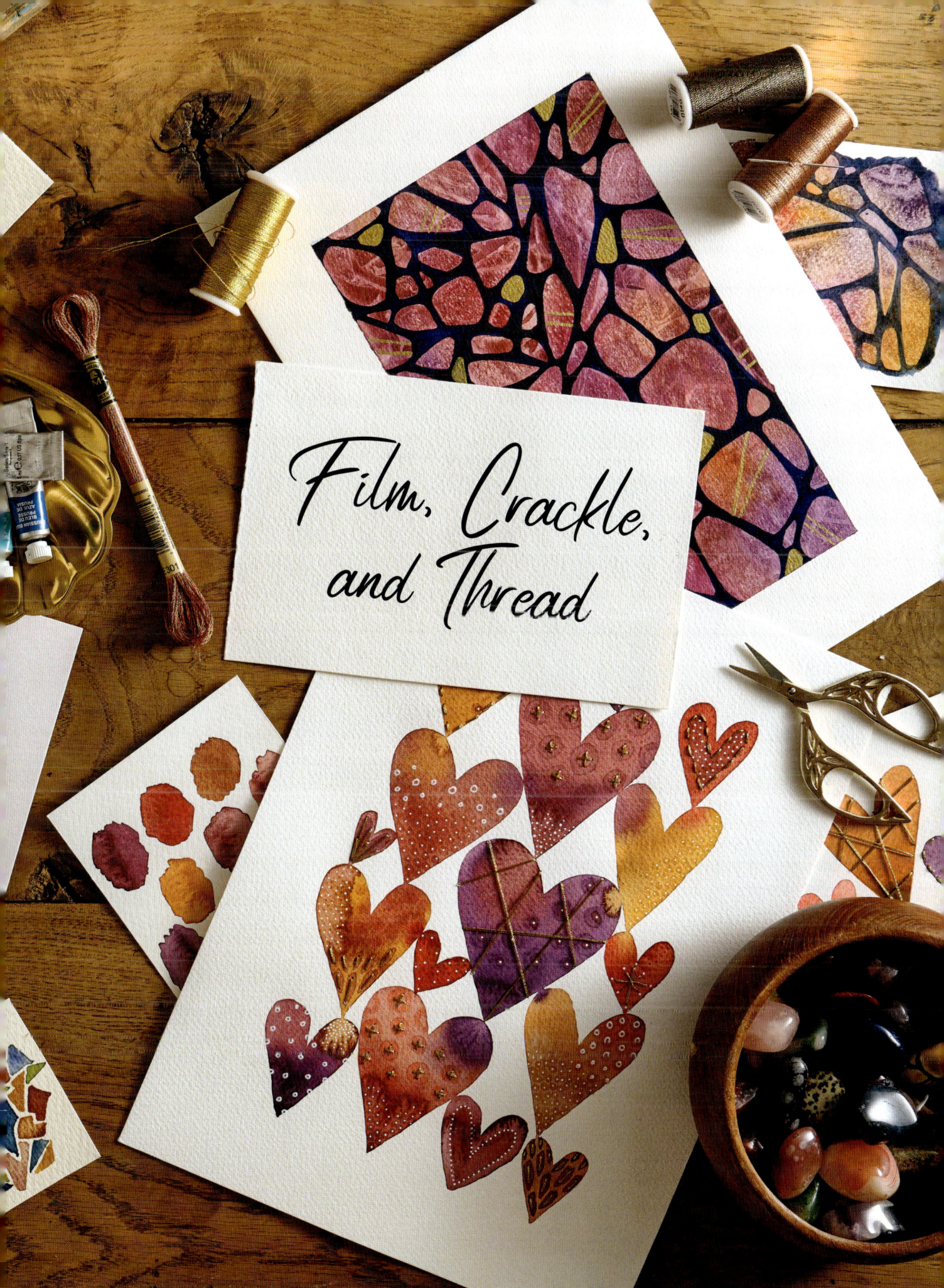

# Film, Crackle, and Thread

# Film, Crackle, and Thread Techniques

While the title Film, Crackle, and Thread trips off the tongue nicely, these are three quite separate techniques that didn't sit comfortably anywhere else – but I just had to include them somewhere in the book! They all hold a special place in my heart, either from memories of my younger artistic days (crackle and thread) or for the creation of my beloved pebble shapes (film). I hope you enjoy these techniques as much as I do.

## GETTING STARTED WITH FILM

Using film (cling film if you're in the UK, or you may know it as Saran or plastic wrap elsewhere) is something quite new to me. I made an exciting discovery on Instagram, where I saw artists laying the film over wet watercolor and allowing it to dry. This created a fun and organic set of shapes, which were then ready to be accented and embellished.

### MATERIALS

- Winsor & Newton professional watercolors
- Artboard or watercolor paper
- Da Vinci Casaneo quill brush – size 2
- Film (cling film/plastic wrap)

### THE METHOD

1. When choosing your paint colors, bear in mind that applying the film will have a 'bleaching' effect on them, so strong colors will ensure the best outcome. Paint your paper/board with watercolors, making sure to work fast so that the paper is still wet in all areas for Step 2.

2. Now to apply your film! Grab a piece that's about double the size of your painted area – you want enough film to allow it to fold and bubble. Lay it down very loosely on the paint, allowing it to form pockets, bubbles, and creases.

3. Once you're happy with the layout, leave the paint to dry completely with the film on top, then you can carefully remove the film to reveal your results.

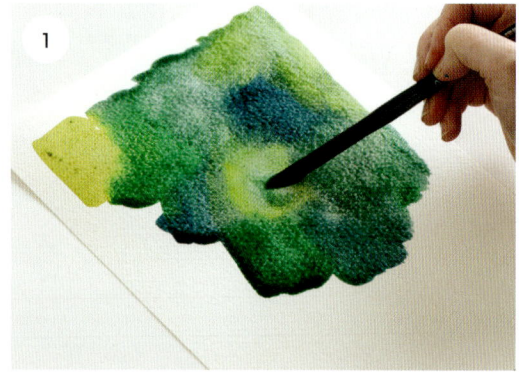

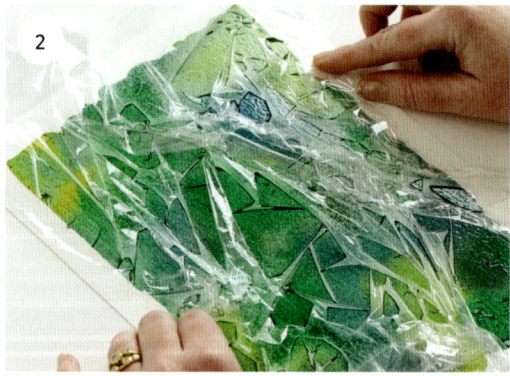

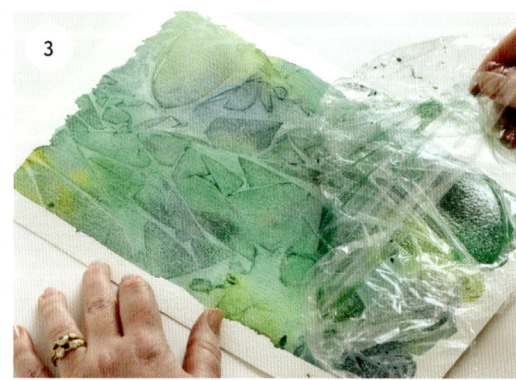

# GETTING STARTED WITH CRACKLE

Crackle is something I've enjoyed using since my student days. Let's start with the basics: what is crackle paste? Well, it's basically a paste with the same consistency as cake frosting that is applied to the surface of your painting and left to dry, creating a fantastic crackled texture. This can be painted with watercolor and, if desired, varnished or sealed.

## MATERIALS

- Crackle paste
- Artist's palette knife (or you can use an old ruler or plastic store card)
- Artboard or canvas

## THE METHOD

1. Open your tub of crackle paste – the brand I use is quite thick and white, and looks a bit like wood filler. Using a palette knife, ruler, or card, scoop up a dollop of the paste and apply it to your artboard or canvas. Cover your working area in a layer of an even thickness and use the palette knife or a ruler to smooth out the surface. You want it to be as flat as possible – imagine you're icing a cake!

2. The cracking process can take anything from a few hours for thinner application to three days for thicker layers. Higher temperatures can speed up the cracking process, but I don't usually apply any additional heat as I worry this will change the organic cracks that form. Obviously, there are natural changes in temperature – everything dries quicker in the height of summer – and the time required will depend rather on the conditions where you are.

3. Once dry, you're ready to paint as you wish!

*Top Tip:* For crackle, you need to work on a thick, rigid structure such as a canvas or sheet of artboard – it won't work on paper.

*Top Tip:* The thickness of the paste applied determines the size and structure of the cracks/platelets. For smaller cracks, apply a thin layer of crackle paste. For larger cracks, apply a thicker layer of the crackle paste.

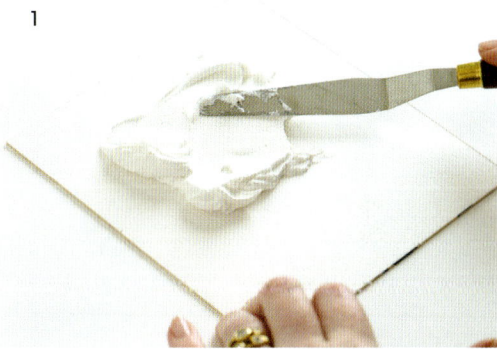

1

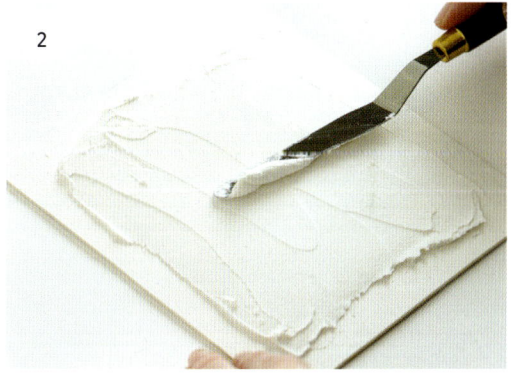

2

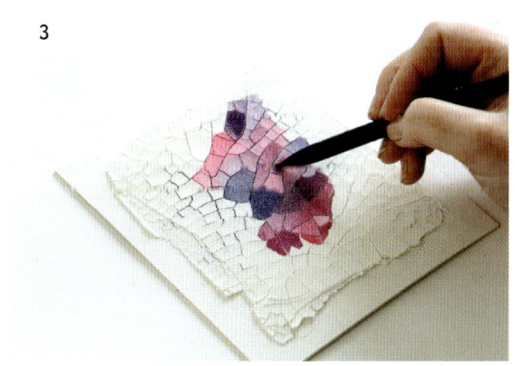

3

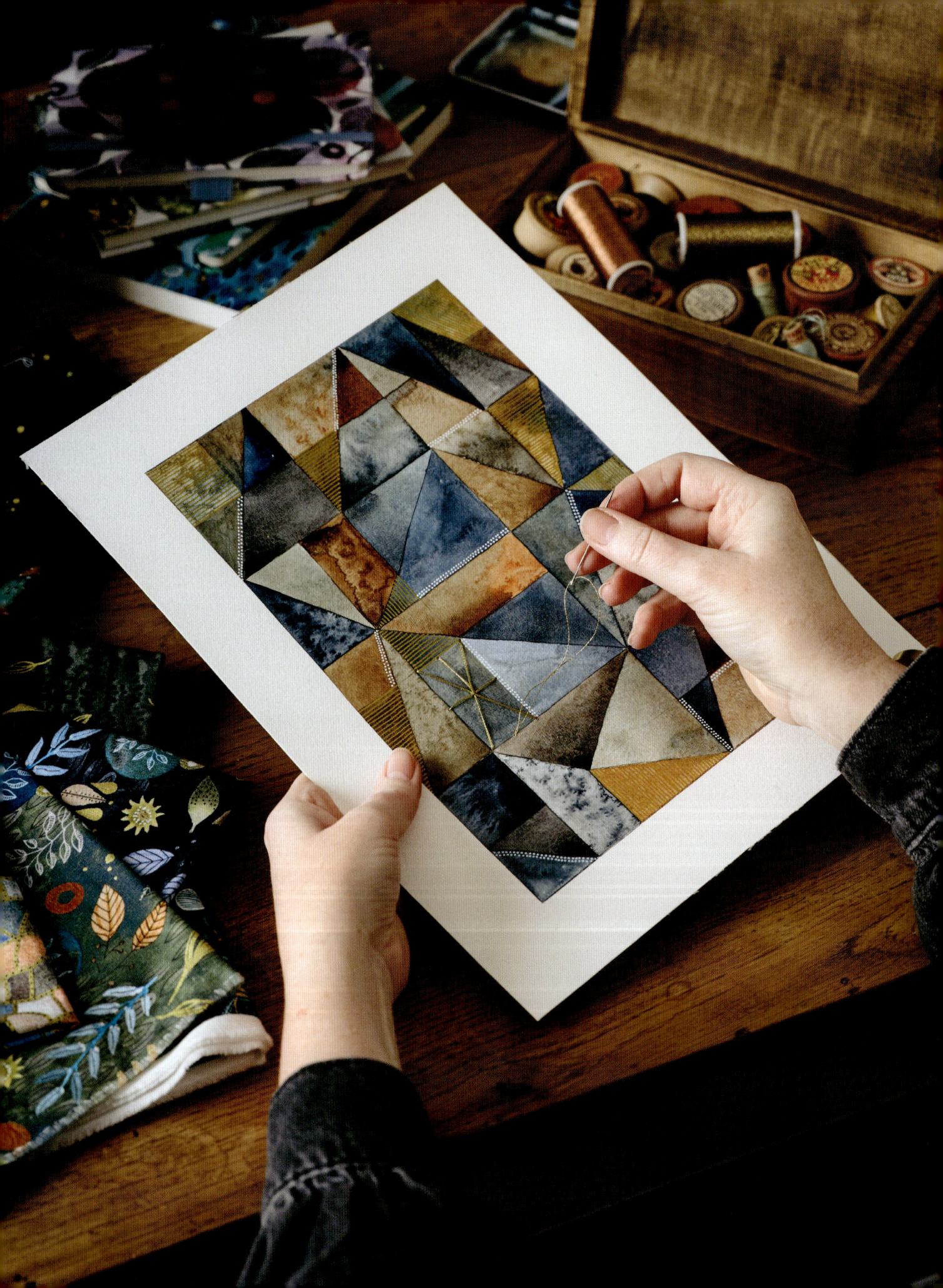

# GETTING STARTED WITH THREAD

Another memorable technique that I've enjoyed since studying textile design is "painting with thread" – whether that be hand stitching or whizzing away doing freehand machine embroidery. These days (many decades later), I no longer have a machine or access to loads of expensive materials, so for my embroidery project you'll see that I've kept things simple – but still effective!

## MATERIALS

- Needle
- Embroidery thread, fine twine, or string
- Large eraser or adhesive putty

## THE METHOD

**1.** As the paper I tend to use is a lovely heavy weight, it really helps to create guide holes for stitching. Decide what area of your piece you want to decorate, then use the needle (unthreaded) to push holes through the paper where you plan to sew (see basic stitches below). Use a large eraser or piece of adhesive putty under the paper, as it will be really easy to push the needle through the paper into it.

**2.** Once you have your guide holes, thread the needle and start to embroider the stitches. I start my thread from the back with a knot at one end.

**3.** After stitching, I finish the other end of the thread at the back of my work using sticky tape to secure it to the paper – if you're a dab hand at sewing, you can finish with another small knot. Cut away any excess thread.

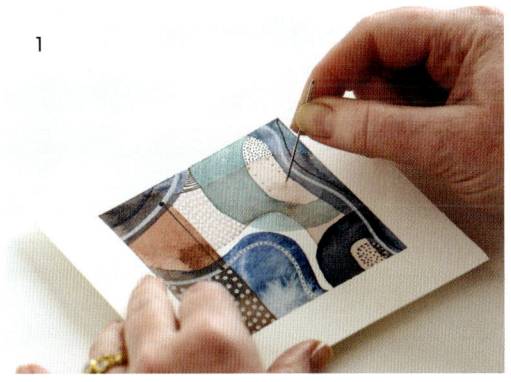

1

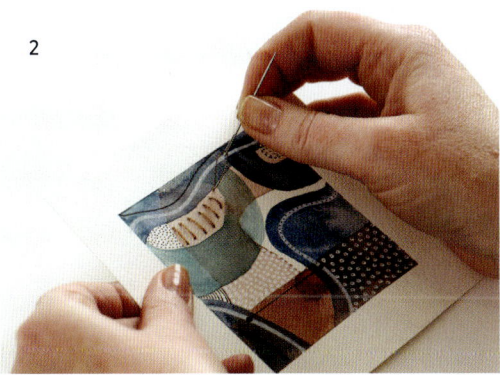

2

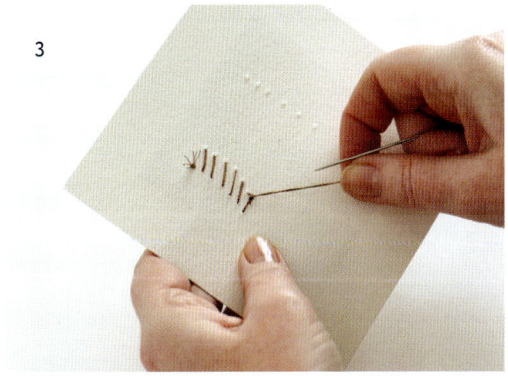

3

## GUIDE HOLES FOR BASIC STITCHES

I tend to use very simple stitches like running stitch and cross stitch to emphasize the key areas of my work.

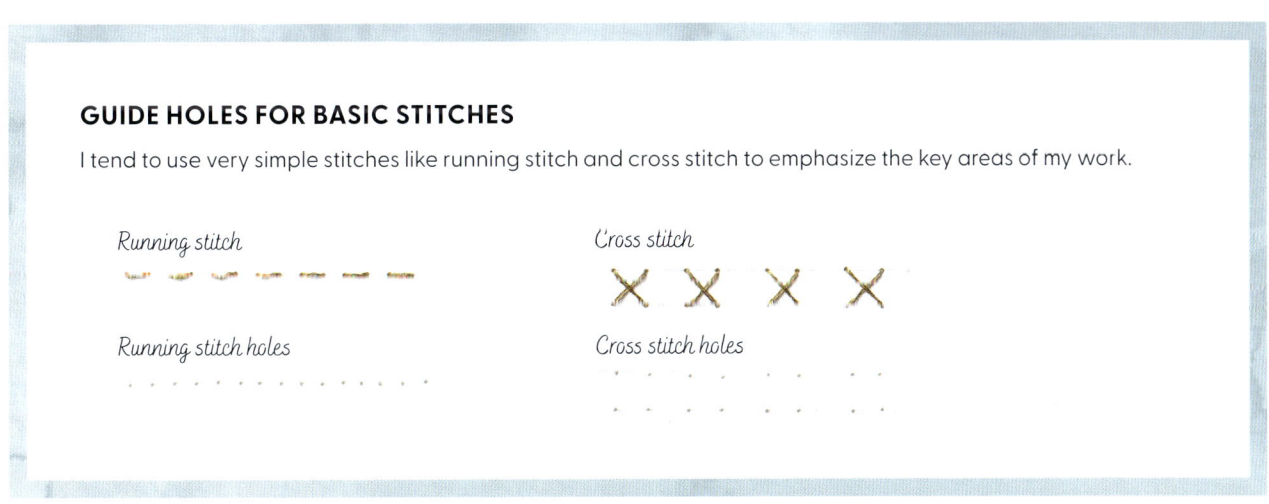

*Running stitch*

*Running stitch holes*

*Cross stitch*

*Cross stitch holes*

# Cling Film Pebbles

Now for something completely different! If you know my work, you'll be familiar with my slight obsession with pebble shapes. Here I'll show you how to create an exotic pebble pattern without any need to think about composition – just let the cling film do the work!

## MATERIALS

- Winsor & Newton professional watercolors
- Daler Rowney Aquafine Artboard
- Da Vinci Casaneo quill brush – size 2
- Winsor & Newton Drawing Ink – gold
- Film (plastic wrap)

## COLOR CHOICES

For this project I knew I'd be using a darker color in between the pebbles to pick out the shapes, so I wanted to keep the color palette for the initial painting stage lighter yet rich. Inspired by my travels, I picked a luxurious palette of rich purples, orange, and red to give a spicy, exotic feel. This piece would work equally well in any colors you fancy, so experiment and have fun!

### WINSOR & NEWTON COLOR REFERENCES

- Alizarin Crimson
- Indigo
- Permanent Magenta
- Winsor Orange
- Winsor Violet (Dioxazine)

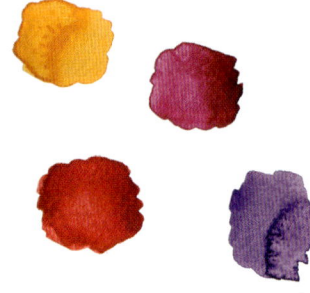

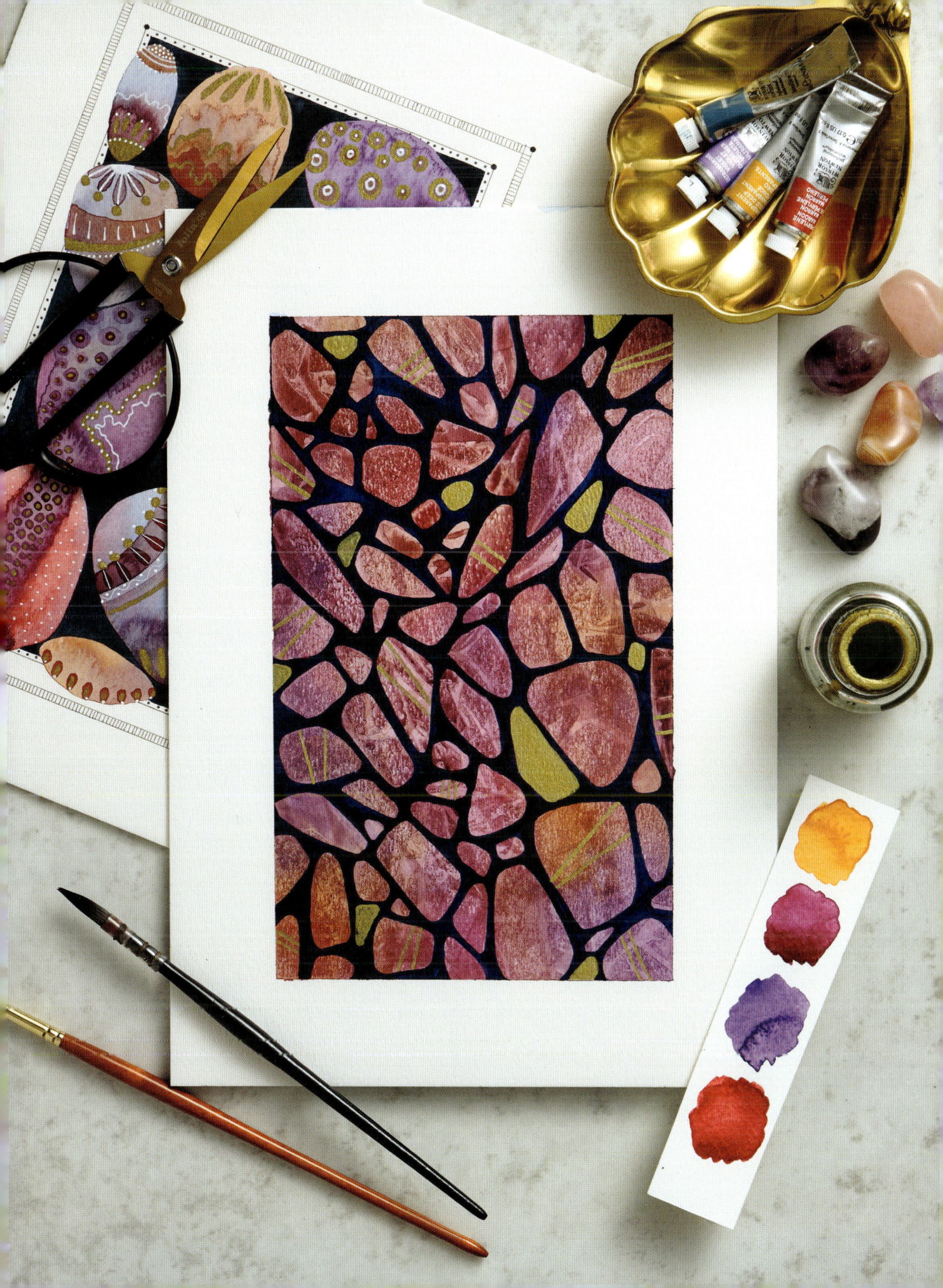

## Step 1: WET PAINT AND FILM

Mask out your artboard to create the area for painting (see Core Watercolor Techniques: Masking Borders). Next, mix up a couple of loose washes of each of your colors: a saturated intense mix and a more dilute softer color, too. Cover your artboard with your paints, making sure that you add different colors next to each other for contrast, so magenta next to orange, orange next to violet, and so on. Don't worry if the colors merge and bloom – this all adds to the organic effect. Once your full page is covered, add a layer of film to your piece (see Getting Started with Film). Make sure the film is large enough to crinkle and crease – this will give fantastic texture once dried.

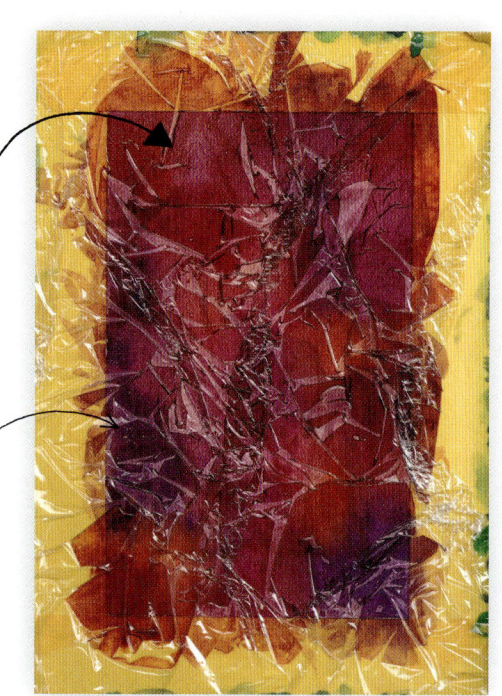

*Work quickly when painting so that the paper is still wet when you add the film. It won't stick to or create texture on any dry areas.*

*Let the clingfilm bubble – don't squash down any raised areas as these will soon become your pebbles.*

*Top Tip:* Don't be tempted to peek under the film until everything is completely dry! Lifting when wet will lose some of the lovely textures caused by the contact between paint and film.

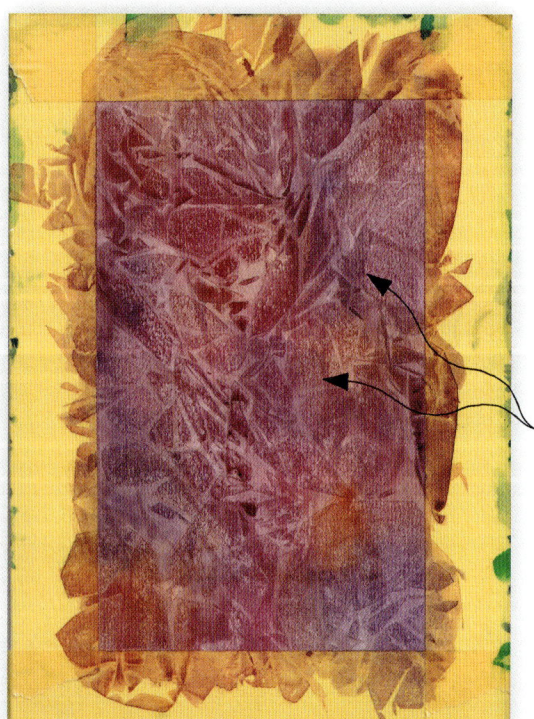

## Step 2: REMOVING THE FILM

Once your paint is completely dry, carefully remove the film to reveal the lovely textures left behind. You'll be able to see rounded and angled shapes where the film has creased and folded. Imagine these creases as the areas between your pebbles – in the next step we'll start to define the pebble shapes by painting in between them.

*Look for pebbles and rocky shapes both small and large. You don't want things to look too uniform, so aim to mix up the scale of your design.*

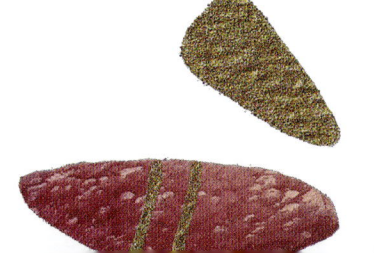

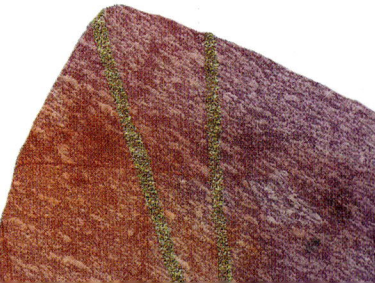

## Step 3: PAINTING AROUND THE PEBBLES

Begin this next step by mixing up some of your Indigo watercolor. This should be quite strong and intense, so add more paint if it looks transparent and watery. Once you're happy with your mix, use your quill brush to carefully pick out the pebble shapes in the textures of the paint, filling in the spaces in between them. Continue until the whole sheet is filled.

*Don't worry if some areas don't have distinct pebble shapes — use some artistic license and create your own in any bare or untextured areas.*

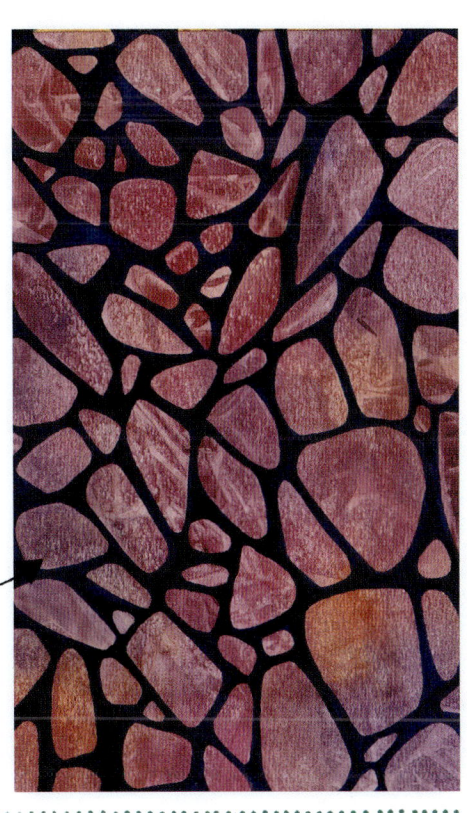

*Rather than completely covering some of your pebbles with gold, you could easily just decorate them, adding textures with interesting mark making.*

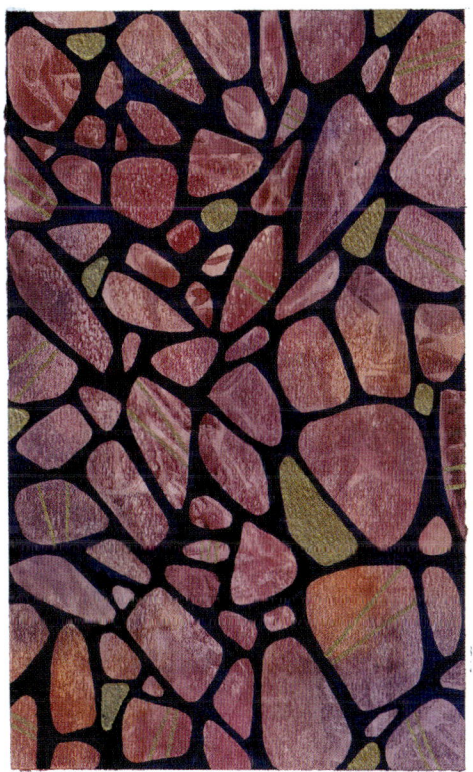

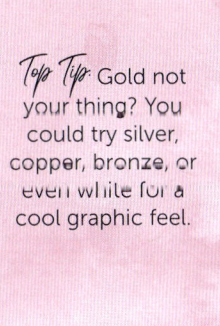

*Top Tip:* Gold not your thing? You could try silver, copper, bronze, or even white for a cool graphic feel.

## Step 4: GOLD EMBELLISHMENTS

Now you should have a lovely piece with textured pebbles on a deep, dark indigo background. I already love the look of this, but feel it still needs something... gold, of course! Pick out some smaller pebbles, making sure they are spaced evenly across the page, then paint them in with gold ink. I also added thin gold lines across some of the pebbles, inspired by the markings you find on pebbles at the beach. Now all that's left to do is remove the masking tape and admire your work!

# Abstract Mosaic

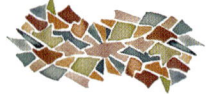

Back in my university days, I often worked in a range of different media, and I recently remembered my beloved crackle glaze, once used with acrylic. I was keen to see if I could use it with my watercolors. After much experimenting with different crackle mediums spread in different thicknesses, I finally found the perfect technique to give me lovely deep crackles that were easy to paint on with watercolor.

## MATERIALS

- Winsor & Newton professional watercolors
- Daler Rowney Aquafine Artboard
- Da Vinci Casaneo quill brush - size 2
- Golden Crackle Paste
- Palette knife (or try using a stiff business card/old loyalty card)
- Clear varnish / decoupage matt medium

## COLOR CHOICES

For this project I was drawn to a slightly autumnal, mid-century inspired palette of subtle but strong colors. People often remark on how crackle looks very organic, so feel free to lean into the colors of nature, or do what I've done and try a range of appealing colors to create a striking pattern.

### WINSOR & NEWTON COLOR REFERENCES

- Burnt Sienna
- Indigo
- Olive Green
- Payne's Gray
- Yellow Ochre

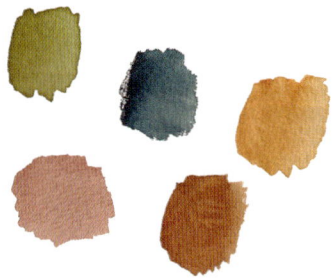

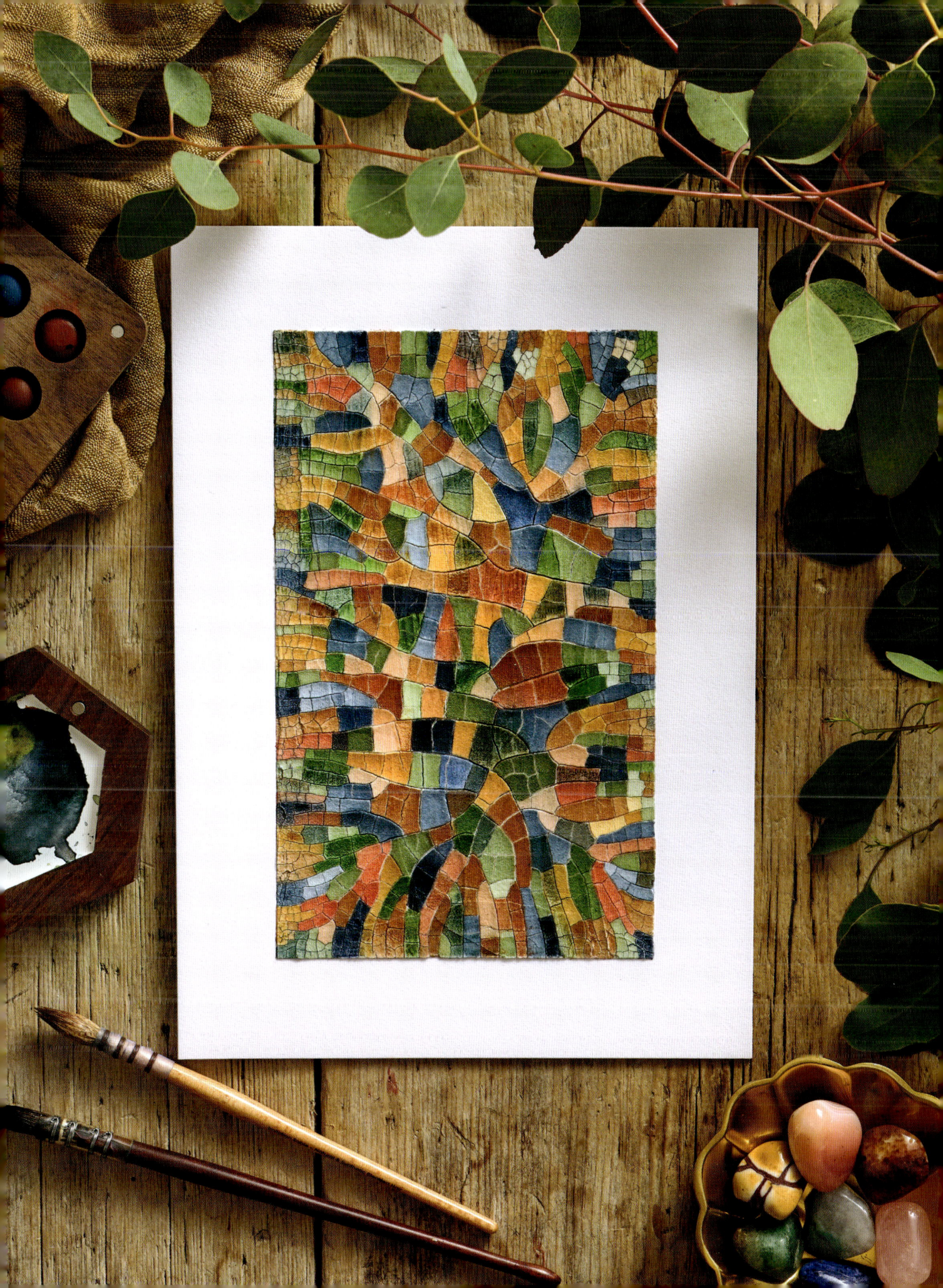

## Step 1: CRACKLE PASTE

To begin, mask out your sheet of artboard using masking tape to protect the border of your piece (see Core Watercolor Techniques: Masking Borders). Once this is done, apply your crackle paste (see Getting Started with Crackle). spreading it out with your palette knife or card to a thickness of about 2mm (1/16in). Once you have a nice smooth layer, remove the masking tape. Now leave to dry completely – large cracks will form, then smaller ones will appear as time goes on. Depending on the conditions in your workspace, this may take from a few hours to overnight. Ideally, leave it for a couple of days to ensure that everything is completely dry and ready to paint!

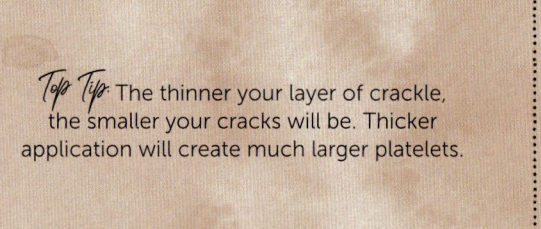

*Top Tip:* The thinner your layer of crackle, the smaller your cracks will be. Thicker application will create much larger platelets.

## Step 2: FIRST LAYER OF COLOR

Now that the crackle paste has dried on your board, you are ready to start painting. Choose your first color and select platelets across the surface to paint. I like to ensure these are evenly spaced across the page to give a nice equal spread of each color.

*The platelets tend to be larger toward the middle of the piece and a little smaller at the edges. Tiny platelets can be fiddly to paint individually, so paint them in small groups to form a block.*

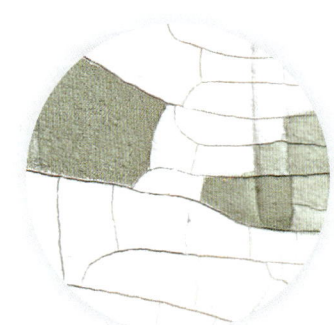

## Step 3: REMAINING COLORS

Continue to paint with the rest of the colors, adding each new mix in turn until you fill your whole piece with a nice, evenly spaced range. Here is where you can intersperse random gold platelets if you wanted some extra shine.

*If you're halfway through and you're not so keen on the overall look, feel free to add a new color – just remember to use it evenly across the piece.*

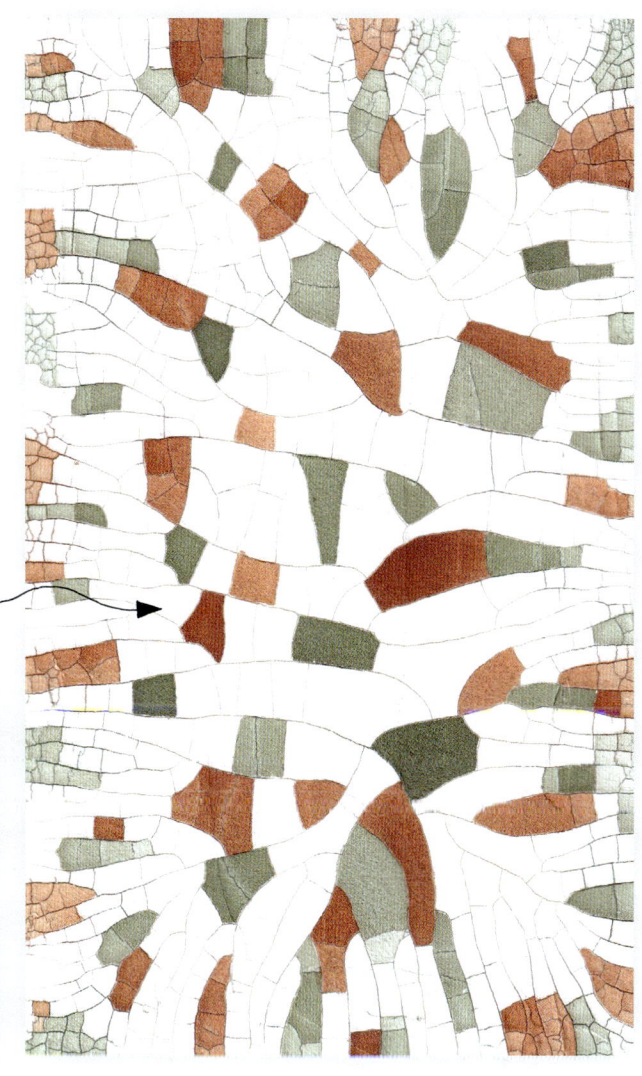

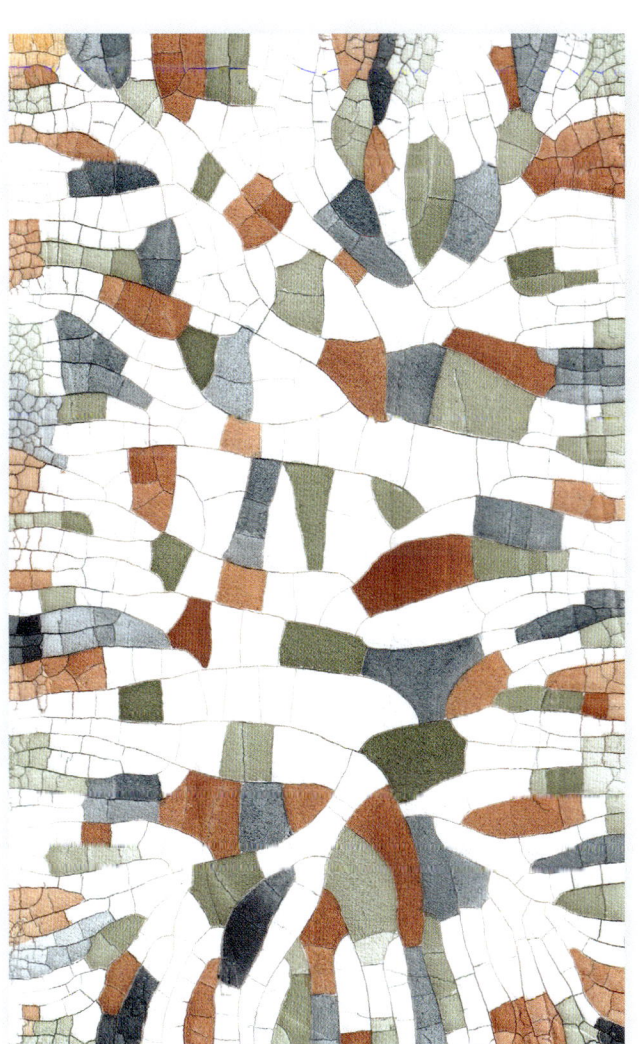

*Top Tip: Want some extra sparkle? Throw a metallic into the mix and add the odd section in gold, silver, or even copper!*

## Step 4: VARNISH

Crackle, by definition, is quite fragile and has a tendency to crack further when moved, or platelets can even come away from the background substrate. Sealing the piece with varnish or sealant helps to protect the crackle texture and holds everything in place (see Mixed-Media Materials).

*I've used spray varnish for an even finish but you can paint varnish or sealant across the piece carefully with a brush if that's what you have to hand.*

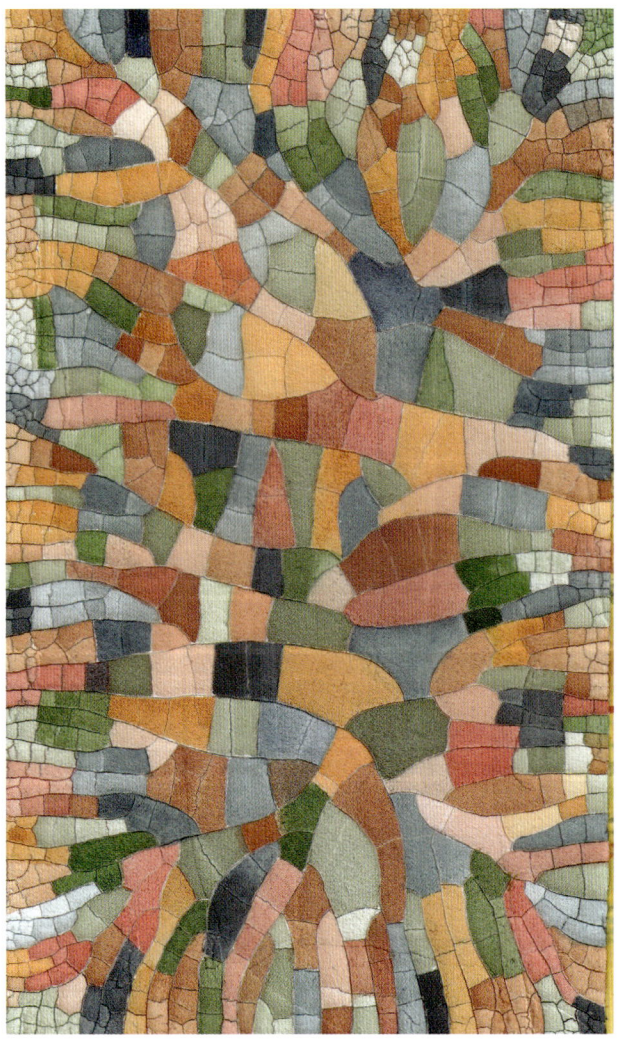

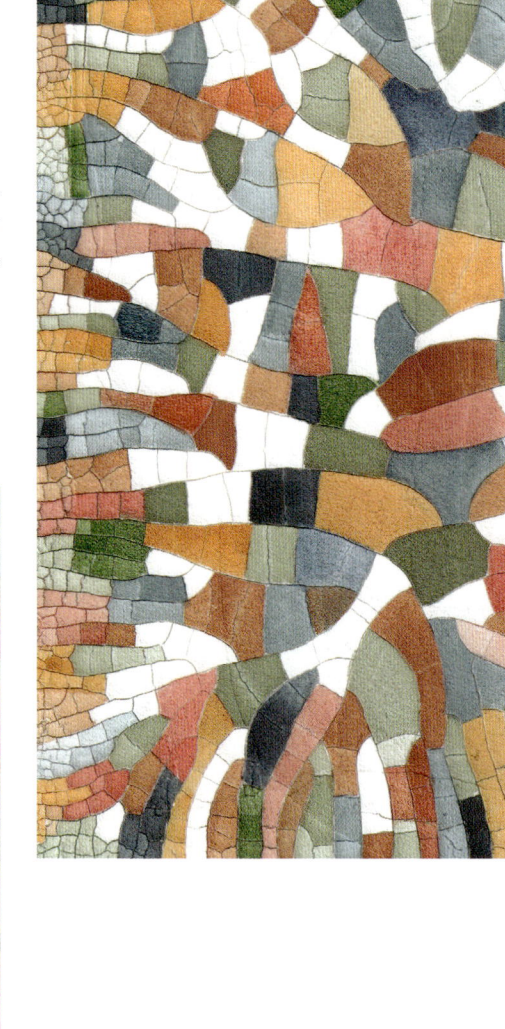

*Top Tip:* Some brush-on sealants and varnishes will disturb the watercolor paint (which can look quite cool) but if you want to ensure that your colors stay separate, try using a spray varnish.

# More Inspiration

Crackle is such a fun technique that I'm always looking for new ways to bring its glorious texture into my work! Here I've split my page in two, using the bottom half of the page for a crackled sea and leaving the top half of the page clear to create a sky using traditional painting techniques.

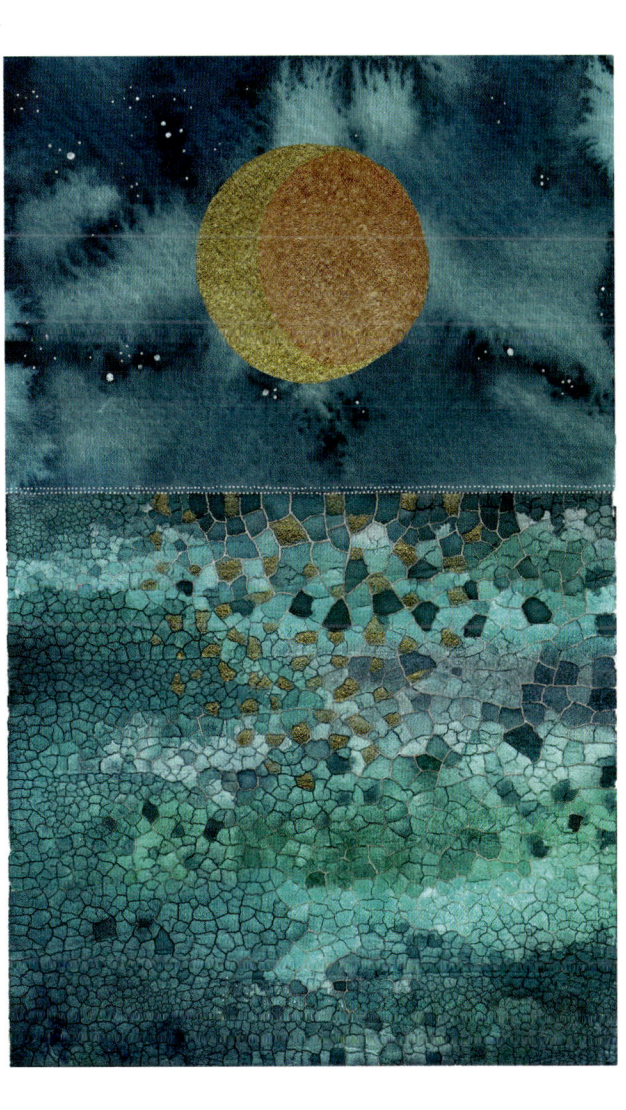

# Freestyle Crackle

Our second crackle project is great fun and uses a very loose watercolor style, washing different harmonious paint mixes across the crackled surface to create a soft blended effect. The result is beautifully soft and organic. The gold border finishes it off nicely and gives a very jewel-like quality to the piece.

## MATERIALS

- Winsor & Newton professional watercolors
- Stretched white canvas or canvas panel
- Da Vinci Casaneo quill brush - size 2
- Winsor & Newton Drawing Ink – gold
- Golden Crackle Paste
- Palette knife (or try using a stiff business card/old loyalty card)
- Clear varnish / decoupage matt medium

## COLOR CHOICES

Here, I've been inspired by a trip to the Maldives. The ocean was an unbelievable aqua blue, which is now one of my favorite colors! In this piece, I've teamed it with some deeper and more saturated blues as well as an emerald green. This abstract design would work in any color palette you can dream up, so have fun and experiment.

### WINSOR & NEWTON COLOR REFERENCES

- Cobalt Turquoise
- Emerald Green
- Indanthrene Blue
- Indigo
- Prussian Blue

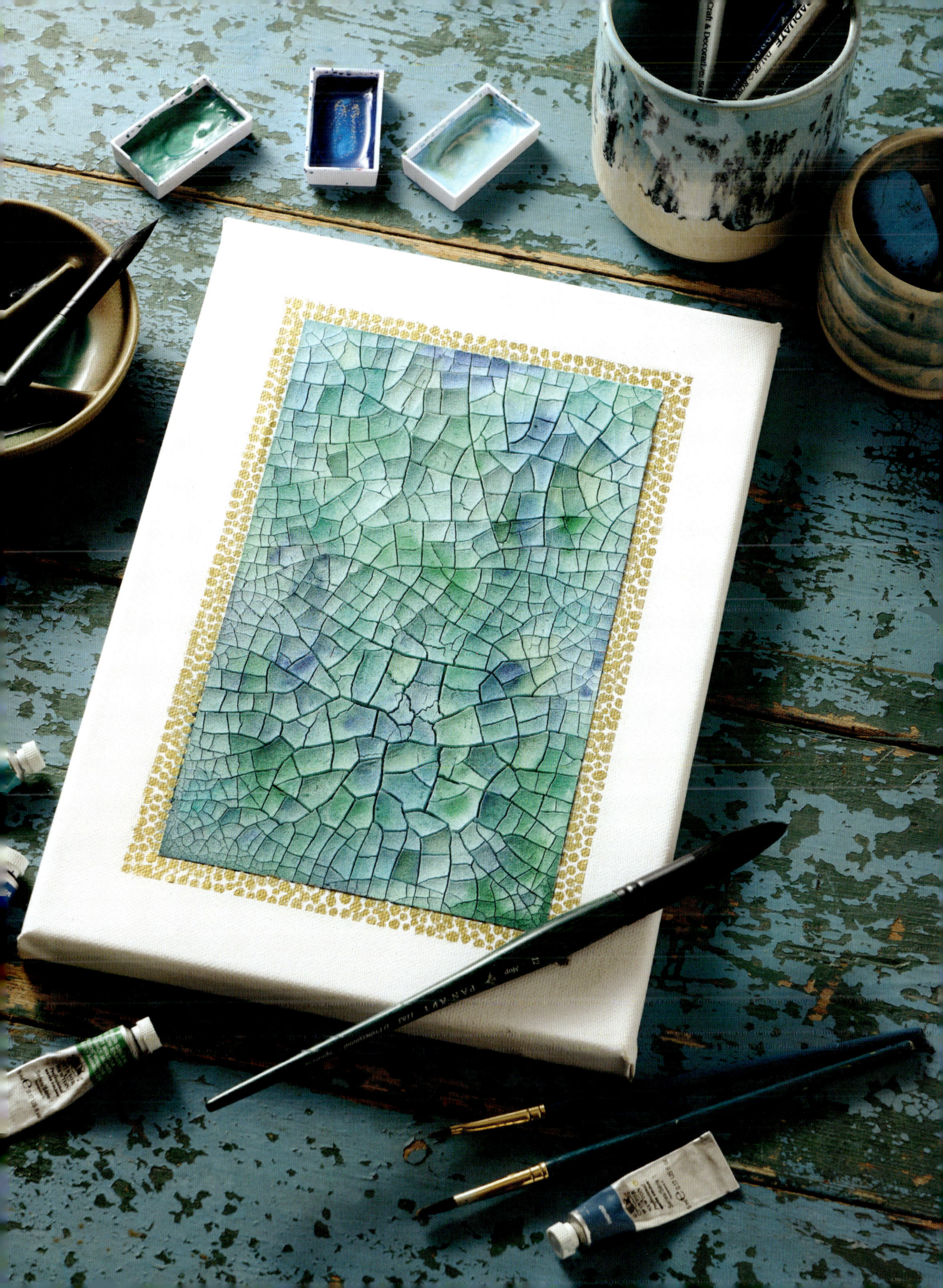

## Step 1: **CRACKLE PASTE**

Mask out the canvas to create your working area and protect what will be your outer border (see Core Watercolor Techniques: Masking Borders). Apply a thin layer of crackle paste (see Getting Started with Crackle). Remove the masking tape, then leave to dry thoroughly – ideally for a couple of days – to allow the cracks to form.

*Remember that the thicker you apply the crackle paste, the larger the cracks and platelets will be.*

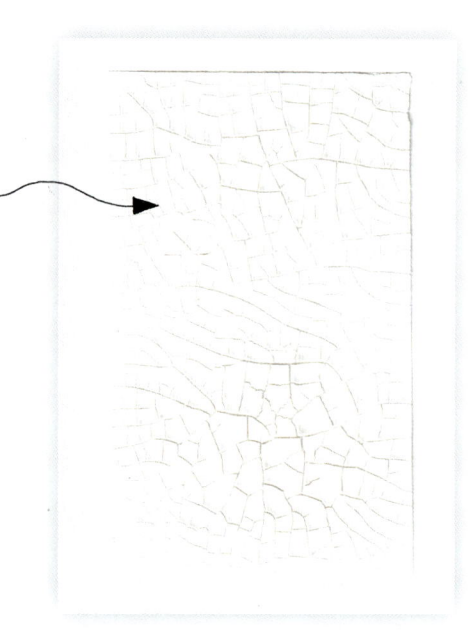

## Step 2: **WET PAINT**

Once your crackle is completely dry, you can start to paint! Begin by mixing washes of your chosen colors so they are ready before you start painting. Be sure to have dark and light washes of each one, as this will create contrast and add interest. Now start to apply a color to each platelet, working from the top corner of the canvas. Allow the paints to merge, blurring the edges so that everything looks soft and organic. Continue until you have filled the page. Even at this stage, you can continue adding color to any areas that you feel require it. When you're happy with the look, leave everything to dry again.

*Load your brush with enough paint so that it floods the cracks as well as the platelets and the whole crackled surface is covered. Sometimes this means working your brush into deeper sections to ensure full coverage.*

*Top Tip:* The crackle paste is quite porous so will "drink in" plenty of paint. Make sure you mix enough of each color at the start of the project so that you can work quickly to allow the colors to merge.

## Step 3: GOLD BORDER

Once your painted crackle is completely dry, you can create a decorative border. For this I masked off the canvas, leaving about a 10mm (⅜in) gap all around the edge of the crackle. This gap is the area we're going to paint. Ensure your masking tape is securely stuck down, then take your gold ink and fill the border with raindrop spots (see Core Watercolor Techniques: Mark-Making Directory). I like to paint right up to the edge of the crackle, then back to the tape. Don't worry if your spots overlap the tape, as you'll get a crisp edge once the tape is removed.

*Use more masking tape to help create the inner border.*

*I will use gold here, but feel free to use any metallic ink or even use a coordinating color for the border if you'd prefer a less sparkly and more graphic look.*

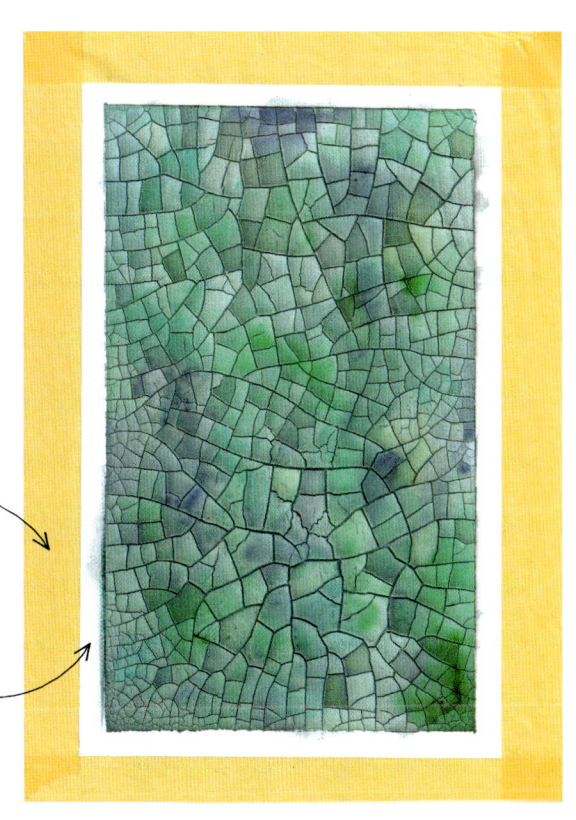

## Step 4: VARNISH

Seal your freestyle crackle piece with sealant or varnish (see Mixed-Media Materials) to protect the crackle texture and hold everything in place.

*Top Tip* Remember when choosing a varnish or sealant that there are options for gloss or matt. This will make a big difference to the final look, so choose wisely!

# Stitched Hearts

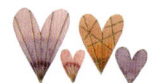

This project looks technical, but uses only basic stitches (running stitch and cross stitch) as, although I'm a trained textile designer, I'm not much of a sewist! Golden thread is a great way to add highlights in a more textural, three-dimensional way than my usual inks and gel pens. The design is a riff on my pebble motifs – simple heart shapes connect through small touch points to allow the colors to bleed and merge into one another.

## MATERIALS

- Winsor & Newton professional watercolors
- Bockingford 300g cold press watercolor paper
- Da Vinci Casaneo quill brush - size 2
- Posca paint pen – white, 0.7mm (Ultra Fine)
- Gold embroidery thread and small needle
- Small scissors
- Sticky tape

## COLOR CHOICES

Call it a cliché, but when painting heart shapes I'm instantly drawn to reds, pinks, and purples! With a lot of my more abstract pieces, there's no need to stick to a particular color palette – use the colors that call out to you. The shapes don't have to be hearts either, depending on your color choice these could be circles, leaves, fish, geometric shapes... you name it, it's possible!

### WINSOR & NEWTON COLOR REFERENCES

- Alizarin Crimson
- Cadmium-Free Red
- Cadmium-Free Yellow
- Winsor Orange
- Winsor Violet (Dioxazine)

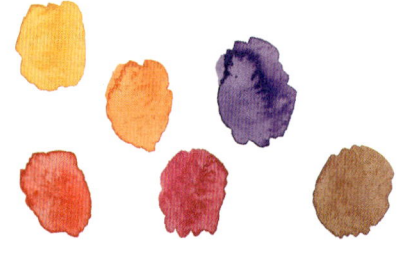

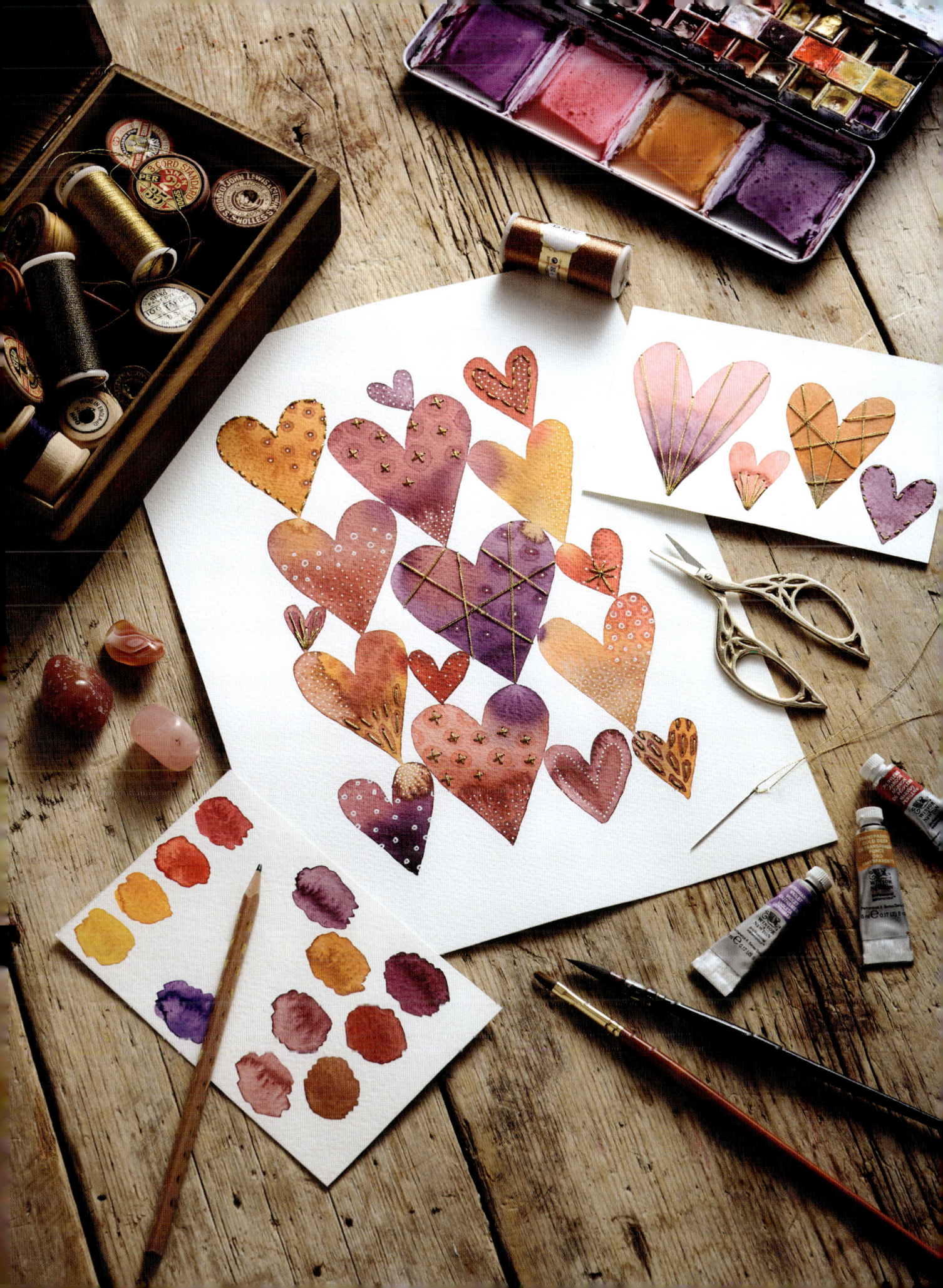

## Step 1: WET PAINT

You don't strictly need to mask off your page for this project, but I like to for two reasons. Firstly it protects the edge of my paper, meaning no marks or splashes of paint. And secondly, it gives me a nice defined area in which to paint. To kick things off, mix up your colors into loose washes, intermixing them until you find the perfect shades for you. I didn't sketch out my design beforehand; I simply started at the top of the page and painted a heart, then continued adding more until the page was full. To ensure you get the lovely bleeds between the hearts, connect them carefully – the smaller the areas of connection, the more delicate this will look.

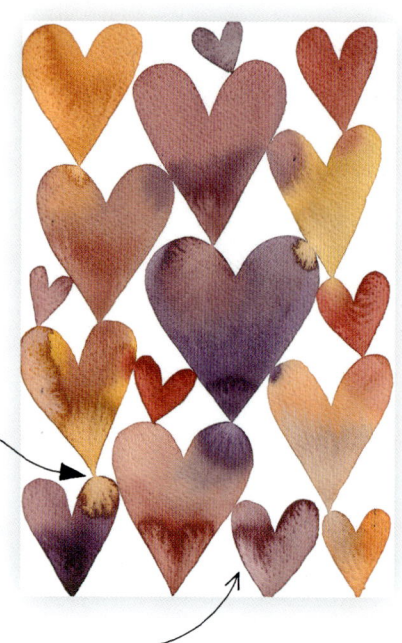

*Top Tip:* To get more runs and bleeds between your hearts, try tilting the paper propping it up a half inch or so at one end (I use an eraser for this).

*There's nothing wrong in giving the colors a helping hand to achieve the bleeds you want. Simply flood the bottom of one heart and push the color through to the heart below, encouraging the paints to merge.*

*Space your hearts and colors out evenly for a balanced look – don't have all your purple hearts in one area, for instance, but use the color across the piece instead.*

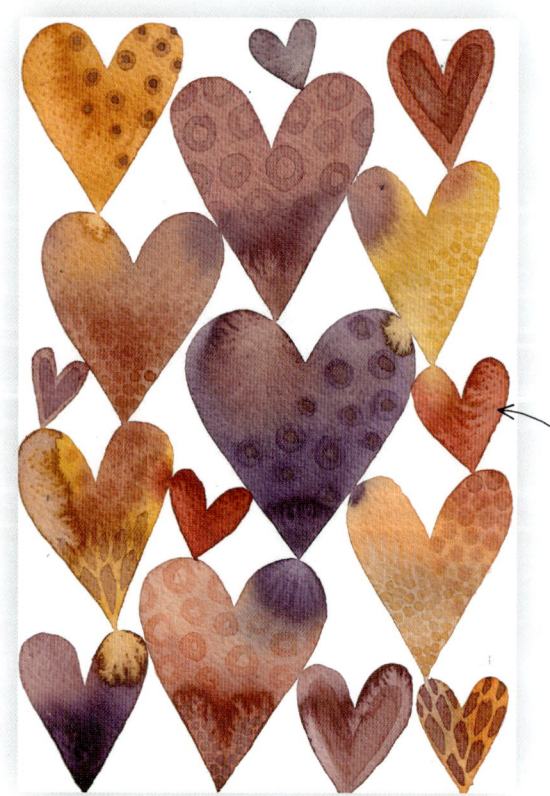

## Step 2: WET ON DRY

Once your first layer of paint is completely dry, assess your work for areas where you want to add some extra details. I felt that some of my smaller hearts were lovely, so I kept them plain; for the larger hearts I used a range of mark making, including brush prints, loose circles, and watercolor dots (see Core Watercolor Techniques: Mark-Making Directory). I wanted to enhance the first paint layer, so I left the lovely merges and water blooms untouched, and worked around them.

*I didn't want to add too much contrast at this stage, so for some marks I used a slightly stronger mix of the same color as the heart to add some texture.*

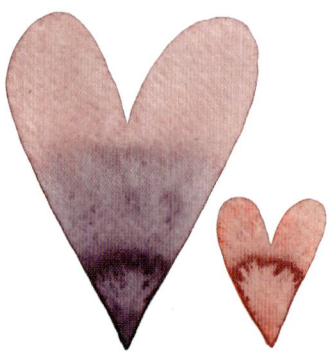

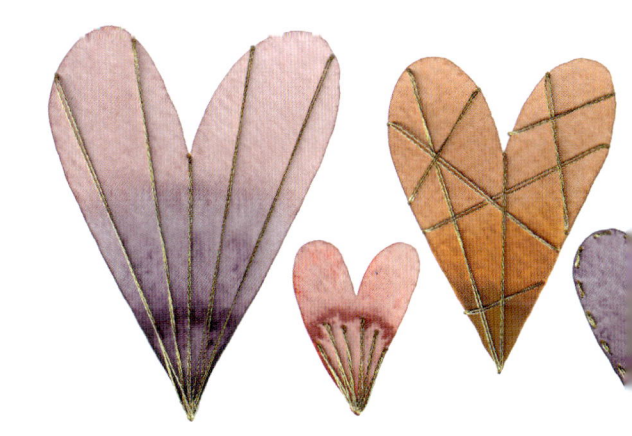

## Step 3: EMBROIDERY

Next up is the super fun part: embroidery! You can remove the masking tape before you start, as we have finished with the paint. Use simple stitches to emphasize the key areas of a selection of hearts – pick the first heart to decorate and work out what embellishment you'd like to add. Push out the guide holes for the stitches with your needle (see Getting Started with Thread). Now thread your needle and work the stitches. I haven't embroidered every heart for this piece, rather I've worked on about half of them evenly across the piece.

I purposely haven't gone too far with the embroidery: simple shapes and patterns scattered across the piece add highlights and areas of interest.

Try to allow the painted composition to guide where you add embellishment. You can see I've added cross stitches into the circles and lines to the brush stamps.

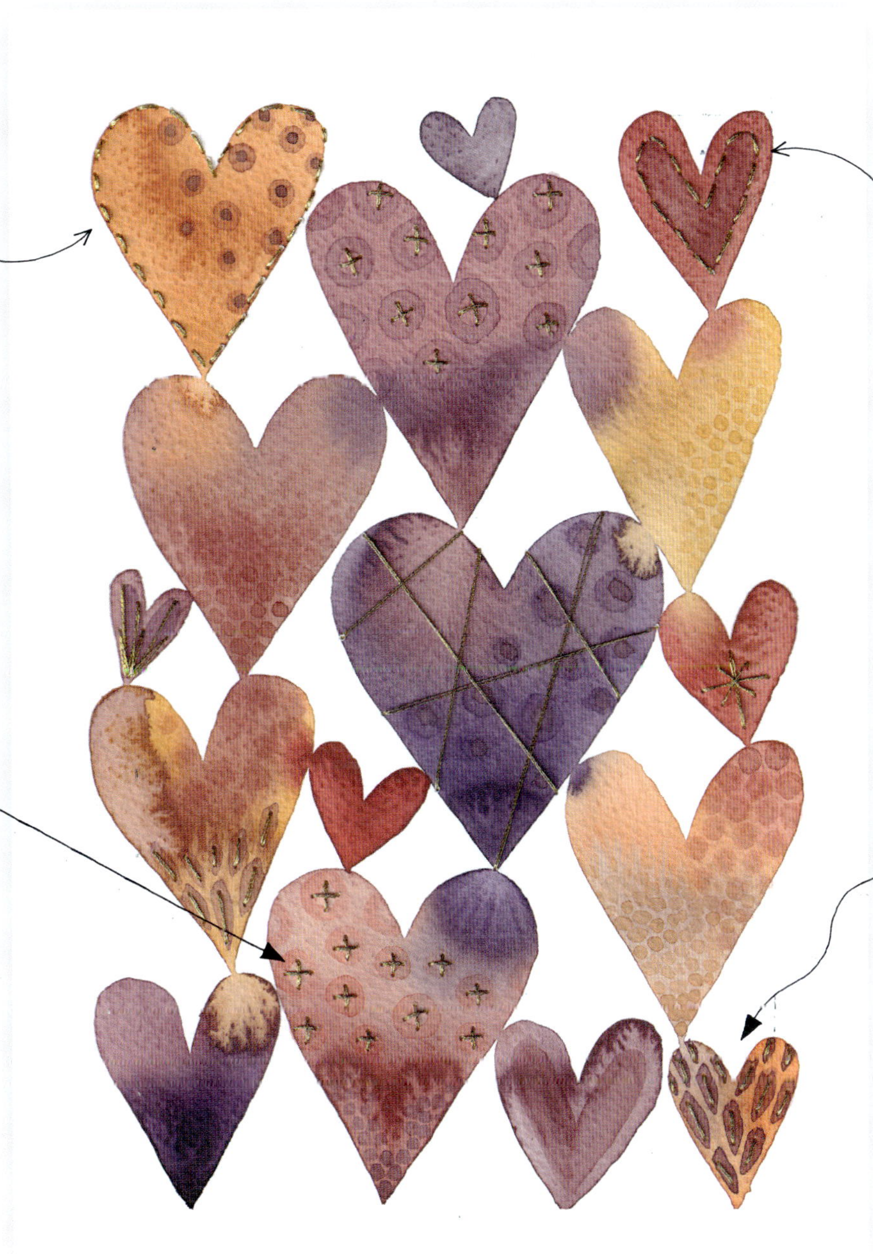

I've used gold thread for this piece but silver, bronze, or copper would also look great and add some metallic sparkle.

I've used straight lines on some hearts and small crosses on others. If you love to sew, try using French knots, chain stitch, or others – they could look really effective.

## Step 4: WHITE EMBELLISHMENTS

Once you've completed your embroidery, it's a good time to stand back and take a look at the piece. What does it need? If your painting is very light and pale you could add black details to create contrast. If, like mine, your colors are deep and vibrant, embellish with white. I've focused mainly on the plain, unstitched hearts and added white marks for interest and to freshen up the darker areas.

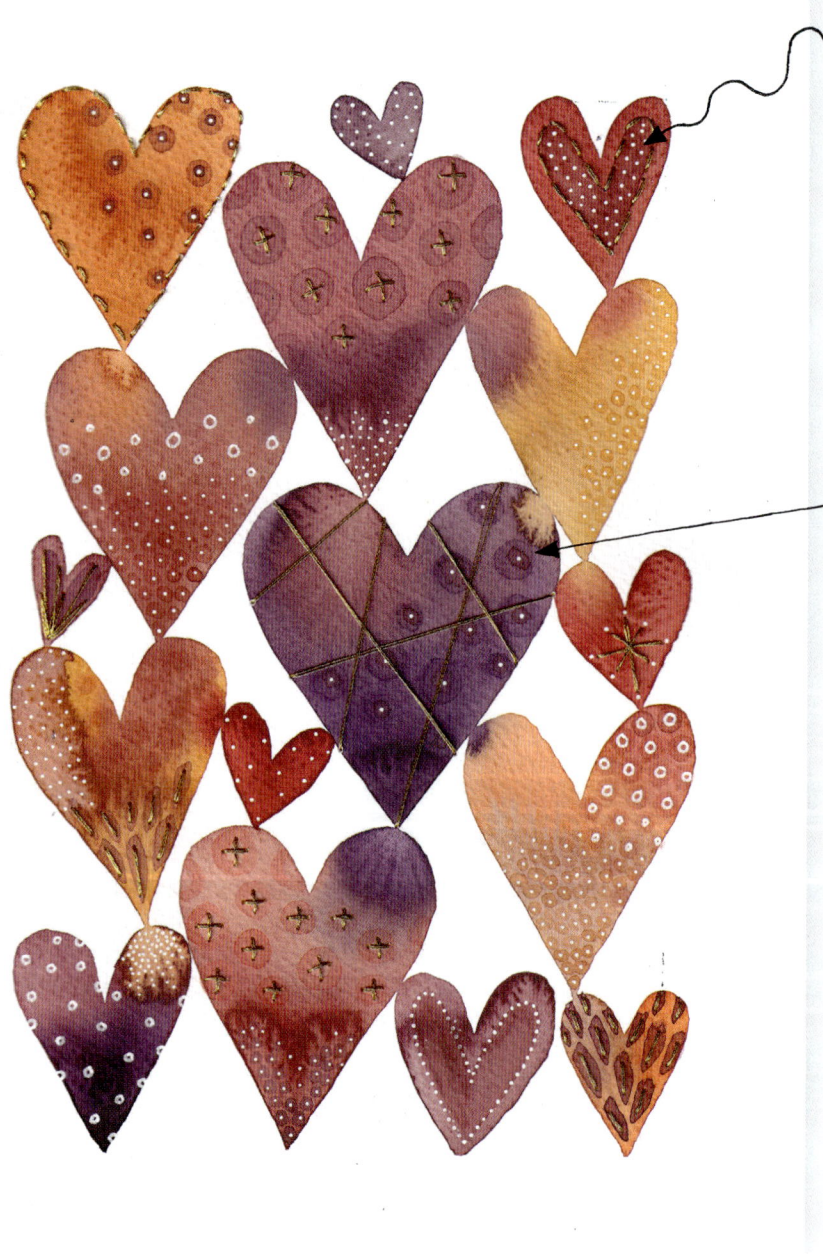

*I have used a mix of circles and dots, depending on the area I wanted to cover.*

*Remember to highlight any areas you really like. For example, I've added a dot to each of the stamped circles here, even though this heart also features stitching.*

# More Inspiration

While I haven't actually embroidered this piece (yet!) it would make for a fabulously fun stitched project. There are loads of lovely straight lines and angles that would lend themselves well to stitching, and the color palette would really pop with some metallic threads.

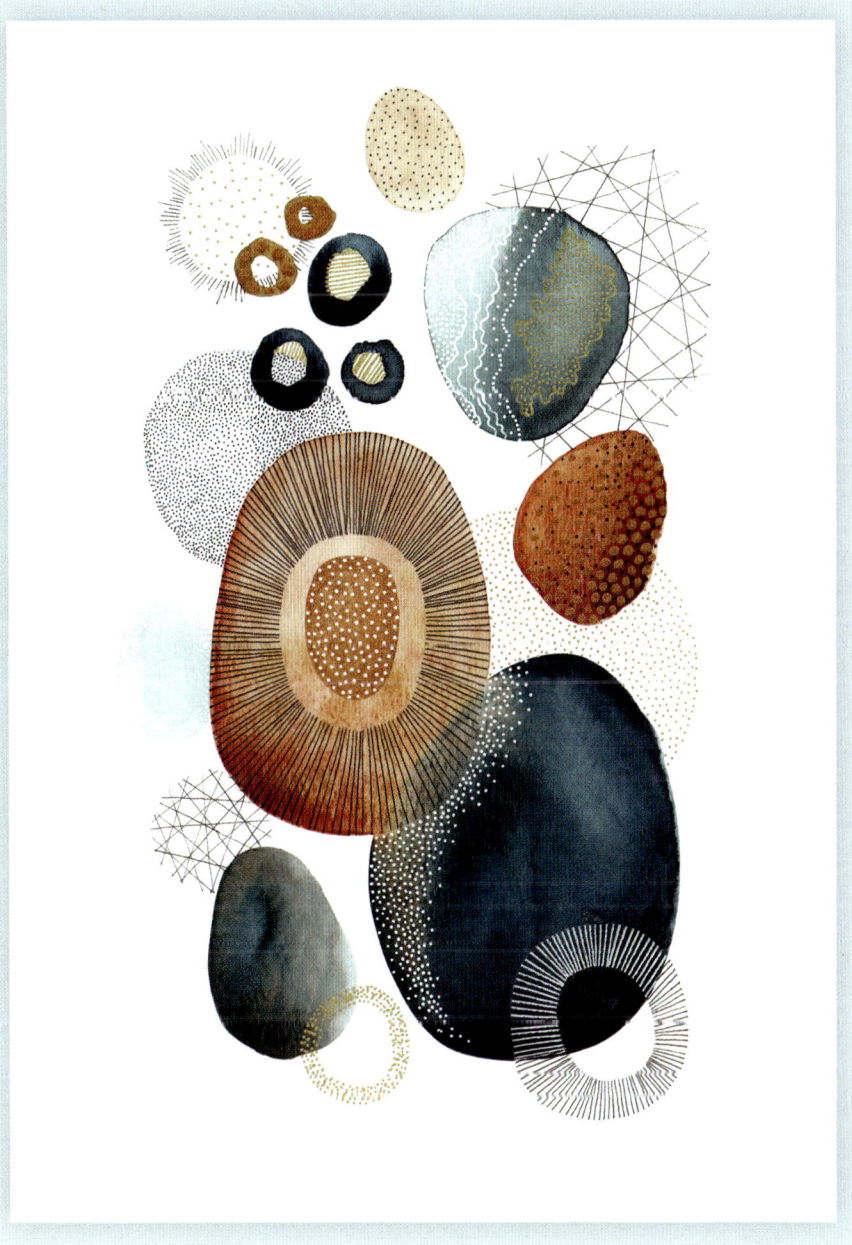

# About the Author

Kate Rebecca Leach is an artist, illustrator and tutor based in Hertfordshire, UK.

She founded her brand, Essoldo Design, in 2020 and since then has been lucky enough to have built a community of over 200,000 social media followers, sold her work in more than 35 countries worldwide, and licensed products across the UK, Europe, and the USA. In 2024, Kate published her first book with David and Charles, *Creative Abstract Watercolor*, which quickly became a bestseller and is set to be published in seven languages. *Creative Abstract Mixed Media* is Kate's second book.

Kate would love to see how you're using the book and your experiments with abstract watercolors. Tag your photos on social media using **#EssoldoMixedMedia** for your chance to feature on her social media channels! You can find out more about Kate and her art here:

**Social media :** @essoldodesign

**Website:** essoldodesign.com

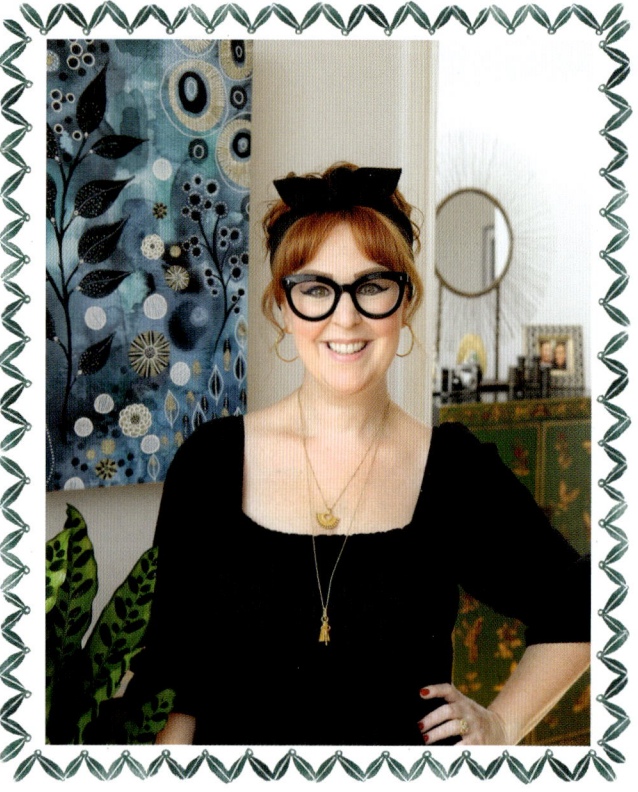

# Acknowledgments

My first, most heartfelt thanks is to the wonderful art community that I've been lucky enough to be a part of for the last few years. From lovely friends and followers over on social media, to the students who attend my workshops, and to you (yes you!) for buying this book! Your support for me personally, my art journey, and my small business have literally made my dreams come true.

No list of thanks would be complete without mentioning my amazing partner, Anthony. From packing orders and accompanying me on trips to the post office, to your creative input and impeccable graphic design skills, this dream wouldn't be possible without you. Thank you for being my right-hand man!

To my wonderful family for always believing in me and for supporting me in this artistic adventure. I'm forever grateful for your advice and love. To my fabulous friends, too numerous to mention (you know who you are!), thank you for the fun and adventures, laughter and love, and for keeping me sane when I'm overwhelmed by it all! To Theresa and Jenny, I wish you were here to see me writing this book. I hope you'd be proud. I miss you.

Finally, I wouldn't be sitting here writing these acknowledgments without Ame and the team at David and Charles. Thanks for taking a chance on me right at the beginning – I'm enjoying this wild ride we're on. Here's to book three!

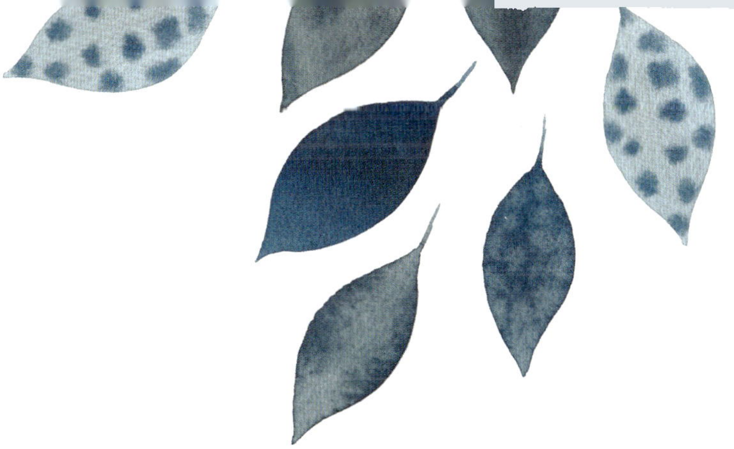

# Recommended Brands

These are the brands I use in my own work, and throughout the book:

**Paints**
- Daler Rowney
- Daniel Smith
- Kuretake
- Skrim Watercolors
- The Art of Soil
- Winsor & Newton

**Paper**
- Arches
- Canson
- Cass Art
- Daler Rowney
- St Cuthberts Mill

**Brushes**
- Daler Rowney
- Da Vinci Casaneo
- Panart
- Pro Arte

**Inks**
- Winsor & Newton Drawing Ink

**Pens**
- Posca
- Pentel Fineliners
- Tom's Studio
- Uni-ball Signo

**Masking fluid**
- Winsor & Newton Art Masking Fluid

**Masking tape**
- Frog Tape Delicate Surface Painter's Tape – Yellow

**Ceramic palettes**
- Muddy Ceramic
- Mud Made Ceramics

**Brush pots**
- The Love of Pots

**Crackle paste**
- Golden Artist Colors

**Printing materials**
- Cranfield Relief Ink
- Essdee – lino ink
- Handprinted – rollers and lino

**Self-adhesive sheets**
- Hobbycraft

**Lever punch**
- Fiskars

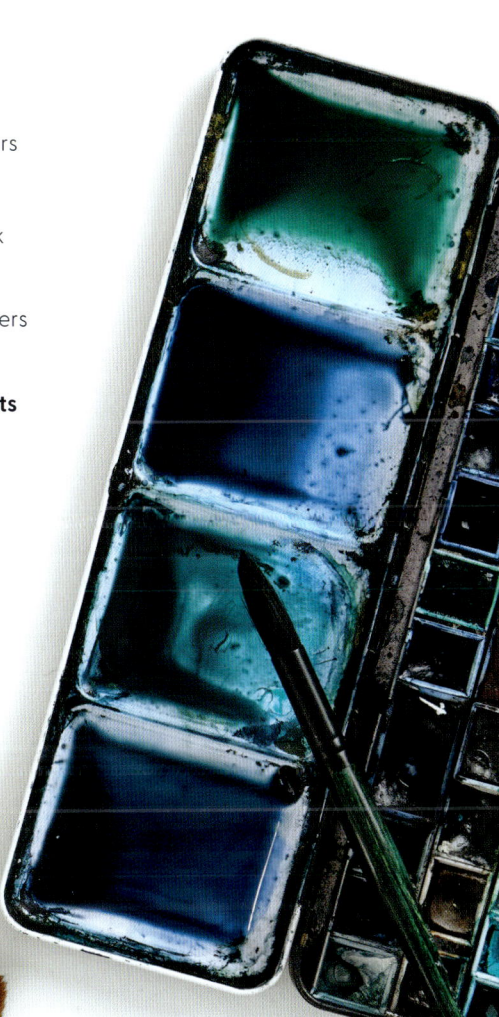

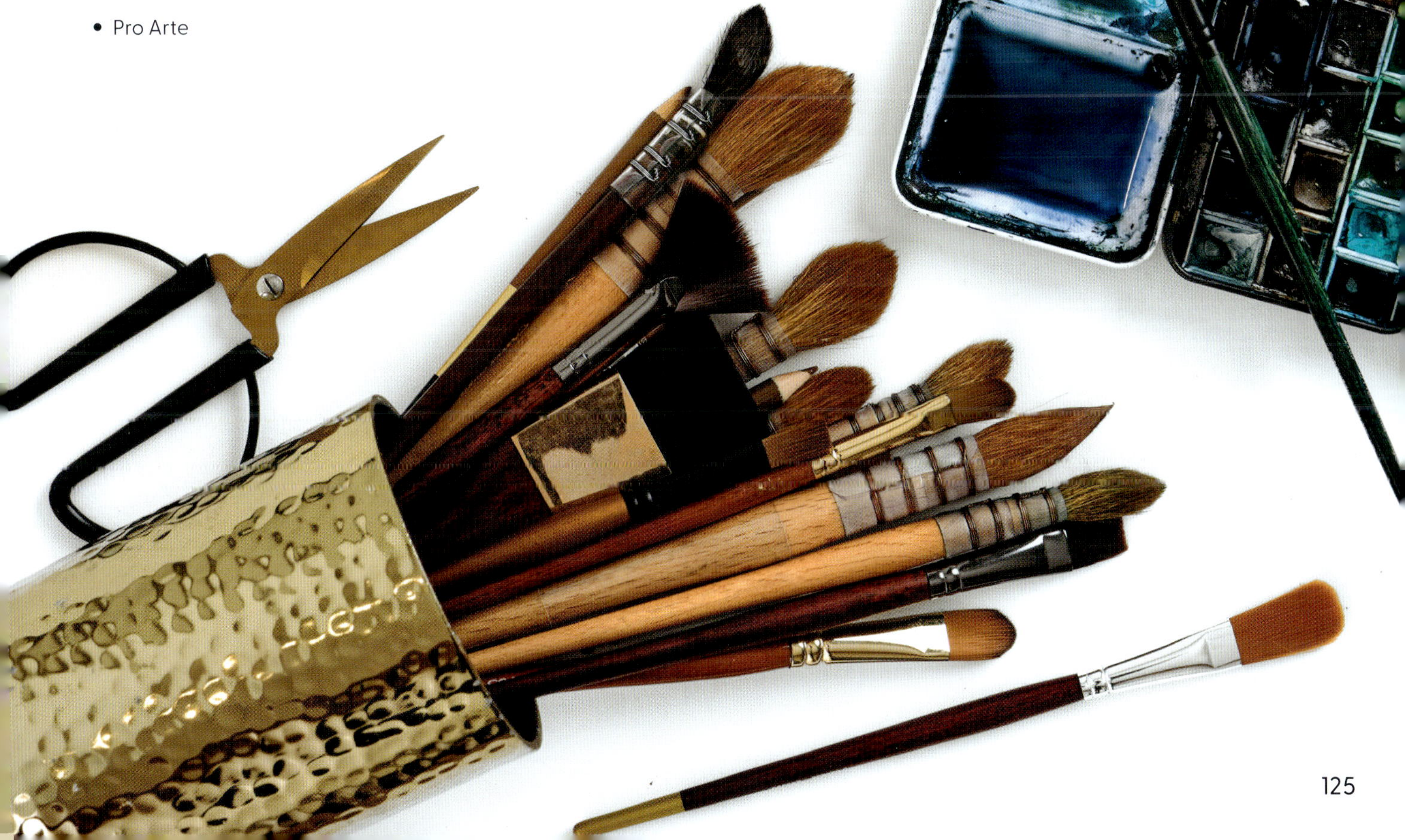

# Index

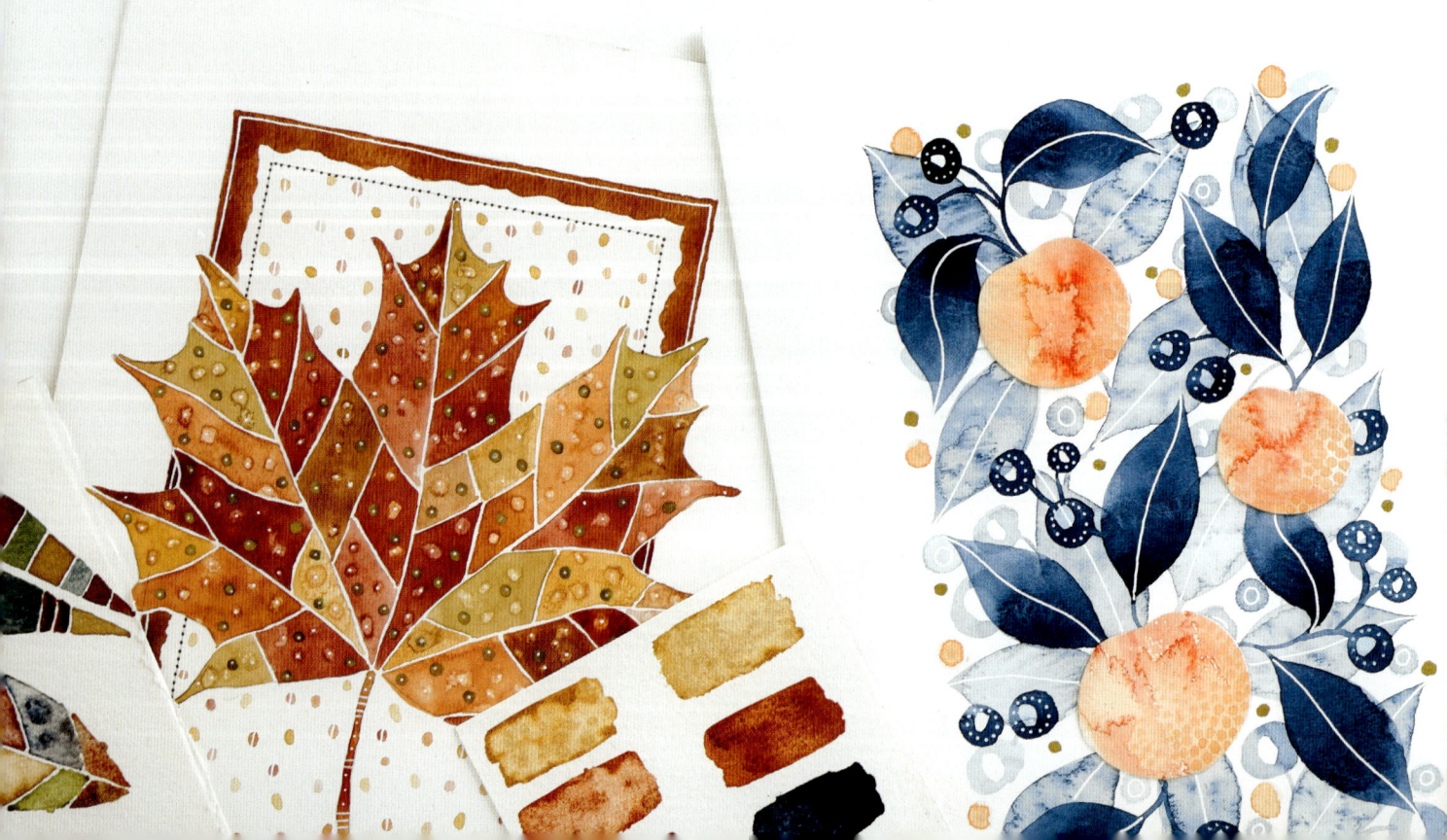

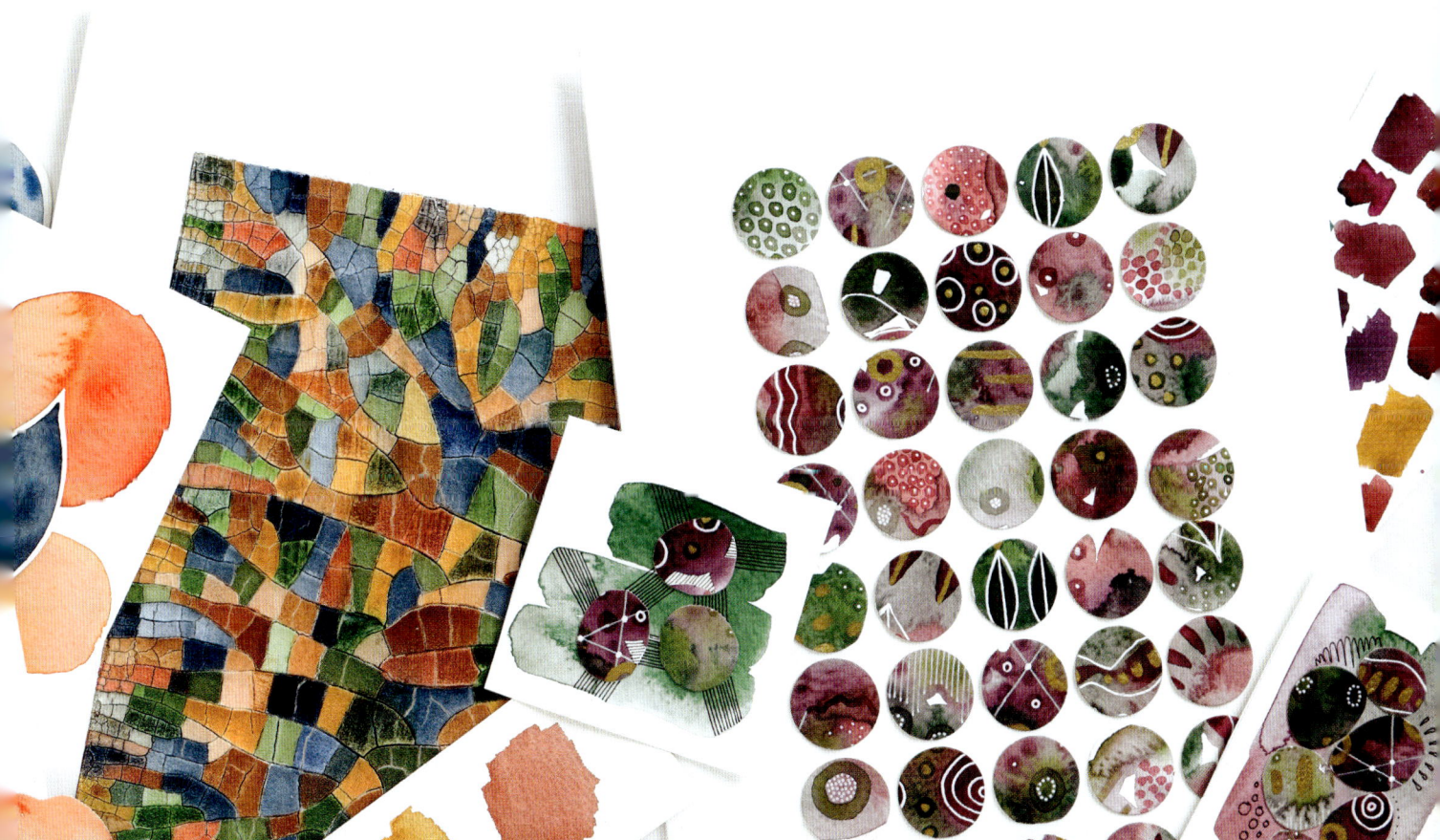

A DAVID AND CHARLES BOOK
© David and Charles, Ltd 2025

David and Charles is an imprint of David and Charles, Ltd
Suite A, Tourism House, Pynes Hill, Exeter, EX2 5WS

Text and Artwork © Kate Rebecca Leach 2025
Layout and Photography © David and Charles, Ltd 2025

First published in the UK and USA in 2025

ISBN-13: 9781446315613 paperback
ISBN-13: 9781446311936 EPUB

This book has been printed on paper from approved suppliers and made from pulp from sustainable sources.

Printed in China through Asia Pacific Offset for:
David and Charles, Ltd
Suite A, Tourism House, Pynes Hill, Exeter, EX2 5WS

10 9 8 7 6 5 4 3 2 1

Publishing Director: Ame Verso
Publishing Manager: Jeni Chown
Editor: Victoria Allen
Project Editor: Claire Coakley
Design: Sam Staddon
Pre-press Designer: Susan Reansbury
Art Direction & Photography: Tom Hargreaves
Production Manager: Beverley Richardson

David and Charles publishes high-quality books on a wide range of subjects. For more information visit www.davidandcharles.com.

Share your makes with us on social media using #dandcbooks and follow us on Facebook and Instagram by searching for @dandcbooks.

Layout of the digital edition of this book may vary depending on reader hardware and display settings.